| Enigmas of Identity

# Enigmas of Identity | Peter Brooks

PRINCETON UNIVERSITY PRESS
*Princeton and Oxford*

Frontispiece and jacket. Paul Cézanne, *The Garden at Les Lauves* (*Le Jardin des Lauves*), c. 1906. Oil on canvas, 25-3/4 x 31-7/8 in. (65.405 x 80.9625 cm.). Acquired 1955. Courtesy of The Phillips Collection, Washington, D.C.

Copyright © 2011 by Princeton University Press

Requests for permission to reproduce material from this work should be sent to Permissions, Princeton University Press

Published by Princeton University Press, 41 William Street, Princeton, New Jersey 08540

In the United Kingdom: Princeton University Press, 6 Oxford Street, Woodstock, Oxfordshire OX20 1TW

press.princeton.edu

Library of Congress Cataloging-in-Publication Data
Brooks, Peter, 1938–
    Enigmas of identity / Peter Brooks.
        p.      cm.
    Includes bibliographical references and index.
    ISBN 978-0-691-15158-8 (hardcover : alk. paper)    1. Group identity.
I. Title.
    HM753.B76 2011
    305—dc22                                    2011005722

British Library Cataloging-in-Publication Data is available

This book has been composed in Garamond Premier Pro
Printed on acid-free paper. ∞
Printed in the United States of America
10 9 8 7 6 5 4 3 2 1

# Contents

| Enigmas of Identity

# | To Begin

Take a nightmare situation evoked by Jean-Paul Sartre to image his childhood sense that he was a fraud, lacking all authenticity. He has sneaked onto a train from Paris to Dijon and fallen asleep, and when the conductor comes to ask for his ticket, he has to admit he doesn't have one. Nor the money to pay for one. Yet he makes the grandiose claim that he needs to be in Dijon for important and secret reasons, "reasons that concerned France and perhaps all mankind."[1] This scenario—in which the conductor remained mute, unconvinced, and the boy talked on and on—could never reach an ending. The higher calling—the salvation of mankind—remained an apology for his ticketless train trip, but not one he could really explain. Somehow the train ride had to continue, but without any certain point of arrival—or justification.

Such, we might say, is life, or at least our sense of personal identity within the world, at once unjustified and, to us, crucially important. That is more or less the question I want to work toward in this book. It was not quite my starting point; it took me some time to understand that "identity" was the concept I was after. In essence, the book had its inception in a course I taught under the title "Character, Person, Identity." I was interested in the fact that "character," so central to our experience of reading novels (or biographies, or watching plays, or voting for elected officials) was very hard to talk about. "Character" has never been given the kind of systematic analysis that other elements of storytelling have received, such as plot or point of view or reader response: it isn't susceptible to formal analysis in the same way. There have been fine books on character, notably Alex Woloch's *The One vs. the Many*, which demonstrates the structural importance of minor characters for the emergence of the protagonist. But the concept (as Woloch and other commentators are aware) stretches beyond any formal definition to encompass much of what we want to include when we speak about "persons," the second term in my trilogy, as entire human beings.

It's fairly easy to talk about "person" in a minimalist way—as a grammatical person in, for instance, the pronouns *I* or *you* or *she*—and in that manner begin to understand at least the structured role of persons as participants in a conversation. The analysis of the ways in which language understands persons can be rigorous, and helpful—but it does not resolve all the issues we want to talk about with "character." I couldn't find any minimal position in regard to person in our fuller understanding of personhood, individuality. As with "character," so with "person" in this larger sense: I couldn't find the terms for an analytic discussion. Character slops over into all our discussions of ethics and morality. Where we now talk of writing a recommendation for someone, for instance, our forebears used to speak of "giving someone a character": doing what was still earlier called his or her "moral portrait." That was in ages that perhaps believed in character as a more definitive and complete conception than we do now. Sigmund Freud and others have seemingly shattered the unitary notion of character—though reading the great nineteenth-century novelists one perceives that they never subscribed to the closed, complete, self-contained, harmonious notion of character or person that we at times ascribe to the Victorians, and which was ostensibly their goal in education and child rearing.

"Character" in fact turned out to be beyond my powers of systematic analysis. Not that one has to bring systematic analysis to the concept, which remains useful precisely because of its semantic range, which starts from writing, inscription; the first meaning recorded in the *Oxford English Dictionary* has to do with engravings on coins: "a distinctive mark impressed, engraved, or otherwise formed; a brand, stamp." Already this "original" meaning has a figural extension: "by characters graven on thy brows...," the *OED* gives us, in a quotation from Christopher Marlowe's *Tamburlaine* (1586). And what is engraved on your brows should ethically correspond to what is in your heart. By the eleventh definition, we have "the sum of the moral and mental qualities which distinguish an individual or a race, viewed as a homogeneous whole; the individuality impressed by nature and habit on a man or nation; mental or moral constitution." That gets it all in, the better and the worse ways in which character has been conceived. By the time we reach definition seventeen, the concept has moved into literature: "a personality invested with distinctive attributes and qualities, by a novelist or dramatist; also, the personality or 'part' assumed by an actor on the stage"—with a reference here to Henry Fielding's *Tom Jones* (1749). All our aesthetics and our ethics converge in "character," in what Aristotle referred to as *ethos*—as opposed to *mythos*, story or plot.

So character was too broad and slippery, whereas person was either too narrow, with too much of a grammatical presupposition, or else as replete and elusive as character. What about "identity"? It dawned on me that questions of character in the modern novel—say, from the time of *Tom Jones* on—very often posed themselves as problems of identity. Tom Jones is a foundling who will eventually be revealed as the natural son of Squire Allworthy's sister. That kind of identity is common in the eighteenth-century novel: a disposition to act nobly eventually is underwritten and "explained" by gentlemanly parentage. The nineteenth-century novel also is full of foundlings, orphans doomed to live with abusive stepparents. But it is less common for them to stand revealed at the end as nobly born. They are much more apt to have to forge their own identities. Who you are—in the sense of what you can legitimately call yourself, and what others call you—seems to have become a problem with entry into the modern age in a way that it wasn't before. There are exemplary cases in Charles Dickens—Pip of *Great Expectations* may be the most striking, since he begins his story by naming himself Pip, and recording this act in the graveyard where headstones mark his dead parents—and in Emily and Charlotte Brontë, and in many others. Orphan status gives one the opportunity for self-definition, including the selection of an ideal parent—or someone taken to be such—that will be so important not only to Pip but to Honoré de Balzac's ambitious young men Eugène de Rastignac and Lucien Chardon de Rubempré, for instance.

Then it came to me that identity is in fact a large problem that stamps not only novels but all sorts of social issues in the nineteenth century, and up to our own time. There would seem to be both public and private issues of identity. In the public sphere, in talk about crime, health, prostitution, urbanism, the identities of those who make up the social body become a problem in a new way. This must in broad outline have to do with the growth of cities, along with the institutionalization and increasing bureaucratization of the modern nation-state. Most European capital cities experienced (in the course of the nineteenth century) a large influx of population from the countryside, with an increasingly anxious concern from the upper and middle classes that they were cohabiting with a crime- and disease-ridden underclass that needed to be kept under control. The rise of the protomodern police force in big cities brought questions of how to identify the criminal, especially the habitual criminal—the "recidivist"—who became the object of much attention in a society that would increasingly be persuaded that criminality was a chronic and even a hereditary condition. Finding out who you are—what your identifying marks and characteristics are—became the business of the state, first for the criminal population and then for the population as a whole. And much of the imaginative literature of the time, from popular melodrama to the novel of high or low ambitions, shows a nearly obsessive concern with disguise, imposture, and the discovery of true identities. Though it should be added that these identities, once discovered, often turn out to be far less defined, far more fluid, problematic, and protean than one at first expected.

And that points us toward the private or inner sense of identity that is at the very center of modern thought and imagination from the dawn of the modern world on—starting with the Renaissance, one might say, though one could push the date back to remarkable innovations from the twelfth century but gaining a new momentum and a new accent in the Enlightenment. Jean-Jacques Rousseau strikes the truly new note in his *Confessions*, and all the literature we attach to the Romantic age and thereafter reworks Rousseau's preoccupation with saying who he is—rather, recounting who he is, since the identity of the self can only be captured in a narrative, in multiple genres and dimensions, from William Wordsworth's inner epic of "the growth of the poet's mind" in the *Prelude* to Marcel Proust's three thousand pages on the finding of his writerly vocation. In fact, art—especially narrative art—becomes largely devoted to the understanding of personal identity in a world where that identity seems ever more important while at the same time ever more threatened by the anonymity of the modern, by the sheer numbers of others among whom one lives. The nostalgia for an earlier time, of life rooted in a native soil, in a small place where each is known to each and all form a kind of organic whole, resonates in novelists such as Balzac and Dickens who are fully aware that they, like their protagonists, are condemned to—and animated by—struggle to survive and to impose themselves in the urban crowd. In an increasingly secular world, these protagonists have only themselves to rely on. They cannot find definition in traditional roles and models. As André Malraux would write in retrospect on the heroes of this time, their ultimate ambition seems to be the deification of the individual personality. But, of course, nothing could be more problematic than that.

In thinking about the enigmas of modern identity, I have often turned to the law, to cases and doctrines developed in the law and its application that seemed to speak to public issues of identification and authentication. It is when the trajectory of an individual identity intersects with the requirements of the law that we often discover the bedrock problems of society. The case of the impostor, for instance, jangles all the legal nerves. More generally, rules of discovery and evidence crucially dramatize the search to know who persons are. Because of the Bill of Rights in particular, American law has produced a long tradition of commentary on crucial issues in the relation of the individual to the state. So it is that American law offers a rich field of study if you want to understand such key issues as privacy in relation to identity. As well as to the law, I found myself having recourse, over and over, to three writers who simply seemed inevitable points of reference on the questions posed: Rousseau, Proust, and Freud. Others writing on this vast and unmanageable subject of identity would no doubt pick other guides, but for me these three are indispensable. Rousseau seems to me the first to make his identity the subject of study in an identifiably modern way, and his obsessive display of his neuroses sounds peculiarly modern. Proust orchestrates the finding of personal identity from childhood forward (Rousseau and the Romantics had discovered childhood) in a particularly full and convincing way: for all its claustrophobic attention to the sensations and thoughts of a single person, Proust's novel encompasses a remarkable range of human experience. Freud, finally, offers one possible systematic thinking through of the questions of identity raised by Rousseau and his successors—among whom he very much places himself. I don't mean to give Freud's thought any particular privilege—for instance, as an "explanation" of Rousseau, Proust, and others—but to see it as a different form of reflection on the same constellation of issues. It's not psychoanalysis as a system—or as a systematic attempt to explain who we are—that interests me so much as Freud's more speculative encounters with identity, especially his own.

What I offer here is in fact far from systematic, and by no means an attempt at exhaustive treatment of identity, but instead a set of explorations into different aspects of the problem. I don't, for instance, treat the question of "identity politics"—using identity as an ethnic or other group marker—which would have led my book in an entirely different direction. On the whole, the chapters tend to alternate between the public and the private dimensions of identity, moving from the external world to the internal, all the while recognizing how closely connected they are. Enigmas of identity remain, to my thinking, just that. The cases and the questions and the writers I look at don't bring us to any firm conclusions other than the fact that identity seems to us a crucial knot of our thinking—a concept as necessary as it is difficult to analyze. What I hope a reader may take away from the book is not systematic, either, but some enhanced understanding of the ways in which the drama of identity unfolds for us moderns—why and how we stand in relation to the problems of saying the self first so insistently proclaimed by Rousseau. Beginning with a very literal form of marks of identity—fingerprints—I move on to thinking about the obsession of modern societies with issues of identity, then veer into instances of individual self-obsession and what these have to say not only about persons but also the society or culture in which they must survive. The case of an impostor then leads to thinking about hiding, revealing, masking, transforming what at its most vertiginous becomes a protean sense of self. Then, autoeroticism as an obsessive theme in several modern writers may suggest a discovery that self-love—narcissism—is the primary and original form of the erotic, which makes the socialization of the individual as crucial as it is difficult and possibly doomed. The question of searches and seizures in the law, and the legal doctrines both protecting the individual and providing for his or her capture by social institutions, images a kind of standoff between the self and knowledge of it. And that, returning to the individual's inner problem of knowledge, in turn suggests the importance of the place of the knower in relation to the known, the narrating *I* to the narrated *I*, when they are one and "the same" person—whatever that oneness and sameness may mean, which in fact turns out to be problematic. Finally, the self facing its extinction may make particularly concerted, wild, mad reactions to the impending nothingness of its identity, in late work of a new, unbound creativity.

If there is one constant here, it seems to be the discovery that self-reflection, the work of memory on the self, the telling of a past self by "the same" self in the present, will always run up against an insoluble problem: Is there any valid distinction between the self known and the self as knower here? The need to postulate their continuity—I am the same as I ever was—and the simultaneous claim of progress, change, and thus the possibility of an enhanced self-understanding, come into conflict, since in the very process of self-knowledge the knowing self obtrudes its presence over, and sometimes against, the self to be known: you can't get to the latter except by way of the claims of the former, which may repress the past self, distort it, make it dependent on its present reinterpretation. In this regard, the way stories of the self are told takes on a new importance—including in law, which often seems to treat stories as if they were interchangeable and unproblematically related to "the facts" that they recount, whereas in truth the telling is crucial to the establishment of the facts—to what law wants to use as evidence in the establishment of guilt or innocence of persons, as markers of their identity.

The inner and the outer dimensions of the effort to know identity coalesce in what we might call the identity paradigm as characteristic of modern individuals and societies: that nexus of issues and inquests, beliefs and techniques of knowing that seems so central to our age and its aspirations and anxieties. More accurate might be the identificatory paradigm, laying emphasis less on what it is that needs to be known than on the process of its knowing, its capture in words and techniques, in statistics and categories. To see the identificatory paradigm at work, in a range of cultural and social contexts—from detective stories to psychoanalysis, from autobiographical self-inquest to policing of searches and seizures, from novelistic character to protean impostor—is to bring to attention something characteristic and important about our lives, singly and collectively.

We know that it matters crucially to be able to say who we are, why we are here, and where we are going. We also know that like the boy in the train Sartre describes as protagonist of his recurring nightmares, when asked by the conductor for our ticket, we can't find it. That doesn't mean we won't keep looking for it, inventing it, producing various excuses for being in our seat on the train. We need to keep saying what our identity might be and where it might lie, and how we might find it authenticated by other identities. I can't imagine a world in which that would cease to be the case.

# I | Marks of Identity

I would guess that we share an obsessive interest in identity, however defined. It's in any case my belief that such an interest is nearly definitional of modern human beings and the societies in which they live. While the notion of identity is not new—especially as a philosophical topic—a widespread concern with one's personal identity, and its relations to "the others" among whom one lives, seems to have emerged with greater intensity with the Enlightenment, and to gain force throughout the nineteenth and twentieth centuries, and into our own time. To the extent that a characteristic of modernity is a new valuation of the individual, the obsession with identity follows almost inevitably. Modernity, confessional discourse, the novel itself as genre, identity as an enigma and an object of quest and questioning: these are all related phenomena, and the coming of psychoanalysis at the dawn of the twentieth century merely confirms a process begun by such as John Locke and Jean-Jacques Rousseau. And it seems to be the case that the individual search to know the self is matched by society's concern to know, to classify, and to order the range of selves that are out there.

My own interest in this topic came into focus a few years ago from an article in the *New York Times* concerning fingerprinting and its status as evidence in the law. A decision from the Federal District Court for Eastern Pennsylvania made the extraordinary claim that fingerprint identification did not meet the standard of scientific evidence set by the Supreme Court decision in *Daubert v. Merrell Dow Pharmaceuticals* in 1993, and therefore could not be used to "prove" the identity of a suspect at trial.[1] It came from Judge Louis Pollak (former Dean of the Yale and University of Pennsylvania law schools), in a case called *United States v. Llera-Plaza*. Pollak noted that other recent federal cases described fingerprint identification as "the very archetype of reliable expert testimony" and "scientific knowledge," but that it failed on the grounds of testability and especially falsifiability. "Scientific methodology today is based on generating hypotheses and testing them to see if they can be falsified," wrote Justice Harry Blackmun in *Daubert* (quoted in *Llera-Plaza*). It is the test of falsifiability that allows one to know not only that a proposition is true a good deal of the time but that it is universally true. Fingerprint identification, while mustering a considerable body of expertise, does not in the final analysis meet this test. It is indeed the final step in fingerprint identification—the determination of a match between two sets of fingerprints—that involves a subjective judgment rather than a scientific procedure. Pollak cites forensic scientist Dr. David Stoney: "The determination that a fingerprint examiner makes . . . when comparing a latent fingerprint with a known fingerprint, specifically the determination that there is sufficient basis for an absolute identification is not a scientific determination. It is a subjective determination standard. It is a subjective determination without objective standards to it" (37–38). Therefore Pollak rules that experts may present analysis of fingerprints, and point out observed similarities between prints, but "will not be permitted to present testimony expressing an opinion of an expert witness that a particular latent print matches, or does not match, the rolled print of a particular person and hence is, or is not, the fingerprint of that person" (69).

Yet if you go to look for Pollak's opinion in *Llera-Plaza*, you won't find it; it has now been "unpublished." Faced with the outcry from prosecutors and police across the land and judicial skepticism in a number of other jurisdictions, in response to the government's motion for reconsideration Pollak took the unusual step of reversing himself two months after the original decision, and, by way of a new evidentiary hearing, readmitting fingerprints as within the realm of technical expertise—comparable to the testimony of an expert on metal fatigue or tire failure, for instance. Our criminal justice system, and our culture at large, are not ready yet to do without fingerprints.

The case of Brandon Mayfield—arrested in 2004 as one of the Madrid train bombers (though he was in Oregon at the time of this act of terror) on the basis of a fingerprint match the FBI called "100% positive" and then later released with apologies and a $2 million damage award when the Spanish police (who had never accepted the FBI "match") found the fingerprints to be those of a much more likely suspect—again shed doubt on a technique whose claim to scientific status is more a matter of cultural myth than tested fact. On the basis of the Mayfield mistake, Judge Susan Souder of Baltimore County, Maryland, recently threw out fingerprint evidence in a capital case on the grounds that it was not certain enough to justify putting the defendant to death. In her memorandum opinion, she summarized succinctly the kind of doubts earlier expressed by Pollak concerning the "analysis, comparison, evaluation, and verification" methodology touted by forensic experts, noting, "Defendant contends that ACE-V is not a methodology which has been subjected to scientific testing. As a result, the error rate in latent print identifications is unknown. Absent an error rate, reliability of the methodology is unproven. A fundamental problem, according to Defendant, is that the subjective comparisons in ACE-V involve psychological phenomena known as 'confirmation bias.' Further, Defendant argues that the 'standards' for latent fingerprint identification are inadequate."[2] The "verification" stage in fact involves another fingerprint technician, trained in the same way as the person who pronounced the "match," confirming the work of someone who is usually his colleague. But Judge Souder's caution is not standard operating procedure for courts. Although the reliability of fingerprint evidence has yet to be given a thorough, probative test (efforts to do so are finally under way) both professional techne and the popular imagination clearly believe that fingerprints are revelatory of identity. Recently, for instance, fingerprint expertise was pitted against art historical savoir faire in the contest over the authenticity of a Jackson Pollock—or not—painting that seems to have a fingerprint on its reverse.[3]

I was struck by Judge Pollak's critique of fingerprint identification because, like most Americans, I grew up believing in its infallibility—though I admit to having always had sneaking suspicions about the claim that every set of fingerprints is absolutely unique to the individual, and unalterable over time. It seemed to me comparable to the proposition that no two snowflakes ever are duplicates. It is, at least, counterintuitive. And as I thought about Pollak's critique, it dawned on me that our belief in fingerprints may most of all represent a will to believe that our very identities are carried in our digital imprints—as an infallible signature of who we are. The unique and invariant fingerprint would correspond to a cultural belief unfolded since the Enlightenment and Romanticism that each of us is unique, irreplaceable, never seen before and never to be seen again.

The initiatory statement of the belief no doubt comes from Jean-Jacques Rousseau, on the first page of his *Confessions*, where he claims that nature "broke the mould in which she cast me."[4] Rousseau here invites comparison to Michel de Montaigne's famous statement, "Each man bears the entire form of the human condition" (Chaque homme porte la forme entière de l'humaine condition); every individual bears the stamp or impress of the common lot, like coins struck from the same die.[5] Rousseau rejects that sense of a common identity, insisting on the uniqueness of his own. The markers of his identity—like that of the unique and invariable fingerprint—belong to him exclusively. The mold used to shape him is broken once Rousseau has been cast in it. Further, it is part of Rousseau's contention that this uniquely characterized individual is essentially invariable over time, despite aging and loss and sorrow and even the attempts of his enemies to present the world with a "disfigured portrait," a lying version of Jean-Jacques. This fear of a false, disfigured identity presented to the world—and especially to posterity—anguished Rousseau during his paranoid later years. The very last page he wrote—the opening to the unfinished Tenth of *The Reveries of a Solitary Walker* (*Les Rêveries du promeneur solitaire*)—insists upon his sameness despite difference. Rousseau begins by noting it is Palm Sunday and exactly fifty years from the day he first met Madame de Warens, a meeting that, he claims, "decided what I was to be for the whole of my life, and produced by an inevitable linkage the destiny of the rest of my days" (décida de moi pour toute ma vie, et produisit par un enchaînement inévitable le destin du reste de mes jours; 1:1098). Madame de Warens fixed, stabilized his mobile adolescent character; without his years with her he might never have known who he really was. It is a moving text in that Rousseau near his end asserts through this anniversary his essential sameness, the "linkage" of his self at age sixty-six to the identity established at age sixteen. Despite the disfigured external portrait, he claims an unaltered identity.

Yet to make that claim, Rousseau demonstrates, requires engaging in an ever-renewed autobiographical project. The self knows itself, as John Locke contends, through its capacity to "repeat the idea of any past action with the same consciousness it had of it at first, and with the same consciousness it has of any present action; so far it is the same *personal self*."[6] Rousseau foregrounds Locke's point that the concept of the self depends on memory, that faculty that assures us that we are the same person as before. And he makes clear that this self is narrative; it must be retrieved from the past, the lines of continuity leading from past to present traced and retraced. Identity—and I think here again Rousseau ushers in our modernity—is a project, an undertaking that requires one to ask in what ways one is the same, and different, and no doubt in most cases to hold on to a sense of one's uniqueness and invariance despite the tolls taken by life. We know that we are not quite "the same persons" we once were. We hope that somehow everything that we vaguely classify as "experience" has made us wiser, perhaps in some sense better. At the same time, we know—through memory, largely—that we are identifiably, to the state and to ourselves, the same as we were. Most of us do not want to think of ourselves as impostors—though imposters are certainly useful in thinking about our common sense of identity.

I shall in chapter 3 evoke a modern impostor's lesson. But think for a moment about a premodern example of imposture, or identity theft. Natalie Davis, in *The Return of Martin Guerre*, shows us that the problem of authenticating, or exposing, the claim to be Martin Guerre by the man who was really (apparently, probably) Arnaud du Tilh is made almost impossible by the lack of socially and legally validated marks and tokens of identity. We are in a time before identity cards, before photographs and fingerprints and—when the persons in question are peasants—portraits and signatures and even mirrors. At the trial of the apparent impostor, only the cobbler—who maintained an "archive" of lasts for making shoes—offers anything that approaches scientific evidence: the pseudo-Martin's feet appear to be smaller than the Martin last on file. The rest of the evidence relies on memory of what Martin looked like many years before, how he spoke, and how adeptly the pseudo-Martin can simulate recall of persons and relations. The evidence of Bertrande, wife of Martin who accepted the pseudo-Martin as authentic, has particular importance because it is judged that she can discern the touch and the intimate bodily details of the man who has arrived in the village of Artigat claiming to be her husband.[7]

If the pseudo-Martin is on the whole easily accepted and assimilated in Artigat it is no doubt because, as Davis argues, he is wanted there: his absence has created a gap, a problem in domestic, kinship, and social structure. And the legal system is on the verge of ratifying the pseudo-Martin's identity precisely because he fills this gap, gives the Guerre household the heir, landowner, husband, son-in-law, and father that it has been lacking. The only thing that keeps the Parlement de Toulouse from ruling favorably on his claim to be Martin Guerre is the sensational last-minute appearance of the "true" Martin, hobbling in on his wooden leg.

It is striking, post-Rousseau and post-Freud, that no one at the trial of Martin Guerre talks about his childhood—so much a part of our modern sense of selfhood and identity. (Think of the "replicants" of Ridley Scott's 1982 film *Blade Runner*, who appear human but have no childhood memories—unless "implanted."[8]) The testing of who Martin Guerre is doesn't seem to involve memories of childhood at all. It has more to do with social and kinship structure than individual psychology. The continuity of selfhood, of an ego present to itself, does not seem to be at issue: the problem is not posed in terms of our claims to our own past. Identity in Rousseau, in contrast, lies in a claim of an inner core of selfhood to self-recognition over time, to the assertion of sameness in apparent difference and temporal change. Like his disciple Freud, Rousseau sees in the recall of infantile affect a determinative sign of the continuity of his being and his knowledge of it. Identity depends on a psychobiography in narrative form. No doubt this continues to be true for our contemporary sense of who we are.

In the nineteenth century—following Rousseau, and in so many ways the first "modern" century—the problem of defining, knowing, and testing identity became more acute and anxious. It activated various pseudoscientific technologies for knowing who people are (as we say). Physiognomy and phrenology—techniques for reading identity from face and skull—gave way to "Bertillonage," the system of cranial and bodily measurements perfected by Alphonse Bertillon that was supposed to identify the criminal recidivist. Photography from the moment of its invention in 1839 was put to use for the police mug shot. This was a time of vast social dislocation, and especially of urban growth. Population density, especially in London and Paris, gave the impression of an innumerable new proletarian population—comprising mostly immigrants from the provinces. As Louis Chevalier pointed out in his classic study, the working classes came to appear, in the eyes of the bourgeoisie, the dangerous classes.[9] Part of the official bourgeois response was to control through classification, to establish new markers of identity.[10] Workers and ex-convicts, for instance, were required to carry passports to move within France. Prostitutes were required to carry a card if streetwalkers, to be assigned a number if in a brothel. Once registered in the police files they could be erased and rehabilitated only with the greatest of difficulty: the whole point, as historian Alain Corbin has shown, was to prevent any confusion between the deviant "marked" woman and the respectable bourgeoise.[11] The fear was that a deviant element might show up under the guise of the respectable. What if the mayor of your town turns out to be a former convict—as in Victor Hugo's *Les Misérables*? Hence a society officially committed to its Inspector Javerts, charged with ferreting out the criminal in disguise.

As the novelist who remains the best guide to this period for France, Honoré de Balzac, repeatedly tells us, in the "stupid" nineteenth century people increasingly look alike. All the men dress in bourgeois black: you can't tell the social status and the identity of someone from his costume alone. There is a generalized semiotic crisis, which means that you need to pay attention to small, apparently insignificant signs: how someone ties a cravat, or how fresh his gloves are, or his gait as he walks in the anonymous urban crowd. Balzac worked intermittently throughout his career on a never-finished "Pathology of Social Life," which is all about the new semiotics of modern urban existence.

Balzac (like Dickens and Wilkie Collins in England) was fascinated, even obsessed, by the problem of criminal identity. There are whole novels that turn on false appearance and mistaken identity. There are secret societies, such as Les Treize (The Thirteen), whose occult action on the world is suspected but never directly seen. His novels are mostly set in the 1820s, though largely written after 1832, the date when the legislature, on humanitarian grounds, abolished the practice of branding convicts on the shoulder. This abolition of *la marque*, as it was known, became to Balzac (as to other writers) a symbolic moment in the semiotic crisis. His representation of the crisis pervades his work, nowhere more than in that shadowy key figure of the *Comédie humaine*, Jacques Collin, alias Vautrin, alias the Reverend Father Carlos Herrera, aka Trompe-la-Mort (Cheat-Death) who is always in disguise, very often hidden from view in an attic from which he pulls the strings of the action on the ground floor, who can speak in many languages including one invented by himself and his criminal associates—an absolutely protean figure who will end by passing from the ranks of crime to those of the police. A key moment of *Old Goriot* (*Le Père Goriot*) involves drugging Vautrin so that he can be slapped on the shoulder, to make the latent mark, the *TF* (for *travaux forcés*, forced labor, to which he was sentenced) reappear, and furnish the police with the evidence they need to arrest the man they know as Collin. Collin's branded flesh again becomes crucial at the climax of the later novel *Glory and Misery of Courtesans* (*Splendeurs et misères des courtisanes*) when the magistrate Camusot is trying to penetrate his alias as the Spanish priest Carlos Herrera. Camusot has Collin stripped to the waist, then tells the bailiff to strike his shoulder with an ebony bat. What emerges from the blow to the shoulder is a confused palimpsest of lines and gouges, holes that result from a gunshot wound (which we know was self-inflicted, to efface the brand) with the dubious trace of letters underneath.

That highly characteristic form of the nineteenth-century imaginary, melodrama, repeatedly turns on questions of marking and identity. The token of identity that permits the eleventh-hour recognitions that establish rightful identities, brand evil, and reward virtue became known as *la croix de ma mère*, from this particularly overused piece of religious jewelry left, most often, in the cradle of an abandoned infant and retrieved at the crucial moment. But there are plenty of other marks of identity, especially ones on the body itself, birthmarks, or intentional markings. This preoccupation with marks on the body—often hidden until the denouement—of course renews a very old tradition: think of Odysseus's recognition by his old nurse Eurykleia, when he returns in disguise to Ithaca, by way of the scar on his thigh that her fingers recognize as she washes his feet; or of the birthmark in William Shakespeare's *Cymbeline*; and countless other examples that fall, generally speaking, in the romance tradition, where disguise and recognition are essential to the plot.

Yet the search for sure indicators of identity seems to become particularly acute and anxiety-laden in the nineteenth century. Moving from Balzac across the Channel to Dickens, think of how, in his most expertly plotted novel *Great Expectations*, every detail planted, from the opening paragraph onward, leads to the great, painful, and life-altering recognition scene in which Magwitch returns and reveals to Pip that all along he has been the occult author of the expectations, indeed of Pip's whole life story—and does so in a pantomime that is all about the revelatory marks and details by which Pip has known, and repressed, this story:

> Even yet I could not recall a single feature, but I knew him! If the wind and the rain had driven away the intervening years, had scattered all the intervening objects, had swept us to the churchyard where we first stood face to face on such differ-ent levels, I could not have known my convict more distinctly than I knew him now. No need to take a file from his pocket and show it to me; no need to take the handkerchief from his neck and twist it round his head; no need to hug himself with both his arms, and take a shivering turn across the room, looking back at me for recognition. I knew him before he gave me one of those aids, though a moment before, I had not been conscious of remotely suspecting his identity.[12]

"No need": the praeterition of the passage, claiming no need for the very details—file, handkerchief, shivering turn—that are called "aids" to identity, may only reinforce the sense of a form of cognition that is cru-cial without being wholly conscious in its process. The veils of reality fall away when certain markers reveal their semiotic properties. Magwitch's identity leaps out from the details—and a moment later what this means for Pip's identity comes "flashing" on him, as a kind of hysterical conversion that makes him "struggle for every breath I drew" (320).

This manner of deciphering identity from the particular, from markings, may belong to the lore acquired over the millennia by the hunter, who learned to "reconstruct the shapes and movements of his invisible prey from tracks on the ground, broken branches, excrement, tufts of hair, entangled feathers, stagnating odors." So claims historian

Carlo Ginzburg, in his notable essay "Clues," in which he teases out the implications of the huntsman's lore for narrative in general, and particularly the kind of narrative exemplified in the detective story—a nineteenth-century invention—that seeks to solve a mystery, discover the hidden. The hunter works from concrete particulars, clues that need to be enchained in a narrative to reach a significant end, which is generally the identification of the quarry. The hunter's lore, notes Ginzburg, "is characterized by the ability to move from apparently insignificant experiential data to a complex reality that cannot be experienced directly. And the data is always arranged by the observer in such a way as to produce a narrative sequence, which could be expressed most simply as 'someone passed this way.' Perhaps the very idea of narrative (as distinct from the incantation, exorcism, or invocation) was born in a hunting society, from the experience of deciphering tracks."[13] In Ginzburg's hypothesis, narrative would be a cognitive instrument of a specific type, one "invented" for the decipherment of details of the real that only take on their meaning when they are viewed as clues, then linked in a series, enchained in a manner that allows one to identify that animal or person who passed this way. This is what Sherlock Holmes's searches are all about: reality becomes semiotic when it reveals that its particulars are clues that can be enchained, in a meaningful sequence, to the end of discovery. "It is so long a chain, and yet every link rings true," Watson admiringly exclaims to Holmes at the end of one of their cases.[14] If plots of recognition are age-old, in modernity they seem to have a predilection for the hunter's knowledge by way of individual clues linked, metonymically, into a specifically narrative solution.

Ginzburg's hunter's paradigm—as my examples from Balzac and Dickens suggest—serves the identity paradigm, the need to know who the "others" of society are. It is a paradigm that is bound up with both legality (the law investigates and polices identities) and with narrative (your identity lies in the story you can tell). In both Balzac and Dickens (and Collins and a host of others) these two prongs of the search to know identities converge: the law becomes the passage through which identity must be known, argued, validated, disciplined. Think of the dominating figure of the lawyer Jaggers in *Great Expectations*—not to mention the whole of *Bleak House*. Balzac's most famous lawyer, Derville, probably appears in more novels of the *Comédie humaine* than any other figure except possibly the moneylender Gobseck. Let me mention briefly one of his cases, in the brilliant short novel *Colonel Chabert*, which concerns the effort of this hero of Napoleon's armies, felled with a head wound at the battle of Eylau, declared dead and buried in the common pit, to reestablish his identity several years later, when things have changed not only in the usual posthumous ways—his wife has remarried, for instance—but changed also through a momentous historical reversal, the coming of a Restoration that wishes to bury the Napoleonic past, to repress it, pretend it never existed, in order to return to a prior state of society. That prior state is embodied by the royal decree the law clerks are reading out loud, in order to copy it, as the story begins: a decree restituting to the old nobility lands expropriated during the revolutionary period, a decree rendered in 1814, initiating the Restoration. The decree forcefully announces an end to the regime in which Colonel Chabert achieved his identity—made, as we say, a name for himself—and the coming of a new world of legalism (represented on the national level by the constitution known as La Charte, "granted" by Louis XVIII to the French people as the basis of an experiment in constitutional monarchy).

Chabert, who began life (like Pip in *Great Expectations*) as an orphan in the Enfants-Trouvés, the orphanage, is a self-made man, created through the army, which during the Napoleonic era was the great social institution for rapid advancement, where one could go from an inherited identity—as humble peasant, for instance—to the achieved identity of general or even marshal and a title of nobility literally in a matter of months. The high mortality rate for officers on the battlefield was an engine of social promotion. Yet Chabert in 1818 must press his claim not on the battlefield but in the law office: what the novel calls a "cavern of litigation." Who he is cannot be proved simply by a cavalry charge; it must be negotiated through the motions and countermotions of the law office and the law court, working toward the desired outcome of a public recognition of his identity and the accompanying civil rights and emoluments.

The situation is oxymoronic. When upon Chabert's first visit to the cavern of litigation one of the clerks asks for his name, he replies:

> "Chabert."
> "Is it the colonel who was killed at Eylau?" asked Huré, who hadn't yet said anything and was eager to add his mockery to that of the other clerks.
> "The same, sir," replied the old man with a heroic simplicity. And then he left.[15]

He claims the identity of a man whose public and legal identity is that of a dead hero, whose final acts of bravery and whose decease have been published in the *Victoires et conquêtes*, the official record of the deeds of Napoleon's Grande Armée. Another of the clerks comments, "Il a l'air d'un déterré." To say that someone looks like a man exhumed from the grave—"a l'air d'un déterré"—is, of course, to use a metaphor expressing his generally ghastly appearance. But what if the metaphor isn't one—since it is literally the case that Chabert has been dug from the grave, has in fact dug himself from the battlefield pit for the dead of Eylau? Chabert's heavy task is to make others believe in the blinding literality of this apparent figure, to unbury himself and establish his continuous identity as Colonel Chabert.

Derville the lawyer is the necessary mediator of Chabert's identity narrative: in the modern world of post-Waterloo legalism—see the decree that is being copied in the opening scene—questions of identity must be proved through litigation, not in battlefield heroics. Derville initiates the needed procedure by asking Chabert to tell his story. That proves to be a wholly gothic tale of coming to consciousness in the pit—in the silence of death—and realizing that he is in fact alive, then using a detached arm of a fallen comrade to leverage himself up from the pile of bodies, to emerge, naked, on the snow-covered plain of Eylau, and then to lose consciousness again. It's macabre, yet also a classic tale of death and rebirth—like Odysseus's descent to Hades, like Sinbad the sailor's entombment and escape. Derville, face-to-face with this relic whose very visage bears the signs of his wounds and of his sincerity, is largely convinced by Chabert's gothic tale but realizes that it has no public currency in and of itself. When Chabert has finished telling his story, Derville responds, "you may have to negotiate a settlement" (Il faudra peut-être transiger). To which Chabert reacts with outrage: " 'Negotiate?' echoed Colonel Chabert. 'Am I dead or am I alive?' " (Suis-je mort ou suis-je vivant? 333). Chabert's absolutism here—dead or alive?—corresponds to his military mentality but also the romantic—we could say Rousseauist—intimate, inward understanding of the truth-value of his narrative of identity. Rousseau wants us to know what he calls his "dispositions intérieures," his inward self. Derville, however, understands that this is not enough, that identity is forged in all sorts of transpersonal networks, intersubjective negotiations. The self, as psychologist Jerome Bruner has argued, is "transactional."[16] Balzac's original title for this novel was indeed *La Transaction*. It is Derville, man of the law, who understands the transactional nature of the self, and particularly the legal nature of the transactions involved.

So Derville decides to stake twenty-five gold *louis* that he has won at the gambling table on the attempt to transact Chabert's story: a commercial transaction that intersects with a narrative transaction, one might say, and makes the negotiation of Chabert's narrative of his existence what is at stake in the novel. This transaction must engage in the first instance the Comtesse Ferraud, Chabert's onetime (and still?) wife. Derville realizes that she, too, has a "buried story" and reasons out the possible consequences of Chabert's return on its development. She is of humble origins—Chabert says he picked her up at the Palais-Royal, indicating she had been a prostitute—and her advancement and enrichment through Chabert, and then Chabert's presumed death, are succeeded by marriage to an impecunious aristocrat. The problem is that with the return of Louis XVIII and the establishment of the Restoration, Comte Ferraud has come into some property of his own in addition to his wife's riches, has developed political ambitions, and has begun to feel he might have made a better marriage. His caste is once again at the summit of society and power, but he is unlikely to be made a Peer of the Realm. If his marriage to the Comtesse Ferraud were to be annulled and he were then to marry the daughter of a peer who had no sons of his own but wished to have his peerage transmitted to his son-in-law: there would lie the path to glory. Thus the position of the comtesse is potentially precarious, and the return of her former spouse, urging his claim to be the real husband, is very threatening to her. The accuracy of Derville's narrative hypothesis is confirmed when he presses the comtesse toward the horrified realization that if she becomes the object of a lawsuit by Chabert she might lose the Comte Ferraud's support, since he might be glad to see his marriage to her annulled. Derville's advice to her, then, is the same as to her sometime spouse: "Transiger."

The rest of the novel is about how and why this transaction fails, and how the comtesse manages to trick Chabert and finally disillusion him to the point where he chooses to give up his claim to his rightful identity and to disappear from society. She lures him to her country estate, shows off the children fathered by Comte Ferraud, and calls upon his generosity not to press his claim. Yet she overreaches when she asks him to give up his identity in a notarized act: using his identity to deny it. She asks him to "recognize that you are an impostor" (365), and plots with her own lawyer to have him locked up with the madmen at Charenton. Yet she gets her way not from a transaction but from Chabert's disgust at her duplicity, and his refusal of the "odious warfare" of litigation. He decides to "rentrer sous terre" (365)—to go back underground. And he in fact disappears, leaving even Derville baffled as to his fate.

The burden of negotiating Chabert's story with that which the comtesse wishes to impose appears to be too heavy: the personal is weighted by the sociohistorical, carrying a freight of political and cultural meaning. For all his willingness to have Derville attempt to turn his dramatic story into a socially acknowledged identity, Chabert remains fixed in the Napoleonic past. The loss of Napoleon, his supreme father, has also brought the loss of *patrie* and *patrimoine*, both irretriev-ably alienated. "Our sun has set, now we are all cold," Chabert says to Derville (Notre soleil s'est couché, nous avons tous froid maintenant; 331): the sun has set on an entire historical epoch, and its irreconcilable partisans now have entered an ice age. There is a continuing absolut-ism in Chabert's understanding of the world, familiar to psychoana-lysts working with patients who will not abandon past affects. His "Am I dead or am I alive?" is his bottom line. He doesn't want to put his watch ahead to Restoration standard time, and he finally gives up on the negotiation, abandoning his title and his very name, Chabert, to reassume simply the name assigned him in the orphanage, Hyacinthe.

The novel ends with an epilogue (added by Balzac on the print-er's proof of his novella), set in 1840, some twenty-two years after the main action. Derville and his associate Godeschal come upon a des-titute Chabert, seated before the old age hospice in Bicêtre, who has "fallen back into infancy" and fearfully denies his identity as Chabert, which has brought him nothing but litigation and trouble in the con-temporary world. "Not Chabert! Not Chabert! I'm named Hyacinth" (Pas Chabert! Pas Chabert! Je me nomme Hyacinthe), he exclaims in a kind of baby talk (372). And we are informed that Derville now tells Godeschal "the preceding story"—making the lawyer in the story the very author of the narrative. At its end, Derville laments that there are three figures in society who always wear black, as if in mourning for all virtues and all illusions: the priest, the doctor, and the lawyer. Of all of these, he says, the lawyer is the most unfortunate since he learns over and over again the worst traits of humanity. And he gives a brief litany of the horrors—culled from other novels of the *Comédie Humaine*—to which he has been privy. It is at the last the figure of the lawyer as novelist that emerges: the black-coated man of the law who knows all of society's sordid hidden stories.

Like the Balzac who invented him, Derville understands that to get at modern stories of personal identity one must make one's way through the narrow passages of the law. And Balzac is, of course, only one of several novelists one could choose in order to make the point;

Dickens is another (and Inspector Bucket of *Bleak House* one of the early police force detectives), and Collins is perhaps the most prominent case in that nearly all his fiction—*The Moonstone*, *The Woman in White*, and *The Lady and the Law* most prominently—turn on detecting identities and giving them legal solutions. Other sensation novelists of the Victorian age, such as Mary Elizabeth Braddon in *Lady Audley's Secret* and such French popular novelists as Alexandre Dumas (especially in *The Count of Monte Cristo*) and Eugène Sue (*The Mysteries of Paris*), explore nexuses of crime, policing, identity, and narrative. As, of course, does what we characterize more literally as "the detective story," from Edgar Allan Poe's invention of the genre in "The Murders in the Rue Morgue" (1841) to the classics of the form in the Sherlock Holmes tales of Arthur Conan Doyle, without neglecting the later French versions of Gaston Leroux (*Le Mystère de la chambre jaune*, 1907) and the creators of the Fantômas novels, Marcel Allain and Pierre Souvestre, who from the first volume in 1911 spun out a total of thirty-two.

As D. A. Miller argues in *The Novel and the Police*, the novel itself in the nineteenth century may be a reflection and an instrument of the policing power of the state, most potent when most hidden from view.[17] The social need to identify, to police, and to classify made the nexus of the lawyer and the policeman crucial, and also made the detective story the most characteristic invention of nineteenth-century literature. My sense of what this all points to finds confirmation in Ronald R. Thomas's assertion, in *Detective Fiction and the Rise of Forensic Science*, that the development of "the state" in the nineteenth century "involved the systematic transformation of the notion of the individual citizen's essential reality from something we call 'character' to something we came to call 'identity.'"[18] The state is not primarily interested in your "character," but it needs to know, to classify, and to keep watch over your identity. Yet it seems to me that the movement from character to identity—or perhaps more accurately, the specification of the most important and knowable aspect of character as "identity"—does not depend exclusively on the needs of the state. Already in Rousseau's self-examination—in the uniqueness of that mold in which nature formed him—we find that the sense of modern individuality points to the importance of the concept of identity: I am that person and not another. In this sense, the individual's sense of his or her identity seems to resist the state's classificatory impulse—which throws individuals into categories. Yet that may be illusory, since the sense that individuals have an identity feeds the need to find systems of classification.

The implications of the intersection of law and identity play themselves out throughout our modernity, and it would be interesting to pursue them all. Consider the single instance of marriage, the legalized form of desire and sexuality that offers the predominant plot structure of the nineteenth century, contract and transgression: the discovery of both desire and the law in adultery, and all the consequences for narratives of inheritance, property, money, sexual identity, self-definition.[19] As in *Chabert*, romance and legalism converge in a relationship that is disciplinary—heroines from Emma Bovary to Anna Karenina discover the wages of transgression—and yet also complicit. The contractual nature of the marriage bond may necessitate its breaking, while that breaking in a sense demonstrates the nature of the bond. All questions of who we are and what we want pass through the narrow straits, the *détroit*, to evoke a Lacanian image, of the law's definitions of the human. Increasingly rigid classifications of sexual identity, for instance, come by the end of the nineteenth century, and are acted out in the trial of Oscar Wilde. Now you must be homosexual or heterosexual: it is difficult to claim a mobile indeterminacy of orientation. The same is true of racial classifications—and here the latent anti-Semitism unleashed in France by the Dreyfus Affair at the end of the century may be the symbolic event, pointing to a dire future. The "identity politics" we now struggle with, and no longer exclusively in the United States, are one long-term consequence of the nineteenth-century obsession with classification and identification: a consequence that can result in the affirmation of diversity on the one hand and the practice of genocide on the other. There are many different, though intersecting, lines of identity to explore here. For now, let us return to the fingerprint story, which will lead us back to—and beyond—our starting point.

"Anthropometry, which is a mechanism for elimination, chiefly demonstrates *non-identity*," wrote Alphonse Bertillon, "while the direct *identity* is established by the peculiar marks, which alone can produce *judicial certitude*."[20] As Simon Cole notes in *Suspect Identities*, Bertillonage involved—as well as its famous bodily and cranial measurements—the careful recording of identifying marks: scars, birthmarks, tattoos, and the like. Though Bertillon reduced the notation of such marks and their location on the body to a precise shorthand, the system fell short of perfection. The recording of its data was painstakingly slow, and demanded rigorous training of its practitioners. Its classification and retrieval also demanded immense care: you had to be able to retrieve not simply by the suspect's name (since he was bound to be sporting an alias) but according to measurements, or ear configurations, or distinctive marks. The system worked, to a fair degree, but it was exasperating—even to its inventor, who railed against its sloppy use by poorly trained operators. The police detectives of Europe were ready for something better. The anthropology of their own criminal classes would be aided by colonial "anthropology."

If identification and triage of a European criminal population was difficult, the problem posed by the subject peoples of the colonies was far worse. To European eyes they all looked the same. They had no identifying marks. It was eventually an official of the British Raj in Bengal who "discovered" fingerprinting. It seems probable that Bengalis had long been using *tip sahi*, a kind of fingerprint signature. Their English rulers, who had been desperately trying to track identities among the population, adapted it to their own uses (then quarreled about which Brit had discovered it). The technique quickly migrated back to Europe. Systems were worked out for categorizing and retrieving prints according to type—here Francis Galton of the composite criminal photographs, who in 1892 published his book *Finger Prints*, was the key analyst and classifier, particularly intent on using fingerprints for social and racial classification. While Galton wanted to use fingerprints "to give to each human being an identity," he also thought they would establish racial identities. He was disappointed when he could not demonstrate hereditary and ethnic patterns in fingerprints, a research program more important to him than the identification of criminals. There is a disquieting historical link between the use of this kind of identificatory mark and racist classifications.[21]

Fingerprinting quickly became the queen of identifying marks, the key to criminology. Western cultures came to believe in those two infallible characteristics of fingerprints—their uniqueness and their permanency—and came to accept these truths perhaps more on faith than on evidence. When fingerprint evidence entered American courtrooms early in the twentieth century (the first convictions on fingerprint evidence seem to date from 1909 in Britain and 1910 in the United States) it was rapidly accepted—no doubt because it was so much needed and wanted—and never truly subjected to scientific testing. By the 1920s, the infallibility of such evidence was no longer in question. As Cole and other legal historians have noted, its acceptance was based on general cultural consensus, anecdotal evidence, and probabilistic statistics rather than on any rigorous testing of the ability of the experts to perform unquestionable identifications of "latent" crime-scene prints with their owners. The error rate in fingerprint identification is essentially unknown, and has never really been tested: the problem that worried Judge Pollak, and led to his first *Llera-Plaza* decision.[22] Fingerprinting continues much in use in forensics. Yet like other forms of evidence once—and still, to most law-enforcement agencies and the popular imagination—held to be infallible, such as confessions and eyewitness identifications, it may well be scheduled to be supplanted by techniques that come closer to our contemporary sense of science, such as DNA identification or optical scans.

Judge Pollak's first *Llera-Plaza* opinion suggested that the process of fingerprint identification belongs to Ginzburg's "hunter's paradigm," not to a harder science. It enchains a series of concrete particulars in a "case," and shows how they are linked to one another toward identification of an animal, or person, who has been there and left traces. We are, as in the detective story or the melodrama, in a paradigm of recognition by way of clues that become significant through a narrative sequencing. The significant bodily detail is, of course, the clue of clues—that which allows the body to "speak." Bertillon, like the Giovanni Morelli who was so important to art connoisseurs and to Sigmund Freud (we shall encounter him again in chapter 5) was particularly interested in ears, and the classification of their varieties, the subject of an elaborate morphology. It was inevitable that Arthur Conan Doyle should write a Sherlock Holmes tale in which two severed ears provide the sole evidence, "The Adventure of the Cardboard Box":

> As a medical man, you are aware, Watson, that there is no part of the body which varies so much as the human ear. Each ear is as a rule quite distinctive and differs from all other ones. In last year's *Anthropological Journal* you will find two short monographs from my pen upon the subject. I had, therefore, examined the ears in the box with the eyes of an expert and had carefully noted their anatomical peculiarities. Imagine my surprise, then, when on looking at Miss Cushing I perceived that her ear corresponded exactly with the female ear which I had just inspected. The matter was entirely beyond coincidence. There was the same shortening of the pinna, the same broad curve of the upper lobe, the same convolution of the inner cartilage. In all essentials it was the same ear.[23]

Miss Cushing is in this manner identified as sister to the woman murdered, along with her paramour, by her jealous husband. Science and detection are at ease with one another, identificatory paradigms unquestioned.

Yet "The Cardboard Box" ends with a curious questioning of the human nature that lies behind the production of such evidence: "'What is the meaning of it, Watson?' said Holmes solemnly as he laid down the paper. 'What object is served by this circle of misery and violence and fear? It must tend to some end, or else our universe is ruled by chance, which is unthinkable. But what end? There is the great standing perennial problem to which human reason is as far from an answer as ever'" (62). Are we to take this as a break in Victorian and

Edwardian confidence about the knowability of the universe, or simply as a rhetorical gesture toward the uncharted regions of human motivation that Freud was beginning to explore? One may want to read it as a sign that the most distinctive bodily symptoms, those most readable to crime detection, while leading with certainty to the identification of the criminal, nonetheless leave unsolved the deeper mysteries of human motivation. Not only does one need to make the body speak, it must be made to speak of that which the individual does not consciously know, the motives that produce criminal behavior that need to be classified and brought under control. The seen, the recorded, the classified has a way of throwing up new material from realms less visible and less directly detectable.

Our culture remains relentlessly visual. Yet perhaps because of the banality of the visible, the most probative clues to identity may lie beneath the surface, in a realm that needs to be pried open by new technologies of knowing. The problem surfaces in the law: do heat-sensing devices that will reveal the presence of heat lamps inside a house—used for growing marijuana, perhaps—require that the police, using such devices from a van parked across the street, obtain a search warrant for the premises?[24] The invention of the X-ray and its use in medical science quickly offered a metaphor for seeing through walls—Superman's specialty—and under the bodily integument, as in Thomas Mann's *The Magic Mountain* (*Der Zauberberg*, 1924), in which patients in the mountain sanatorium exchange not photos but X-rays of one another's chests. The scene in which Hans Castorp enters the radiology lab and views the beating heart of his cousin Joachim holds a powerful metaphorical significance—running the gamut from physiology to romance—of our understandings of "heart." It is a dramatic and prescient moment in a cultural movement beyond that which can be seen to a hidden, and possible truer, source of vitality, yet one now conceived not in the manner of Balzac's occult sources of power and energy but as an organ, however mysterious to most of us.

I mean to suggest that the identificatory paradigm may be shifting. We now tend more and more to believe that "truth" lies beyond the visual, in the evidence discovered through heat-imaging sensors, or in the codes read in DNA. The work of the Innocence Project at Cardozo Law School in freeing prisoners under mistaken conviction for crimes has offered a dramatic demonstration both of the new forensic technologies and of the suspicion that should be directed to the old, largely visual paradigms of identification. The visual alone no long satisfies us. Yet we have not moved out from the old visual paradigm—as the outraged reaction to Judge Pollak's attempt to demystify fingerprints shows. We are waiting for the development of a new paradigm in which we can have faith.

Yet faith in reassuring identificatory principles has always been contested, at least implicitly, by those who stand in the Rousseauian tradition of narrative self-inspection, who, like Rousseau himself, discovered that the encounter of knower with object of knowledge unsettles both, and casts the classic premises of identity into question. The most self-conscious of the modernists, such as Mann, reflect consciously on the problem—as, of course, does Freud, and also another master of modernist epistemological questionings, Marcel Proust. The opening pages of Proust's *In Search of Lost Time* (*A la Recherche du temps perdu*), to which I shall come back later on, are all about the unspecifiability and unlocatability of the *I* who speaks to us, who is analogized to the sleeper awakening in a strange place and posture, not knowing who or where he is. Proust deliberately confounds the protagonist *I*, "Marcel," and the narrating *I* by moving vertiginously in time, refusing to tell us when he is speaking from. And where it comes to knowing others the problem is compounded, since we never can quite gain access to the place in which identity—inner identity—establishes itself. Knowledge of others is made more complex by the phenomenon of sexual "inversion," as Proust calls it, appropriately since such a sexuality turns everything around, gives new valence to all social encounters, new identities that revise those we thought we knew. And such knowledge is made impossible by the very force of desire that it sparks. Of the dozens of passages that speak to this in Proust, let me cite only Marcel's first encounter with Albertine, who is part of the "*petite bande*" of girls in flower who materialize along the seafront in the Norman coastal resort, Balbec; it is an encounter that immediately provokes the question of what kind of cognizance she takes of her observer: "If she had seen me, what might I have represented to her? From the depths of what universe did she discern me?" He—"Marcel" and/or the narrator—continues,

> If we thought that the eyes of such a girl were merely two glittering sequins of mica, we should not be avid to know her life and to unite it to ours. But we sense that what shines in those reflecting discs is not due solely to their material composition; that they are the dark shadows, unknown to us, of the ideas that that person creates for herself about the people and places she knows . . . shadows also of the home she'll return to, of the plans that she is forming or that others have formed for her and above all that it is she herself, with her desires, her sympathies, her revulsions, her obscure and incessant will. I knew that I should never possess this young cyclist if I did not possess also what was in her eyes. And it was consequently her whole life that filled me with desire; a painful desire because I felt that it was not to be fulfilled, but an intoxicating one because, what had hitherto been my life having ceased of a sudden to be my whole life . . . offered me that prolongation, that possible multiplication of oneself, which is happiness.[25]

To know someone's identity on this model would require taking up residence in the place of the other's consciousness, inside her skull, a couple of inches behind her eyes. Marcel will eventually have to make Albertine his prisoner, and subject all her movements to something like police surveillance, in order to know her—but even that won't work. The possible multiplication of self called happiness is constantly undermined by the dark shadows, by the fact that knowledge of others, like their possession, always needs more to satisfy it, and in the process of searching for the more, opens itself to constant revision, to a fluidity that the *Recherche* enacts throughout.

Yet the impossibility doesn't kill Marcel's passionate, obsessive need to know, to perform again and again acts of voyeurism that use the identificatory paradigm to the hilt as they may also put its uses into question. The linkage of this kind of knowing to the revealing detail— the clue—and to narrative is in full display in Proust. While the glory of modernism, and even more the hero of our postmodernism, Proust also stands at the conclusion of an essentially Romantic tradition of self-knowledge inaugurated by Rousseau. As we await the coming of a new paradigm—if there is to be one—we may find ourselves at the tail end of that romantic tradition that wants to see our identities stamped, even indelibly and unalterably, on our fingertips.

As coda to the story so far, or perhaps more as poetic envoi, I am tempted to reach back to a Romantic poet, to John Keats and his poem "This Living Hand," probably the last lines he wrote, proffering, as to eternity, the reality of his fingertips as his identity, as poet and biographical person:

—see here it is—
I hold it towards you.

A powerful image to carry away—yet as a proof of identity, not enough. The anxiety, I think, is there behind Keats's haunting gesture: what's really to establish, to "prove" his identity?

There is a question about ourselves—which we roughly gesture at with the term "identity"—which cannot be sufficiently answered with any general doctrine of human nature.

—Charles Taylor, *Sources of the Self*

# 2 | Egotisms

Clues to who we are: that has long—at least since the time of Jean-Jacques Rousseau—been an object of our introspective imagination. John Locke, in his *Essay Concerning Human Understanding*, may be the first thinker to address the issue of our personal identity in a way that resonates with our modern conception. The *principium individuationis*, says Locke, is "existence itself"—that is, the continuous sameness of an entity or combination of particles throughout time.[1] What assures us as humans of a personal identity is our consciousness of our having had experiences in the past that we can recall as happening to us: "since consciousness always accompanies thinking," notes Locke, "and 'tis that that makes every one to be what he calls *self*, and thereby distinguishes himself from all other thinking things; in this alone consists *personal identity*, *i.e.* the sameness of a rational being: and as far as this consciousness can be extended backwards to any past action or thought, so far reaches the identity of that *person*; it is the same *self* now it was then; and it is by the same *self* with this present one that now reflects on it, that that action was done" (302; emphasis in the original). So that—and this will be crucial in all the authors under discussion—the sameness of the present self reflecting on the experiences of the past self is fundamental to the concept of identity, though it will pose its own problems.

Locke continues, "[I]t is by the consciousness it has of its present thoughts and actions, that it is *self* to *itself* now, and so will be the same *self*, as far as the same consciousness can extend to actions past or to come; and would be by distance of time, or change of substance, no more two *persons*, than a man be two men by wearing other clothes to-day than he did yesterday, with a long or a short sleep between: the same consciousness uniting those distant actions into the same *person*, whatever substances contributed to their production" (303; emphasis in the original). What we call personhood, then, derives from this pres-entness of the self to itself by way of consciousness that enables the extension back to a past self.

To quote Locke one more time,

> it is plain, consciousness, as far as ever it can be extended, should it be to ages past, unites existences and actions very remote in time into the same person, as well as it does the existences and actions of the immediately preceding moment: so that whatever has the consciousness of present and past actions, is the same person to whom they both belong. Had I the same consciousness that I saw the Ark and Noah's flood, as that I saw an overflowing of the Thames last winter, or as that I write now, I could no more doubt that I who write this now, that saw the Thames overflowed last winter, and that viewed the flood at the general deluge, was the same *self*, place that *self* in what substance you please, than that I who write this am the same *myself* now whilst I write (whether I consist of all the same substance, material or immaterial, or no) that I was yesterday. (307; emphasis in the original)

If Locke in this manner lays out the program of modern self-knowing as an act of consciousness uniting present to past selves, his bracing common sense will not be shared by all his posterity, many of whom will find that common consciousness of the present and past selves to be problematic, and the recovery of the sense of identity an active searching. Memory becomes a faculty as troubling as it is necessary. For David Hume as for Rousseau, selfhood is inconceivable without memory. Before coming back to Rousseau—and Sigmund Freud and Marcel Proust—consider for a moment the exemplary case of someone situated on the divide between the Enlightenment and the Romantic era for whom self-understanding was a constant imperative. Henri Beyle, aka Stendhal, repeatedly admonished himself in his diaries and other personal writings, usually in Latin or in Greek: *nosce te ipsum*, *gnothi seauton*: know thyself. He was trained by his enlightened grandfather in a tradition that believed knowledge of the human psyche—*la connaissance du coeur humain*—was the ideal of all analytic thinking. But it turned out not to be so easy.

At the outset of his fullest attempt at an autobiographical self-knowledge, Beyle describes standing on the Janiculum Hill in Rome one October morning in 1833 and discovering that he was about to turn fifty: "I am going to be fifty, it would be a good time to know myself."[2] Returning to his lodging in the Piazza Minerva that evening, Stendhal removed his belt and wrote inside it, "J. vaisa voirla5"—an encryption of the type he was so fond, easily deciphered as, "Je vais avoir la cinquaintaine" (I'm about to turn fifty). It's significant that the message to himself—a kind of Post-it note written on the available surface, then hidden from view—is encrypted and that it is written. As he says in an earlier autobiographical effort, he needs to make his "examination of conscience" with "pen in hand."[3] That is the way to know what you have been and who you are. Any available writing surface will do, but one that turns inward toward your body may be he best of all. Stendhal's pen also plays games with itself: as in the broad spectrum of pseudonyms he invented for himself over he course of his life, he turns to codes that both conceal and reveal.

In the very next chapter of *The Life of Henry Brulard*—the title intentionally misnames Henri Beyle, though again in a somewhat transparent encryption—we find him still thinking about writing his account of himself, now walking on the banks of Lake Albano. He inscribes in the dusty soil a string of initials: "V. A$^a$. A$^d$. M. M$^i$. A$^l$. A$^{ine}$. A$^{Pg}$. M$^d$. C. G. A$^{ur}$. (Mme Azur, dont j'ai oublié le nom de baptême)": initials of those he had loved, including at the end the doubly encrypted "Mme Azur"—in reality, Alberthe de Rubempré, whose first name he says he has forgotten. He then tells us that he had sex with only six of the list—numbers placed under their initials identify which ones—and proceeds to debate where his greatest passion lay: among Mélanie Guilbert, the first M. in the list, an actress whom he loved when in his twenties; Alexandrine Daru (A$^{ine}$); Métilde Dembowski (M$^i$), the aching passion of his Milanese years who would never give in; and Clémentine Curial (C.), the wildest of his loves (nine times in one night, he elsewhere recorded), the passionate countess who left him for a military officer, causing him the maximum pain of his love life—or was that instead Métilde's refusal to say she loved him? In any event, the string of letters in the sand plunges him into a reverie over the "astonishing stupidities and idiocies they made me commit (I say astonishing for myself, not for the reader, and moreover I don't regret any of it.)" (544).

Ordering the list—in the manner of the mathematician he once considered himself to be—is a way of taking control, and seeking to "destroy the charm, the *dazzling*" (in English) of his experiences with these women (544). But that control isn't really what Beyle wants. He wants to know himself, and that can only be accomplished through writing. When finished, in two or three years, only then will he finally be able to say who he is. That is a remarkable addendum to Locke: self-knowledge will come only after the completion of one's autobiographical exploration. The writing of self is critical. Yet it poses another problem: how to address a reader who will pick up your book—if anyone has published it—only fifty or more years after your death. "This is new for me; to speak to people whose cast of mind one doesn't know in the slightest, nor the education they've had, nor the prejudices, or the religion! What an encouragement to be *truthful*, and simply *truthful*, that's all that matters," Beyle writes (536–37). The descent into the self—into one's past to say who one is now—makes no sense unless it is pursued in the mode of absolute candor and freedom from hypocrisy. And yet Beyle at once reminds himself, "How many precautions are needed to avoid lying!" Often, he says, it's not the thing itself he remembers from his early life, but the memory of the image that he formed of the thing from the first narratives of it told to him (578): a kind of anticipation of Freud's notion of the "screen memory."

A first reading of *The Life of Henry Brulard* always provokes astonishment at the number and the importance of the line drawings, the sketches that Beyle intersperses in the text, in order to orient himself in the past scene he would evoke. And as he proceeds on the attempt to put together a coherent narrative of his past, it is another pictorial image that comes to represent the problem of memory: the frescoes of the Camposanto (the cemetery) of Pisa, where large portions have fallen away, leaving only incomplete figures: "I see images, I remember the effects things had on my heart, but as to causes and physical appearance, nothing. It's always like the frescoes at Pisa, where one perceives perfectly well an arm, and where the piece next to it that represented the head has fallen off. I see a series of *very clear* images but without their physiognomy other than that they had in regard to me. Even more, I see this physiognomy only by way of the memory of the effect it produced on me" (705; emphasis in the original). Again and again, he comes upon a fallen piece of fresco—where to fill in would be to become a novelist rather than a historian of the self. So that by the "end" of this book that does not end—that simply breaks off without reaching any satisfactory state of organization—Beyle notes, "All this, these are discoveries that I make in writing. Not knowing how to represent what happened, I give the analysis of what I was feeling at the time" (958). Retrieval of the past appears to be doubly mediated, through evocations of the emotions provoked by past happenings, by the discovery of those emotions, related to happenings, in the process of writing.

Those names of women loved, given in their initials, are an important measure of and counterweight to another problem of the script in pursuit of self-knowledge: the need to say *I* and *me* all the time. If the idea of writing his life pleases him, Beyle is put off by the consequence, "this fearsome quantity of *I* and *Me!* It's enough to put off the most benevolent reader." To be sure, one could use the third person—but then, "how to give an account of the inner motions of the soul?" he asks (533). Those pseudonyms that sign all of Beyle's writings—he never signed with his "own" name—may seem like a way out of the problem of egotism represented by the *I* and the *me*.[4] Beyle's earlier attempt at an autobiographical memoir bears the title *Recollections of Egotism* (*Souvenirs d'Egotisme*) as if precisely to own up to the problem of the self recounting the self. "What kind of a man am I?"(Quel homme suis-je?) he asks on the first page of *Souvenirs*. To answer this question the *I* needs to confront itself, or perhaps play tricks on itself, seeking through self-disguise to trick the self into self-betrayal. The most impressive modern novelist in the tradition of the quest for self-knowledge, Marcel Proust, will make a first assay of his narrative in a third-person account, *Jean Santeuil*, then return to the first person in *In Search of Lost Time* (*A la recherche du temps perdu*)—but a first person that turns out to be strangely disjointed, split between writer and actor in ways that purposely dissimulate the difference. To distinguish the knowing *I* from the *I* that is to be made known turns out to be both a necessary and an impossible task. The writing *I* keeps encountering itself—as in the young Rousseau's adventure with the apples and the spit, and the pen held by the older self (about which more later). Beyle writes in the final sentence of chapter 1 of *Henry Brulard*, "Mais je m'égare" (I wander from my track, I digress; 538). That will be a leitmotif: digression becomes a kind of literary form, a way to avoid a direct narrative of his life, which even if possible would seem irrelevant. It is the digressions of self-consciousness, the wanderings from the straight path of memory, that matter.

As for the frescoes of the Camposanto of Pisa, they return as a warning to stick to what can actually be seen in the eye of memory, not to reconstruct in the manner of an overambitious art restorer. Perhaps it is symptomatic that the first time he mentions the frescoes, he leaves a blank where the word *camposanto*—cemetery—should stand, as if in forgetful avoidance of what the cemetery represents, though the next time he mentions the frescoes *camposanto* is there, underlined. It is interesting also that Beyle, connoisseur of Italian art, didn't like these frescoes. Yet he chooses them—over other examples of semidestroyed artworks that might have been available—to represent the problems of memory struggling with the restoration or reconstruction of the past. Their very unpleasantness may be important—and may make one want to think ahead, to Freud's "forgetting" of the name of the artist Luca Signorelli, creator of the terrifying frescoes of the *Last Judgment* in the Duomo of Orvieto.⁵ The self-knowledge game is dangerous: it seems somehow to cohabit with the end of life, the extinction of the ego. The Pisa frescoes included work by Taddeo Gaddi, Spinello Aretino, and Benozzo Gozzoli—but even more impressive, by an anonymous fourteenth-century artist known as "The Master of the Triumph of Death," for the much decayed but in Beyle's time still striking representation of death's dominion. The composer Franz Liszt was inspired by it to compose—more or less on the spot—his *Dance of Death* (*Totentanz*). Would it have been a consolation to Beyle to know that the frescoes were destroyed by an Allied bombing raid on July 27, 1944? Probably the opposite.

Stendhal's worries about the effect of too much *I* and *me* on his readers may point to an insuperable problem in that the most basic definition of the self may be simply: the person who says "I." In Locke's words again, "since consciousness always accompanies thinking, and 'tis that that makes everyone to be what he calls *self*; and thereby distinguishes himself from all other thinking things; in this alone consists *personal identity*, *i.e.* the sameness of a rational being. . . ." The notable French linguist Émile Benveniste argues that human subjectivity is in fact constituted in language: it depends on the capacity of the speaker to say "I". "Is 'ego' who *says* 'ego.' Here we find the foundation of subjectivity, which is determined by the linguistic status of the 'person.' "⁶ But this *I* is not conceivable without a listener to whom it speaks, an interlocutor: *I* implies *you*, and when *I* falls silent and the interlocutor speaks, the *you* becomes *I* and the *I* takes on the role of *you*. So that subjectivity, in its linguistic understanding, is at bottom intersubjectivity, a correlation of two grammatical "persons." For Benveniste, the person represented by the pronoun *I* is not a concept; it has no signified, only a referent—which is simply that of the person currently speaking, who appropriates for the moment the language system to his own discourse, then surrenders it to whoever else takes the floor, or "takes the word," as the French expression has it.

Benveniste's structuralist and minimalist definition of the ego as founded on the use of pronouns in situations of speaking (and listening) has a kind of bracing quality when set beside various Romantic anguishes about the self, its knowledge, and its fate. At the same time, Benveniste's minimalism may confirm Stendhal's perception that the self can unfold to itself only in the process of writing, in a kind of interlocution of a present *I* and a past *I* that, for the occasion, assumes the position of *you*. Stendhal's cryptograms on his belt and in the dirt of the lakeshore figure the need for an actively discursive *I*, a writing *I*, to go after the *I* of the past. Memory itself, the guarantor of our self-sameness, depends on an active self-construction.

Stendhal's complex egotism would show him to be, if we didn't know it from other declarations, a thorough reader of Rousseau. When Julien Sorel, near the start of *The Red and the Black* (*Le Rouge et le noir*) is asked whether he will accept a position as tutor in the upper-crust family of the Rênal—his start on the path to glory and self-destruction—his first reaction is, "Whom will I eat with?" (Avec qui mangerai-je?). He needs the assurance that he will dine with the family, not the domestic servants. This reaction, we are told, is not natural, but instead a result of reading Rousseau's *Confessions*, one of his principal optics on reality, along with Napoleon's memoirs. The reaction shows a good understanding of Rousseau, who is perpetually finding himself dining with the domestics, claiming that he is out of his rightful place, and seeking ways to reclaim it—operating always with a slight disjuncture from what he sees as his "true" identity. He falls in love, for instance, with daughters of noble houses in which he is a servant.

The reclamation of his rightful place—in the eyes of posterity if not of his contemporaries—is a principal motive for Rousseau's writing of the *Confessions*. Stendhal's paternalistic narrator, both censuring and affectionate toward Julien, criticizes a worldview derived from Rousseau. And Stendhal's own enthusiasm for Rousseau was more and more tempered by his critique of Rousseau's *emphase*, his overstatement, his rhetorical overkill. Stendhal's writing has a cool that is quite alien to Rousseau. And yet, despite the critique, Rousseau remains a touchstone of true emotion. At the end of Stendhal's unfinished novel *Lucien Leuwen* (written between *The Red and the Black* and *The Charterhouse of Parma* [*La Chartreuse de Parme*]), Lucien flees the important political position he's attained in Paris to seek solitude—and love—on the banks of Lake Geneva, and visits the sites made famous in Rousseau's one novel, *Julie, or the New Héloise* (*Julie, ou la Nouvelle Héloïse*). And in *The Charterhouse of Parma* also, the phrase in which Clélia Conti admits to her passion for Fabrice comes straight from Rousseau's novel: "You have a beautiful soul" (Vous avez une belle âme), she tells him; the beautiful souls, who have so much trouble getting together on this earth, derive directly from Rousseau's theories of the human heart, and when Stendhal forgets to be the ironist, he signs on to this romantic knowing.

Where Stendhal is appalled at the profusion of *I*'s and *me*'s required in the introspective enterprise, Rousseau defiantly displays his egotisms from the very first words of his *Confessions*: "I undertake an enterprise that has never had a precedent and will never have an imitator. I wish to display to my fellow men a man in all the truth of his nature; and that man will be myself." Note the movement from "fellow men" (mes semblables) to "a man," to "that man" and, finally, "myself." Think, in contrast, of Alexander Pope's lines in his *Essay on Man*:

Know then thyself; presume not God to scan.
The proper study of mankind is man.

Rousseau's optics of the study of mankind zooms in, perversely, on a single man, who turns out to be *myself, I,* the speaker of these words.

This movement is repeated in the next paragraph: "Myself alone [Moi seul]. I feel my heart, and I know other men. I am not made like any of those that I have seen; I dare believe that I am not made like any other being. If I am not more worthy, at least I am other. Whether nature did well or ill in breaking the mould in which I was formed is something that can be judged only after having read me."[7] Here, I think, is the very fountainhead of modernity. Rousseau's audacious claim to know other men by way of knowing his own feelings opens up a new epistemology that has been variously viewed as dangerous or revelatory by his follow-ers—as I think we all still are, whether of his camp or that of his most bitter opponents, who are as right as his apologists in claiming that the modern insistence on the individual personality (in a gamut run-ning from human rights discourse to narcissistic self-absorption and self-justification) derive from Rousseau's insistence on his own right to the interpretation of others in a perspective starting in his own truth as known in his inward feelings.[8] He is unique—which seems a strange grounding for the claim to know others, but will prove nonetheless a durable claim to the right to one's own perspective in the interpreta-tion of life and the pursuit of happiness (Stendhal's definition of char-acter: the way someone goes about the pursuit of happiness, *la chasse du bonheur*).

The image of the broken mold, like the sculptor's mold (the story of Pygmalion, from which Rousseau made an opera, may lie in the background here), evokes, as I mentioned earlier, a famous phrase from a famous precursor in self- examination, Michel de Montaigne. "Each man bears the stamp of the whole human condition" (Chaque homme porte la forme entière de l'humaine condition), he wrote, in a fine ex-pression of the Renaissance humanist's creed. But to Rousseau, the creed is false. The stamp—as in an impress, on a coin perhaps, which takes us back to etymological meanings of the word *character*—that implies sameness, interchangeability, falsifies for Rousseau the essen-tial difference of each human being. The similarities of human animals are real enough, and allow us to coexist—to form a social contract, for instance, in which each of us surrenders some autonomy in order to contribute to the general will—but they don't erase the uniqueness of each individual alive, or who has ever lived. What could be more characteristic of the beliefs on which modern liberal societies—and their educational philosophies—are founded? Even in the utopian world of fiction, in *Julie*, where Julie d'Etange forms around herself at Clarens a society of *les belles âmes*, it cannot endure. It is always on the verge of being undermined by a more individual claim to happiness—by a world-annihilating eros. As Julie reveals in her testamentary letter, the repression required to keep the social compact going is more than she can stand. Death seems the better option. We are already underway toward Richard Wagner's *Tristan und Isolde*, the world kicked aside in *Liebestod*.

Rousseau's egotism next (returning to the first page of his *Confessions*) stages a future encounter with his maker, the Eternal Being whom he will meet on the Judgment Day—with this book, his *Confessions*, in hand. This surely is the first moment in history when someone invokes the right to present himself at the Last Judgment with a book that he claims will justify him—that will show, at least, that he is no worse than his fellow human beings. And that claim, we are told, is based on the transparency of what he has presented in his writing: the total unveiling of himself before his reader—who is pressed into service as a kind of precursor or anticipation of that Eternal Being. If the Protestant Reformation brings with it a new bookishness, a sense of communion with oneself often expressed in the spiritual autobiography or allegory—John Bunyan's *Pilgrim's Progress* (1678–84) is the best known—I don't think anyone before Rousseau claimed that the book he had written would serve as self-justification before the throne of God. Here, too, we are at the very origins of the modern sense of the self and its claim to autonomy and justification through sincerity. The aesthetics of transparency that are crucial to Rousseau's enterprise—"I would like to render my soul transparent to the reader's eye," he tells us in book 4 of the *Confessions*—are themselves the justification of the confessional enterprise. To be able to say everything—this ambition to *tout dire* becomes a leitmotif of the book—about yourself, to lay bare your shortcomings and indignities, your thefts and your sexual aberrations, becomes for Rousseau the very criterion of *authenticity*, as a later generation would name it. And I think we still today subscribe to this notion, with however many reservations and world-weary acknowledgments that authenticity only get you so far. Still, if the characteristic ideology of the present moment is a concern with global human rights, one must say that the very basis of the concern is the Rousseauian notion of the irreducible individual identity.

The Lockean account of personal identity, which might be said to undergird both Rousseau's affirmation of unchanging selfhood and his anxiety about its possible loss, has been criticized, and may no longer be the standard account: Bernard Williams, for instance, defends a bodily criterion of personal sameness, and Derek Parfit argues that the problems that result from thinking about any account, psychological or physical or any variant thereof, suggest the unimportance of the question.[9] As another philosopher, Eric Olson notes, it is hard to say what our identity over time consists in: "Of course, we are the beings we refer to when we say 'I,' or more generally the beings that our personal pronouns and proper names refer to; but it is unlikely, on this view, that our personal pronouns succeed in referring to just one sort of thing. Each utterance of a personal pronoun will probably refer ambiguously to many different candidates: to various sorts of psychologically interrelated aggregates, to an animal, and perhaps to others as well. That would make it indeterminate which things, even which kind of things, we are."[10] This may confirm the minimalist view of Benveniste while also arguing that some version of Locke's account, however modified and fluid, remains useful. Any further attempts to answer take one deep into metaphysics.

There would be more, much more, to say about Rousseau, the *Confessions*, and his other autobiographical writing, but I want to postpone that in order to bring to bear on the notion of individual identity, what it is and how we know it, a latter-day disciple of Rousseau who acknowledges his debt to his precursor only in somewhat marginal ways:

Sigmund Freud. Perhaps the most obvious place to look for the place of identity in Freud might be in what he has to say—throughout his career—about the ego, and particularly what he calls, in the key essay *The Ego and the Id* (1923), the "dependent relations of the ego"—that is to say, in particular, its far from easy relations to the id and to the superego.[11] The id, from which the ego originally emerges, is the realm of drives that push, lawlessly, to their own ends. The superego is "the heir of the Oedipus complex" (*Standard Edition* 19:36), by which Freud means that it represents the internalization of the child's passage through the oedipal drama, very much including internalization of paternal authority as interdiction ("thou shalt not have the mother"). In Lacanian language, what's at issue is "the name of the father": the father as the forceful abstraction we call law. It is the realm of "morality," but a morality that can be censorious and punishing, representing an unbridgeable gap between ideal and actual performance.

Freud images the relation of the ego to the id as a rider on a horse—controlling the force of the more powerful animal, but at times only apparently so: "Often a rider, if he is not to be parted from his horse, is obliged to guide it where it wants to go; so in the same way the ego is in the habit of transforming the id's will into action as if it were its own" (*SE* 19:25). The ego, that is, exercises its control only by acting as if it wanted what in fact the id demands. Two other images extend this view of the ego in relation to the id later in the essay. First, "in the matter of action, the ego's position is like that of a constitutional monarch, without whose sanction no law can be passed but who hesitates long before imposing his veto on any measure put forward by Parliament" (*SE* 19:55). The very existence of a constitutional monarch depends on his popularity with the parliament—to lock horns with the parliament would be to risk exposure of the monarch's fundamental weakness. This political situation suggests Freud's subsequent image for the ego: "In its position midway between the id and reality, it only too often yields to the temptation to become sycophantic, opportunist and lying, like a politician who sees the truth but wants to keep his place in popular favour" (*SE* 19:56).

These are fairly harsh judgments of the place and the power of the ego in its own house, so to speak—in relation to the forces it must deal with every day. The judgments offer an approach to what may be the most famous of Freud's statements on the subject of the ego: "Wo es war, soll Ich werden" (Where id was shall ego come to be). The phrase has been interpreted—especially in American ego psychology, focused on strengthening the ego in its conflicts with id and superego—as an optimistic humanist affirmation. Ultimately, the statement seems to suggest, we can become masters in our own house—make the ego take over control from the id. Things may not be so simple. Take, for an example to work on, Freud's fullest statement of the dogma, from his *New Introductory Lectures on Psychoanalysis* (1933), in lecture 31 (which is indeed derived from *The Ego and the Id*):

> Wo es war, soll Ich werden. Es ist Kulturarbeit etwa die Trockenlegung der Zuydersee.

> Where id was, there ego shall be. It is a work of culture—not unlike the draining of the Zuider Zee. (*SE* 22:80)

I am sure that Freud expected his readers to register an allusion here to part 2 of Johann Wolfgang von Goethe's *Faust* in which the restless, striving hero turns from the private to the social world and undertakes a vast project of reclaiming land from the sea by way of dikes and drainage. Faust here overcomes the metaphysics of personal fulfillment in a social project, in a piece of *Kulturarbeit* that enlists the ego in larger human benefaction. And yet, his reclamation of land from the sea is also a project executed with a certain brutality and disregard for human consequences. And in a sardonic aside, Mephistopheles makes it clear that holding the sea in check is ultimately a futile enterprise. The waves will return to conquer the land.

The mention of *Faust*—a text Freud cites more often than any other, though more usually in part 1 than part 2—again suggests that the "cultural work" achieved by the ego has a somewhat unstable and uncertain status. Freud's conception of the human subject is deeply Faustian.

In what may be his boldest essay on the life of that subject, *Beyond the Pleasure Principle* (1920), he analyzes with skepticism what is often seen as a drive toward perfection in human beings, claiming that it is really a dynamic created by the difference between the instinctual pleasure we demand and that we achieve: the result is "the driving factor which will permit of no halting at any position attained, but, in the poet's words, "presses ever forward unsubdued" (ungebändigt immer vowärts dringt; *SE* 18:42). It is not insignificant that the words cited belong to Mephistopheles (part 1, scene 4). Freud is usually most at home in the role of Mephistopheles, proposing what we might almost call a "deconstructive" reading of human claims to perfection, mastery, and culture.

Jacques Lacan, in his glosses on Freud, repeatedly makes the case for a darker, gloomier reading of the "Wo es war" dictum. I have noticed three different translations Lacan proposes for the dictum (there are further variations I've passed over). They are not without a certain teasing interest. First, in 1955, in the essay "La chose freudienne" (The Freudian Thing): "Là où c'était, peut-on dire, là où s'était, voudrions-nous faire qu'on entendît, c'est mon devoir que je vienne à être." I paraphrase rather than attempting (a very difficult) translation: "There where it was, one could say, there where being was, one should understand, it is my duty to come to be." The hooker here is *s'était*, using the verb "to be" in a kind of impossible reflexive construction, to suggest the mere presence of the self's coming into being. Then, in 1957, in another essay, "L'instance de la lettre" (The Agency of the Letter): "Là où fut ça, il me faut advenir" (There where it [id] was I [ego] must happen [or: emerge]). Lacan uses the old Latinate verb *advenir*: to arrive, to come upon, to happen, to emerge. Finally in 1965, in "La Science et la vérité" (Science and Truth): "là où c'était, là comme sujet dois-je advenir" (there where it was, there as subject I must happen).[12]

So it is that Freud's dictum may be read (as in ego psychology) as a rationalist-humanist declaration of the work of ego as cultural progress and mastery: the ego over the id; or, as in Lacan, as a recognition of the need imposed on the subject—the *I*, the ego—to "happen" in the place marked out by the id, by this impersonal other(ness) of the *ça*, the "it"—to emerge, to come to being where the id has dictated. I would argue that many, perhaps all, of the most probative attempts at understanding the self in our culture—the ones that matter most to us—make something like this discovery, in some form. The individual comes into being, into its identity, in a system that preexists his or her existence: a system that can at one end of the spectrum be considered the ensemble of biological forces (including the inevitable death of the organism), and on the other end the elaborate cultural system we call language, in all its properties. We come into being in a language that already has its rules, and to the extent that we can make a personal utterance, it must conform to those rules—or break them only in comprehensible ways. The place for self-invention may be wholly real but quite limited. We are spoken by the language that we speak: we are creatures of its rules and systems, as we are of biological necessities.

This oscillation and ambiguity in the interpretation of relations of ego and id is not to be evacuated or explained away: it is central to Freud's thought, and the Kulturarbeit accomplished by the ego is always exacted at a high cost (here *Civilization and Its Discontents*, 1930, ratifies the findings of *Faust*, part 2), and always threatened by the pressure of instinctual forces, drives—as the First World War so amply demonstrated to Freud. "All individual moral acquisitions are obliterated, and only the most primitive, the oldest, the crudest mental attitudes are left," he writes in *Thoughts for the Time on War and Death* in 1915. War returns us to a primitive dichotomy in which we wish death on our enemies and deny its relevance to ourselves, to the point where Freud asks whether we need to give into the cultural "regression" brought by war: "Should we not confess that in our civilized attitude towards death we are once again living psychologically beyond our means?" (*SE* 14:299). In his most disillusioned moments, Freud tends to see Kulturarbeit as a grim illusion, a dike that can't keep the flood waters out for long, and moreover demands a further price because of its very illusiveness, its tricking us into thinking we are masters where we aren't.

Freud's repeated recourse to quotation from Goethe and other of the "poets and philosophers" he claims were his true precursors suggests that his response to the tenuousness of identity, and of the culture in which it comes into being, is one that has made a special claim to attention since the Romantics, and maybe found its most ardent spokesman in Friedrich Nietzsche: the claim, as Charles Taylor puts it, of the "Romantic ideal of self-completion through art."[13] If we can attempt to complete ourselves through art, this may include the aesthetic mastery of our own existence and identity: the capacity to relate the story of the self in a coherent and meaningful narrative. As Freud noted as early as his case history of *Dora* (1905), his patients came to him with broken-down narratives, stories that did not make sense of their lives, stories that were noncreative. The stories told by neurotic patients, he writes, "may be compared to an unnavigable river whose stream is at one moment choked by masses of rock and at another divided and lost among shallows and sandbanks" (*SE* 7:16). The connections among events are faulty, the narrative glue that should hold them together intelligibly has disintegrated. The modern sense of individual identity puts this burden on us: that we must negotiate a certain intelligibility of the self from birth to imagined death in order to affirm its coherence. Those who have best understood their own egotism—such as Stendhal, Rousseau, and Proust—have seen it as a negotiation of ego, id, and superego rather than as the superficial claim to ego mastery that in fact simply unleashes aggression within societies, the will for power over others.

The modern issue of identity came for a time to focus on what Erik Erikson named an "identity crisis"—and this form of the problem still is with us. Developed originally during the Second World War (as Freud's deepest insights derived from the First) to describe the experience of veterans who had lost "a sense of personal sameness and historical continuity," the term expanded to refer in particular to a life stage, the adolescent's encounter with the problem of selfhood.[14] For Erikson, as for Freud, the issue of identity is both individual and cultural. Explaining why the problem of identity "is so all-pervasive and yet so hard to grasp," Erikson writes, "we deal with a process 'located' *in the core of the individual* and yet also *in the core of his communal culture*, a process which establishes, in fact, the identity of those two identities."[15] There is a version of Benveniste's intersubjectivity here, as of Taylor's claim that the self emerges from "webs of interlocution."[16] To Erikson's foregrounding of the psychic and cultural problem of identity one may add Robert J. Lifton's reflections on "the protean self": the human capacity to undergo transformations that may be destructive or renewing, and particularly human resilience in the face of necessities for transformation.[17]

As representatives of the need to write the story of the self in order to understand its identity, Rousseau and Stendhal both show to a high degree the work of the shaper on the shaped: the presence of the retrospective narrator and creator of the tale of the self. Rousseau's doubts about the total recovery of the past tend to be met by his arrogant but unconvincing assertions of reliability. Trust me, he implicitly says over and over, that in the essentials I have told you everything, and that it all hangs together as the story of a human being in all his imperfections—which indeed stand as guarantor of its truth and authenticity. Stendhal, who spent some years of his life living as a "dandy," exercising aesthetic mastery of his appearance and style in living, also and more durably spends much of his time contemplating the self-knowledge project: noting that it is time to know himself, sketching in the dirt the names that form the chain of his affections and erotic attachments, making diagrams of places and events, returning again and again to the very process of remembering and memorializing: "Je m'égare": I wander from the point—if the point can be defined as a step-by-step narrative of his life. But the wanderings are, of course, a large part of the point, as Proust's narrator will come to understand. If the self would tell its story to and for itself, that story will end up being as much about the narrator as the narrated, as much about the creator as the created.

This instance of egotism, this self-reflexiveness and self dramatization of the speaker, may, as Stendhal most acutely senses but Rousseau and Freud are also aware, have to do with the newness, the lack of precedent of their enterprise. All three might be characterized as what Alain Badiou has called "antiphilosophers," along with such others as Søren Kierkegaard, Nietzsche, and Saint Paul. For Badiou, "it is of the essence of antiphilosophy that the subjective position figure as a decisive factor in the discourse."[18] Such speakers cannot rely on a tradition to support them since they represent a break in tradition. "For an antiphilosopher," Badiou continues, "the enunciative position is obviously part of the statement's protocol. No discourse can lay claim to truth if it does not contain an explicit answer to the question: Who speaks?" I think it is precisely because Stendhal, Rousseau, Freud (and also Proust) are deeply committed to persuading us of the truth claim of their probes into the self that they must face explicitly the question of who speaks—most pertinently in the form, Who writes?

This returns us to the status of the *I* in discourse evoked, in different ways, by Locke and by Benveniste. Rousseau, Stendhal, Freud, and Proust all write in a high awareness of the position of that *I*, in relation to a listener/reader, as well as to its earlier manifestations, the *I* being written about. Stendhal is clearly embarrassed by this form of egotism—he'd rather not write *I* and *me* all the time, but he recognizes the necessity if he is to make himself known. Rousseau, for whom confessing is often an exhibitionist act, doesn't mind. In fact, the confrontation of *I* with *me* constitutes much of the drama of the *Confessions*, the challenge to dare to know and to say all. For Freud and Proust, as we shall see, there may be a more complex game of hiding and revealing who writes. But for all of them, the question Badiou raises about the apostle Paul remains key: their enterprise depends on an acute awareness and a staging of "Who speaks?"

Odysseus when he returns to Ithaca must be discovered, revealed—by his old nurse Eurykleia recognizing his ancient scar under her fingertips as she washes the feet of this apparent stranger, and then by the test of the making of the marriage bed set by Penelope. He knows who he is; he simply must make it clear to others. He belongs to a world in which heroes, when they meet on the battlefield, begin by proclaiming their patronymics: they can say who they are by way of the lineage they are called upon to illustrate. For Rousseau and the moderns, the process is one of self-discovery, self-recognition, self-declaration, and a tenuous holding on to identity within temporal flux. Freud very much situates himself in this tradition.

Yet Freud will also reach back, again and again, to the Greek culture—or, more accurately, the nineteenth-century European version of Greek culture that dominated his education—to anchor his "scientific" discoveries about human behavior in mythic creations. Here again, we sense that Freud is best characterized as a kind of tragic humanist: he is drawn to texts that tell of the limits of human freedom. "He solved the riddle of the sphinx, and became a man most mighty": so read the inscription on the medal presented to Freud by his followers on his fiftieth birthday—a presentation that made him go pale and nearly lose consciousness. He had indeed been searching for the riddle of the sphinx. But to be identified with the riddle-answerer Oedipus implied the rest of that story, too: What good is such knowledge—the chorus puts it to us—when it leads only to suffering? And indeed, to knowledge of the self's identity as unutterably confused, at once son and husband, father and brother, sower where he himself was sown:

> loathed by the gods, son of the mother I defiled
> coupling in my father's bed, spawning lives in the loins
> that spawned my wretched life. What grief can crown this grief?
> It's mine alone, my destiny—I am Oedipus![19]

Wisdom not only comes with suffering: when it comes, it is radically unusable. Freud finds his bedrock for human identity in certain stories that seem fated, inevitable, a pattern of human existence—especially the story of Oedipus of Thebes.

Freud is a tragic humanist, at one with the long tradition in Western culture that dissents from any facilely optimistic understanding of human identity. In his discovery, provoked by the tragic betrayal of European civilization of the Great War, that we may be living "psychologically beyond our means," he implicitly asks whether egotisms have any lasting value, whether they are not simply illusions. Eventually, in 1930—as Europe began its slide toward a yet darker abyss—Freud came back to what we might call the poorly regulated economics of the self in culture in *Civilization and Its Discontents. Das Unbehagen in der Kultur*: Freud's title is in reverse of its English translation: "Malaise in Culture" would be a more literal (though less good) translation. It may today be the book of Freud's most widely read outside professional psychoanalytic circles: a favorite of college curricula, and for good reason: its message seems to have been largely confirmed by world history in the three quarters of a century since its publication.

That message is in essence that civilization, or culture, itself says no to the egotisms it encourages and fosters. The need for instinctual renunciation on which society and culture are founded exacts an enormous toll, substituting for the immediate gratification of the senses a "higher" goal that may be illusory. Indeed, exacting a toll becomes an active function of the superego. Conscience is not simply the product of renunciation; renunciation creates conscience, which then in its turn demands further renunciation. The punishing aggression of the very agency of civilizing, of law-making—the superego—creates a superabundance of guilt, which to Freud becomes the central issue of civilization, and the possibilities of its survival. As he writes in the summary he provides at the end of his next-to-last chapter,

> Since civilization obeys an internal erotic impulse which causes human beings to unite in a closely-knit group, it can only achieve this aim through an ever-increasing reinforcement of the sense of guilt. What began in relation to the father is completed in relation to the group. If civilization is a necessary course of development from the family to humanity as a whole, then—as a result of the inborn conflict arising from ambivalence, of the eternal struggle between the trends of love and death—there is inextricably bound up with it an increase of the sense of guilt, which will perhaps reach heights that the individual finds hard to tolerate. (*SE* 21:133)

Freud has worked himself into one of those paradoxes, those knots, that his thought so often produces: the civilization that ought to be the solution to human aggressivity becomes its enabler and its condition.

We are in many ways back with Rousseau—especially the Rousseau of the *Discourse on the Origin of Inequality* (*Discours sur l'origine de l'inégalité*) and *The Social Contract* (*Du contrat social ou Principes du droit politique*)—in the perception of the divide between what we want as human animals and what we are required to want as members of civilization. Rousseau's mythic "state of nature"—a thought experiment for explaining how people entered a law-governed social compact and then suffered from it—comes to appear as an ideal over and against the poor track record of cultural progress in promoting happiness. As Freud writes in the final chapter of *Civilization and Its Discontents*, "It almost seems as if the creation of a great human community would be most successful if no attention had to be paid to the happiness of the individual" (*SE* 21:140). Rousseau made the same claim, and drew the political consequence: that the social contract requires the renunciation of that which would make us happiest as unsocialized egos.[20] When the Jacobins who claimed him as their inspiration sought, during the most radical moment of the French Revolution, to create their "Republic of Virtue," it was on the understanding that the discontents of virtue as defined must necessarily be purged from the social body. There could be no room for individual wills outside the general will. As Maximilien Robespierre's lieutenant—and the most eloquent of the Jacobin orators—Louis de Saint-Just put it in lapidary style: "The Republic has for its principle virtue; or if not, terror."[21] To which he appends the rhetorical question, "What do they want who want neither virtue nor terror?" Happiness, maybe, but of a type unthinkable within the Republic of Virtue.

I do not mean this as one more attempt to pin Jacobin terrorism on Rousseau, who after all argued that pity, or empathy, should be considered a primary human instinct or drive along with self-preservation and who would surely have found the reign of the guillotine a horrifying perversion of his thought. It is more interesting to ask what Rousseau would have thought of the footnote that Freud appends to his statement that advance in civilization is accompanied by a loss of happiness through the heightening of a sense of guilt: "That the education of young people at the present day conceals from them the part which sexuality will play in their lives is not the only reproach which we are obliged to make against it. Its other sin is that it does not prepare them for the aggressiveness of which they are destined to become the objects. In sending the young out into life with such a false psychological orientation, education is behaving as though one were to equip people starting on a Polar expedition with summer clothing and maps of the Italian Lakes" (*SE* 19:134, n. 1). More optimistic than Freud, perhaps, Rousseau in his *Émile* traces an education designed to produce a young man who will learn sexuality only quite belatedly, and whose aggressive instincts will be well mastered in order that he be a productive citizen. But Rousseau would, I think, have recognized the truths of Freud's comment.

*Civilization and Its Discontents* ends with the tragically prescient recognition, "Men have gained control over the forces of nature to such an extent that with their help they would have no difficulty in exterminating one another to the last man" (*SE* 19:145). This, a little over a decade before the Manhattan Project would unleash the means of extermination in undreamt of potency. Freud has at this point been examining the "most recent of the cultural commands of the superego, the commandment to love one's neighbour as oneself" (*SE* 19:143)—to conclude that this rule cannot be obeyed. In the debate about whether the advance of civilization has been worth the unhappiness it caused— and whether the "advance" was in any case inevitable, or on the other hand could have taken a different course—Freud can offer no answer. Nor can he act the "prophet" to his fellow humans: "I bow to their reproach that I can offer them no consolation: for at bottom that is what they are all demanding—the wildest revolutionaries no less passionately than the most virtuous believers" (*SE* 19:145).

Freud is unable to sign on to the consolations offered by socialism and communism—and by religion. His refusal of religious belief— omnipresent in his thought, but most fully explored in *The Future of an Illusion* (1927) and, at the very end of his life, *Moses and Monotheism* (1938)—marks him off from Rousseau, who precisely in *Émile* introduces his Savoyard pastor to reveal the religious underpinnings of nature. Freud's ultimate reflections on Moses, monotheism, guilt, and ethics will be worth returning to. In terms of egotisms, both he and Rousseau would understand and censure what we find Stendhal proposing in the figure of his hero Julien Sorel. That might be described (I refer here to some suggestive comments by André Malraux) as the attempt at the deification of the individual personality.[22] It responds to the satanic temptation: Ye shall be as gods. Julien undertakes a kind of self-mastery that is heroic—though not necessarily of itself productive of happiness, which demands more *naturel*, the capacity to enjoy the pleasure one has conquered. Yet the self-conquest is imperative to conquering that place in which happiness might occur. But Julien Sorel is decapitated on the guillotine, and the presentation of his trial and execution in *The Red and the Black* seems the very triumph of the superego, the victory of a repressive social formation and the triumph of the law of the father—of Sorel *père*, whom Julien has always detested, and repudiated through the hypothesis of illegitimacy. But the elder Sorel by the end literally inherits from his son, when Julien goes to the guillotine. If Stendhal is an obsessive analyst of egotisms, he as much as Rousseau and Freud is aware of the small place accorded to their real needs for happiness—as opposed to their aggression—in what Freud calls the "pathology of cultural communities." Like the dandy that he was for a period of his existence, Stendhal attempts to take himself out of community pathology, to live in devotion to "the happy few" to whom he dedicates all his books. But his imagined heroes, his fictional selves, do not end their lives in happiness.

Malraux's diagnosis—presented in analysis of the Vicomte de Valmont and the Marquise de Merteuil in Pierre Choderlos de Laclos's *Les Liaisons dangereuses*, whom he sees as precursors to the concerted, voluntaristic heroes of Stendhal—could no doubt be applied to many of the heroes of modernity (including Malraux's own, and himself). The aspiration to deification of the individual personality, the immortalization of one's personal identity, resound as the frustrated aspiration of moderns. The frustration itself no doubt has something to do with the revival of religious belief that seems to be part of contemporary global culture. Neither Stendhal nor Freud (nor Malraux, for that matter) would subscribe to faith as a solution, but both would certainly recognize the problem that calls it forth as the only apparent solution in the bind that egotism and civilization have got themselves into. Yet both would argue that false consolations are to be rejected—that modern heroism consists precisely in facing the void. The only consolation to be offered is understanding, and to the extent that understanding takes an aesthetically convincing form—when you can call it art—one may confer on it something of a redemptive power. Yet that art is like the frescoes of the Camposanto in Pisa: large hunks of it are destined to fall away, leaving blanks beneath. Art may deserve more than Freud's characterization of it as "regression in the service of the ego"—it may make us accept culture as somehow worth the cost. But it can't save you. Recall Stendhal's definition of beauty: *la chasse du bonheur*, the pursuit of happiness. As a novelist who had the greatest of troubles with endings, Stendhal may want us to pronounce the phrase with a principal emphasis on the pursuit, not its point of arrival.

The world is crowded with "as if" personalities, and even more so with impostors and pretenders.

—Helene Deutsch, "The Impostor: Contribution to Ego
   Psychology of a Type of Psychopath"

# 3 | The "Outcast of the Universe"?

In 1935, the Supreme Court of Minnesota had to deal with the case of Ira Collins Soper—to give him what the court assumes to be his real name. Justice Julius J. Olson, writing for the majority, begins, "Ira Collins Soper, a native and resident of Kentucky, was the central figure in the drama now to be depicted. In October, 1911, he and plaintiff Adeline Johnson Westphal were united in marriage. She was a widow with three young daughters, the issue of her first marriage. She and her daughters lived with him until August, 1921, when he suddenly disappeared, not be heard of again by his wife during his remaining lifetime."[1] We learn that the Sopers' family life was said to be happy, though Mrs. Soper had difficulties with which to contend, since Mr. Soper occasionally went on drunken sprees, sometimes with unannounced out-of-town trips. But the disappearance in 1921 was more spectacular, as "he studiously and almost fiendishly made his disappearance take on the character of a suicide. He wrote several suicide notes to his wife, one of them ending with this significant statement: 'If there is any hereafter may meet you again.' His car was found at the bank of a nearby canal and so were his hat and portions of his clothing.

Pinned to his business card and left in his car was a note reading: 'This belongs to Mrs. Soper'" (428).[2]

There was an earthly hereafter for Ira Soper. He managed to slip out of Louisville without leaving a trace, convincing everyone that he had indeed committed suicide. Instead, he traveled to Canada, and then to Minneapolis. By now he was no long Ira Soper but John W. Young, and would continue as such until his death—from a real suicide this time—in 1932.

He was a business success in Minneapolis, founding with a partner the Young Fuel Company. In 1922, he married a widow, Mary Christopher, "and they lived together as husband and wife and were so known until she died in 1925" (428). He must have had a way with widows (though Mary Christopher, it turns out, committed suicide): "In May, 1927, he married defendant Gertrude Whitby, another Minneapolis widow, with whom he had been acquainted and had kept company for some six or eight months prior to their marriage." With his business partner, Karstens, he devised a stock insurance scheme, which included compensation for the surviving wife after the death of either partner. And from this would arise the issue at bar.

Soper's "performances," as Justice Olson calls them (428), kept reminding me of a story read long ago—which I eventually identified as Nathaniel Hawthorne's "Wakefield"—that begins, "In some old magazine or newspaper, I recollect a story, told as truth, of a man—let us call him Wakefield—who absented himself for a long time, from his wife. The fact, thus abstractly stated, is not very uncommon, nor—without a proper distinction of circumstances—to be condemned either as naughty or nonsensical. Howbeit, this, though far from the most aggravated, is perhaps the strangest instance, on record, of marital delinquency; and, moreover, as remarkable a freak as may be found in the whole list of human oddities."[3] Wakefield leaves one day on what he claims is to be a short journey—and then takes lodgings in the next street over from his own house and there "without the shadow of a reason for such self-banishment, dwelt upwards of twenty years. During that period, he beheld his home every day, and frequently the forlorn Mrs. Wakefield." Then after twenty years he reenters his home one evening, "quietly, as from a day's absence, and became a loving spouse till death."

This end to the story is, of course, much too simple, and precisely the kind of enigma that elicits Hawthorne's restless interpretive imagination. His narrator apostrophizes Wakefield on his first night absent from home: "Go quietly to thy bed, foolish man; and, on the morrow, if thou wilt be wise, get thee home to good Mrs. Wakefield, and tell her the truth. Remove not thyself, even for a little week, from thy place in her chaste bosom. Were she, for a single moment, to deem thee dead, or lost, or lastingly divided from her, thou wouldst be woefully conscious of a change in thy true wife, forever after. It is perilous to make a chasm in human affections; not that they gape so long and wide—but so quickly close again!" (292–93).

This sounds possibly less like Ira Soper/John Young's case than that of Martin Guerre, who left his young wife, Bertrande de Rols, in the village of Artigat, in southwest France, to become a soldier—returning only some eleven years later to reclaim his place in the village economy and in his wife's bed. But in that story of sixteenth-century French peasants, so artfully told by Nathalie Davis in *The Return of Martin Guerre*, Martin Guerre's place has been taken by a man, Armand du Tilh, who will eventually be exposed as an impostor—and will at the last confess his imposture, though he and Betrande long maintain his identity as the true Martin. Unlike the chaste Mrs. Wakefield, Bertrande seizes the opportunity to have a replacement husband—though one assumes she must at some early point have realized he was not identical to the departed Martin—who seems in most ways more satisfactory and likable than the original (who was unable to consummate the marriage for several years, and then left it without warning or explanation). The assumption by the "true" Martin that he could simply resume his place in Artigat and in Bertrande's affections is not much explored in Davis's account—there is really nothing for the historian to work with here, whereas with Bertrande and Arnaud there are records of long interrogations and confrontations with witnesses. One can imagine Martin

Guerre as somewhat in the mold of Wakefield, someone whose egotism or narcissism makes him incapable of understanding the human consequences of his actions. The transformation that his leaving home works on Wakefield, in a single night, "is a secret from himself" (294).

Wakefield, at any rate, does return one rainy night, after his twenty years' absence, when he stands wet and chilled before his former home, and makes the "unpremeditated" decision to cross the threshold. And the story comes to its close: "We will not follow our friend across the threshold. He has left us much food for thought, a portion of which shall lend its wisdom to a moral; and be shaped into a figure. Amid the seeming confusion of our mysterious world, individuals are so nicely adjusted to a system, and systems to one another, and to a whole, that, by stepping aside for a moment, a man exposes himself to a fearful risk of losing his place forever. Like Wakefield, he may become, as it were, the Outcast of the Universe" (298). Any regular reader of Hawthorne will recognize the obsessive theme: egotism, "the bosom serpent," as one of the tales puts it, the effects of isolating oneself from fellow mortals. Wakefield returning home may find himself the "outcast of the universe," unable to reclaim the place in society that is woven of human relations and affections. As psychologist Jerome Bruner has put it, selves are "transactional," created by way of what Hawthorne calls "systems"—of interlocution and interrelation, not through simple acts of self-fashioning.[4] The suppleness of the Renaissance courtier's adjustments of self in order to please and seduce others encounters limits, precisely when one passes into what the law sees as fraud. I imagine, too, that many readers of the case of Martin Guerre ask themselves by what right the "true" Martin, hobbling back from war in the Low Countries, can claim to reenter the systems of kinship, property, and affection that he has seemingly abrogated by his absence. It is perhaps most of all, paradoxically, the presence of the man claiming his place—the impostor Arnaud, the fictive husband supported in his role by Bertrande—that allows the assertion of Martin's claim. You can try to make this other person in turn "the outcast of the universe"—and indeed Martin succeeds in sending Arnaud to the gallows.

The lessons of Wakefield, Martin Guerre, and Arnaud du Tilh are problematic in their application to Ira Soper. His "performances" make him most resemble Arnaud, the trickster with the protean ability to take on different identities. Yet there must be something of Wakefield in him as well. He knew of the existence of the first Mrs. Soper, though apparently without the intention of ever resuming his identity as her husband. He was now after all John Young, setting up an insurance trust for his wife Gertrude. As Justice Olson writes, "The trust officer who dealt with the parties was informed that the relationship between Young and Gertrude was that of husband and wife, likewise that of Karstens and his wife. No one except Young knew anything about the first wife. She was to all intents and purposes, as to all arrangements and engagements heretofore related, entirely out of the picture" (429). Yet she will not remain out of the picture. Several months after "Young's" estate has been settled, and his wife Gertrude made the beneficiary of the insurance scheme, "Mrs. Soper, the true wife of Young, put in her appearance." Justice Olson's laconic statement elides what must have been a moment of drama not unlike the return of Martin Guerre, hobbling into court on his wooden leg. His statement indeed teeters on the brink of a kind of Wakefieldian incoherence: "Mrs. Soper, the true wife of Young." We might want to say "the true wife of Soper," because Young does not exist.

Yet Young has clearly successfully refashioned himself in the context of Minneapolis to the extent that the court refers to him as Young, though it recognizes equally that Gertrude Whitby Young cannot truly be his wife. So the issue before the court, as summarized by the plaintiff on appeal to the Supreme Court of Minnesota, is this:

> The essential issue, as it really presented itself at the trial, was this: granting that Mrs. Whitby was not the deceased's wife, could not be his wife, was not his heir, did not have and could not have any rights of inheritance, statutory or otherwise, did Soper, by some valid, clear, effective supervening instrument, valid as a will or as a present deed or conveyance inter vivos,

shut off and determine, in her or in some one else's favor, the
clear rights which his wife and heir would otherwise plainly
have had? And further, if it first be found that he actually did
execute a valid instrument which clearly and unmistakably has
that effect, to deprive his wife of her rights, did he have the
power to do that, without his wife's consent, under our law?
(429)

These arguments appear powerful. But Olson here proceeds to establish Gertrude's innocence of wrongdoing and her good faith in entering
into marriage with Young. Yet he concedes that by the laws of descent,
she has no right of inheritance from Young. The way out, for Olson, is
to declare the insurance trust scheme devised by Young and Karstens to
be nontestamentary. He argues this point over several dense columns,
to conclude that "Gertrude neither did nor could take anything as the
'wife' of Young. As a matter of law, she never became such. But this
conclusion does not solve our problem because she does not lay claim
to the insurance merely as his lawful wife, but as the person intended
to be the beneficiary under the escrow agreement as fully as if her name
had been written into that contract instead of the word 'wife'" (431).

The plaintiffs, Olson notes here, claim that the agreement "is not
subject to construction," that its perfectly plain meaning is that the
money should go to the lawful wife of the deceased husband, whether
he be called Soper or Young. But Olson is not going to be such a tex-
tual literalist, and introduces "parol evidence"—oral history—to the
effect that Gertrude was considered by all and sundry to be Young's
wife and the intended recipient of the insurance funds, though he in-
serts in the middle of his argument the concessionary sentence, "True,
Young knew otherwise, but that he did not intend his real wife to take
anything as beneficiary seems obvious." Perhaps, the plaintiff's brief ingeniously argues, not so obvious: by designating "my wife" as the beneficiary on most of the stock certificates (only one of them is made out
to "Gertrude Whitby"), Soper as Young may have intended the court
to understand that he was attempting, posthumously, to make amends

to Adeline—and give the money to his "true wife."[5] But Olson needs to infer a less ambiguous intention on the part of the ambiguous Soper/Young to produce a legal judgment.

Here, though, Olson's argument becomes interestingly problematic—one is almost tempted to say postmodern. The agreement with Karstens, he says, "points to no one else than Gertrude as Young's 'wife.' To hold otherwise is to give the word 'wife' 'a fixed symbol,' as 'something inherent and objective, not subjective and personal.' Dean Wigmore, in his excellent work on evidence . . . has this to say: 'The ordinary standard, or "plain meaning," is simply the meaning of the people who did not write the document. The fallacy consists in assuming that there is or ever can be some one real or absolute meaning'" (431). In lawyerly terms, he is arguing for the validity of parol evidence in identifying the relevant "wife" in this case—that is, to resort to evidence that lies outside the language of the contract itself. As he writes further (citing precedents from the Minnesota Supreme Court),

> if there be need for resort to extraneous aids to construction, it is immaterial whether such need arises from an uncertainty in the instrument itself, or that being clear, standing alone, it ceases to be so, and a[m]biguity arises when the contract is applied to its subject-matter. In either case construction must follow, and resort must be had to the aids furnished by extrinsic circumstances. . . .
>
> The question is not just what words mean literally, but how they are intended to operate practically on the subject-matter. (432–33)

In dissent, Justice I. M. Olsen (we are in Minnesota, where all justices seem to be of Scandinavian descent) tersely rejects Justice Olson's musings on the need for construction of language ambiguous in its application to reality. For him, the case has only one, simple truth:

> A man can have only one wife. If, while married, a man fraudulently and in violation of law, goes through a marriage

ceremony with another woman, she does not become his wife, however innocent such woman may be of any wrongdoing. . . .

The contract in this case designates the "wife" as the one to whom the money was to be paid. I am unable to construe this word to mean any one else than the only wife of Soper then living. (433)

Justice Olsen, we might say, subscribes to J. L. Austin's theory of speech acts (not yet published in 1935): since there was a first Mrs. Soper, any subsequent "I do thee wed" uttered by Soper/Young simply has no validity—it is a "misfire," in Austinian terms—and the designation of "wife" to anyone other than Adeline Soper is inoperative.[6] To Olsen, "wife" is indeed a "fixed symbol" in that it can refer to only one person at a time. Ambiguity is not relevant to the designation of wifeliness.

This means, of course, that Olsen—unlike Olson—doesn't accept Soper's self-fashioning into Young. That is not something he will deal with. In fact, he uses the last full paragraph of his dissenting opinion to explain why Soper had to do away with himself, his metamorphosis on the verge of collapse, noting, "Soper's suicide is readily explainable. He had committed two felonies in this state. One was bigamy and, assuming that the clerk of court did his duty, perjury was committed in obtaining a marriage license here. About two years before Soper's suicide, his brother had discovered that he was alive and in Minneapolis. There was constant danger of his situation becoming known and being investigated. He was an educated man, had been a teacher in a commercial school, and was a good business man. He was fully aware of what he had been doing" (433). Olsen returns Soper to the status of con man, without any of the interpretive subtleties of the majority, and in so doing makes the claim to restore Adeline Soper as beneficiary of the insurance money. Since that is a lost cause, one has the impression he is most interested in showing up Soper for what he was. Had he been a judge in the Parlement de Toulouse, he would clearly have chosen to hang Arnaud du Tilh. As Hawthornian narrator, he would characterize Soper as "outcast of the universe."

The case seems to me interesting in part because it suggests less than clarity in response to the impostor. There is no doubt that Soper "studiously and almost fiendishly" created a false impression of suicide in order to resurrect himself as Young, and in that role to take on two further wives. (Though there is evidence, from a contemporary newspaper account and her later testimony at trial, that Adeline Soper herself was not wholly convinced of Ira's "suicide"; she evidently knew the man.)[7] The majority of the court, while recognizing what he has done, is willing to let him posthumously carry out what one assumes—though possibly with some residual doubts since Soper is a slippery being—was his intent: to benefit Gertrude. It's a bit like the Parlement de Toulouse declaring Bertrande de Rols's children by Arnaud du Tilh to be legitimate descendents of Martin Guerre because she believed at the time of their conception that Arnaud was Martin. One can say that in both cases we merely witness the law wishing to preserve a certain orderliness in human affairs: the most obvious reading of a contract (despite the fact that Gertrude can't be Soper's "wife"), the legitimation of children and inheritance. Yet in both cases the law must, then, operate on a kind of knowing fiction. It must to some extent validate the metamorphoses worked by the con artist.

*In re Soper's Estate* and "Wakefield" suggest some of the fascination and anxiety set up by the trickster who so successfully changes identity that we can't entirely negate or eradicate the effects of his trickery. In fact, we may always have been fascinated by the master or mistress of identity changes, just as we have been continuously interested in cross-dressing and sexual impersonation. Think of William Shakespeare's young women (played, of course, on the Elizabethan stage by young men) who disguise themselves as men, to create in the wake of disguise complex socioerotic patterns; *Twelfth Night* might be the best possible example. But as we reach modernity—especially the world of the nineteenth and twentieth centuries—it seems to be the disguised con artist and even criminal who interests even more than the transgendered (though our own times may have reversed the emphasis again).

To say that a great deal of our literature is about disguise, false identities, and mistaken impressions—and eventual recognitions of where the truth lies—is merely to reiterate Aristotle's original understanding, in the *Poetics*, that the most basic plot structure has to do with recognition and reversal: *anagnorisis* and *peripeteia*. I have already suggested in chapter 1 how much the romance and melodramatic finding of the mark of hidden identity characterizes the history of our most dramatic literature, perhaps including our mental life in general when one considers the melodrama of Freudian discovery. As the cases of Ira Soper and Arnaud du Tilh and Wakefield suggest, within the general plot of disguise and misprision there may be a special place for the imposter, the willful trickster who would have others believe he or she is another. The imposter is a bit different from Viola or Rosalind disguised as a young man in *Twelfth Night* or *As You Like It*. They are protecting themselves and testing love—and the scenario is replayed with the appropriate cultural differences in the nuanced comedies of Pierre Marivaux and the operas of Wolfgang Amadeus Mozart—especially *Così fan tutte*. Soper and Arnaud are trying to bring off something else, what we might now call "identity theft," or a complete metamorphosis in which a past self has been buried and a new one manufactured. While literature in the picaresque tradition—especially in Spain and in England, I think—is full of tricksters, "counterfeit ladies," and other protean personages—Daniel Defoe's *Moll Flanders* gives a prime example—the impostor may take on a darker coloration in Romantic and post-Romantic literature, particularly in the masked figure intent on vengeance, from Alexandre Dumas's Edmond Dantès in *The Count of Monte Cristo* to Batman, with an attendant focus on the interplay of assumed and "real" identity, as in André Gide's *The Counterfeiters* (*Les Faux-Monnayeurs*), or the recent *The Untouchable*, John Banville's remarkable novel based on the life of the art historian and spy Anthony Blunt—remarkable in part because it is narrated in the first person, from behind the mask, as it were, in a forced intimacy with a person both seductive and loathsome.

The moral drama of the mask receives something like definitive treatment at the start of the twentieth century in Henry James's novella *The Beast in the Jungle*, where John Marcher's mask for his own sense of his true destiny may be said eventually to mask himself from himself: "What it had come to was that he wore a mask painted with the social simper, out of the eye-holes of which there looked eyes of an expression not in the least matching the other features. This the stupid world, even after years, had never more than half-discovered. It was only May Bartram who had, and she achieved, by an art indescribable, the feat of at once—or perhaps it was only alternately—meeting the eyes from in front and mingling her own vision, as from over his shoulder, with their peep through the apertures."[8] The masked man peering out at the world through a dissimulated identity becomes in James's tale the very ruination of identity. Marcher's identity is of failure and self-destruction, as only May Bartram, somehow aligning her vision with his "eye-holes," comes to understand—until the final melodramatic scene of recognition as self-destruction, when Marcher throws himself on May's tombstone. Marcher is quite explicitly James's reprise of Hawthorne's "outcast of the universe."

I find it interesting to juxtapose James's description of Marcher behind his mask with the way John Banville's narrator, Victor Maskell, describes his own experience as a spy for the Soviet Union in Britain:

Let me try another tack. Perhaps it was not the philosophy by which I lived, but the double life itself—which at first seemed to so many of us a source of strength—that acted upon me as a debilitating force. I know this has always been said of us, that the lying and the secrecy inevitably corrupted us, sapped our moral strength and blinded us to the actual nature of things, but I never believed it could be true. We were latter-day Gnostics, keepers of a secret knowledge, for whom the world of appearances was only a gross manifestation of an infinitely subtler, more real reality known only to the chosen few, but the iron, ineluctable laws of which were everywhere at work.

This gnosis was, on the material level, the equivalent of the Freudian conception of the unconscious, that unacknowledged and irresistible legislator, that spy in the heart. Thus, for us *everything was itself and at the same time something else.*[9]

If this is in part an apologetics for the Marxist-Leninist doctrine that made the Cambridge spies believe they were on a higher mission—not so much betraying their country as saving the world—it also gives an interesting image of what the psychic world of any double agent or impostor must be like. That "spy in the heart" is the knowledge that everything is both as it seems and something else altogether, that reality indeed is dual.

It is this interior distance that may most fascinate us in impostors, whether viewed from the inside, as in Banville's novel, or dramatized from without, as in John Guare's play *Six Degrees of Separation*. It's an interior distance that can be made the stuff of high drama and tension, as in Patricia Highsmith's *The Talented Mr. Ripley*, and the two film versions made from it, or Hari Kunzru's *The Impressionist*, about a young Anglo-Indian who learns he can pass as either ethnicity and in the process loses a sure grounding of identity. Or it can simply be left to the imagination of an outside observer, a "narratee," as in Rudyard Kipling's tale *The Man Who Would Be King*. Highsmith's novel well captures the anxiety of living as someone else that must characterize the experience of most impostors—an anxiety probably at once exhilarating and draining, and perhaps ultimately the very raison d'être of imposture. It has been dramatized in a number of novels about 1960s radicals who went underground following an act of violence, to reemerge with a false identity that eventually collapsed, most convincingly in Dana Spiotta's *Eat the Document*.

The version of the impostor most familiar in the popular imagination may be the spy, especially the double agent. In the masterwork of novelist John Le Carré, *A Perfect Spy*, Magnus Pym's first wife, Belinda, declares, "He was a new man every day. He'd come home one person, I'd try to match him. In the morning he'd be someone else."[10] Or as another of Pym's women more strikingly puts it, "'He's a shell,' Kate said. 'All you have to do is find the hermit crab that climbed into him. Don't look for the truth about him. The truth is what we gave him of ourselves'" (235). The self as shell into which various crabs can crawl: this suggests that the spy offers a version of our worst fears about the instability of our selves, our proteanism as a certain hollowness.

Psychoanalyst Helene Deutsch became interested in what she called "as-if" personalities who only tentatively inhabit one identity. She cites the case of an impostor, Ferdinand Demara, who passed himself off as a professional in several fields—including medicine—under another man's name. He managed to obtain the credentials of an expert in the field and made good use of knowledge—up to a point, when he was exposed, always "by accident." Deutsch writes, "Reading his life history, one sees that he was perpetually in pursuit of an identity which would do justice to his narcissistic conception of himself in terms of 'I am a genius,' and which at the same time would serve to deny his own identity."[11] In other words, imposture allows you to live out a life according to your fantasies without attributing this life to yourself, since you know your "true" identity isn't up to the fantasy.

There may, of course, be impostors simply motivated by gain, as in the famous case of the Tichbourne inheritance, where an inconsolable mother's loss of her son created the conditions in which she would accept as authentic even an implausible claimant to being that son. But something more seems to be at issue in the most interesting cases: some version of Sigmund Freud's "family romance," the child's decision that he or she does not really belong in the family and the place in life mistakenly assigned to him or her, and therefore must invent another—a problem for Jean-Jacques Rousseau, as we have seen, and I think a common thread in the impostor's imagination. That is what both Le Carré and Deutsch, in their different vocabularies, suggest. A case of mass delusion in the face of imposture, as in the claim of Anna Anderson to be Anastasia Romanov, Tsar Nicholas's daughter murdered by the Bolsheviks, must have something to do with our collective family romance, our wish for a more glamorous historical reality, one capable of meeting the demands of our melodramatic imagination. If only history did produce such romantic foundlings and claimants to the throne our psychic lives would be more satisfactory. As Jorge-Luis Borges writes in his story of a real world effaced by a more perfect (and totalitarian) world invented by the human mind, "Almost immediately, reality gave way on more than one point. The truth is that it hankered to give ground."[12] Our fascination with—as well as our anxiety at—the impostor surely has something to do with the inadequacies of reality to the imagination. To rewrite the self: that is a temptation, though one that most of us confine to idle day-dreaming.

The fictional impostor most demanding of our attention, because of the breathtaking claims made on behalf of his power and importance, may be that most influential figure in Honoré de Balzac's *Human Comedy*: Jacques Collin, alias Vautrin, also known as Cheat-Death (Trompe-la-Mort). Balzac's sense of the grandiose in his fictional creation allows him to concentrate in the figure of Collin much of emergent modernity's anxiety about the impostor. In his movement from ex-con disguised as at least marginally respectable citizen, to his reincarnation as a Spanish priest, to his final incarnation as high administrator in the state police, Collin injects a kind of tracer dye into a society that doesn't know what kinds of identity to reply on, and how to know them.

Rather than examining the multiple novels in which Collin makes an appearance, it may be instructive to look at his biographical entry in the *Dictionary of Fictional Characters* that scholars have compiled, precisely as a "Who's Who" of Balzac's *Human Comedy*.[13] You might ask yourself, first of all, whether *Collin, Jacques*, is the right rubric to search under. You could also try *Vautrin*, the name by which most readers first encounter this character, in Balzac's most-read novel, *Old Goriot* (*Le Père Goriot*). Or else you might use the name by which he is familiarly known to the criminal population, and the police: *Trompe-la-Mort*, or Cheat-Death. Or you might go to *Herrera, Reverend Carlos*, the name under which he appears to his most important protégé, Lucien de Rubempré, and which he will keep for more pages than any other. And there are some shorter-lived identities: *M. de Saint-Estève* and *William Barker*, for instance. His career, through these many changes of name, takes us from crime, both the petty and the violent, to his final incarnation as chief of the undercover police, as well as through a range of amorous infatuations with beautiful young men.

We think we know that Jacques Collin is his "real" name, the one he was baptized with, though it's hard to be certain. The *Dictionary of Fictional Characters* tells us he was born in 1779, but at once admits that this is conjectural. It's based on information from the time he is living as Vautrin, in the Pension Vauquer where *Le Père Goriot* opens. In 1819, we are told he is forty; but other extrapolations from what he says to other characters, or from the age of his aunt Jacqueline, who is five years older, would give birth dates of 1776 or even 1773. They do seem less plausible, given our sense that the Collin we encounter as Vautrin is in the prime of his vigorous maturity—particularly apparent at the moment the police arrest him, when he resembles Milton's Satan, at war with authority and society. We learn much later—not in our reading of *Le Père Goriot* but when he has made himself into Father Carlos Herrera, Spanish priest on a mission from the pope—that he was schooled by Oratorian monks. Plausible enough, but there is no confirmation of this pious education other than his capacity to act the role of priest effectively. It is through this later reading—of the four-part *Glory and Misery of Courtesans* (*Splendeurs et misères des courtisanes*; 1838–47)—that we learn also that he was convicted in 1812 (thus, in his early thirties) for forgery, and given five years at hard labor—which became seven after an attempted escape. But then we learn that the forgery was in fact committed by someone else—by a beautiful young Italian man whom he was in love with and wanted to spare the rigors of prison. We may be able to identify the Italian as Colonel Franchessini, which might explain why he agrees to serve Collin's (at this point, Vautrin's) interests by provoking a duel with the young Victor Taillefer, whom he dispatches with his sword, in order that Victorine Taillefer become an heiress who will bring an immense fortune to Eugène de

Rastignac, Vautrin's young protégé of the moment, handsome, ambitious, but penniless, whom Victorine adores. If we go so far as to read a passage that was in the first edition of *Le Père Goriot* but later deleted by Balzac, we learn that this Franchessini is the love of Lady Brandon, née Augusta Willemsens, one of the most elegant women of Paris—though her life is shadowed by her adulterous affair—who with the colonel presents a picture of ideal beauty.

We never quite learn how Collin, in prison, became the convicts' banker. He seems at first to carry the title of "treasurer of the three prisons," then cashier of the Ten Thousand and of the Grands Fanandels, a society founded in 1816 that brings together the aristocracy of convicts. But all this comes later—our knowledge of Collin's early years largely (but never more than fragmentarily) reaches us over the course of *Splendeurs et misères*, a very long novel in four parts. It's the Faulknerian aspect of Balzac: often we don't learn of characters' careers in a linear chronology, or in a full presentation. We are obliged to piece fragments together. The *Dictionary of Fictional Characters* has normalized things, given us that *Who's Who* that in Balzac's day existed only for the peerage (and even there, the creation of a Napoleonic peerage complicated the problem and made it harder to know the "real thing"—the ancient nobility considered everything done by Napoleon as an imposture). Let's on this basis assume he's come alive, and treat him as what we call "a real person."

So it may make sense to start where most readers tend to do, with Collin as Vautrin, in *Le Père Goriot*—which would have been the entry point for contemporary readers, since that novel was published in 1834 and the other novels in which Collin figures prominently came in the 1840s. We meet Vautrin as a lodger in Madame Vauquer's famous pension—famous because it has been singled out as a place of special importance in the rise of the realist novel, the place where environment and character are decisively presented as mutually determinative.[14] But Vautrin's presence in the Pension Vauquer is, of course, part of his cover. His first presentation is as "a man of about forty, who wore a black wig, dyed his whiskers, said he was a former salesman, and was called Monsieur Vautrin."[15] In our later retrospect it's clear that the sentence opens all sorts of possibilities for doubting the veracity of the announced identity, though many of the other lodgers also seem to be hiding something of their past. And indeed, the story of the young hero of the novel, Eugène de Rastignac, begins one night when he is spying on his neighbor, Old Goriot, who is turning silver dinner service into ingots in his room, when he hears Vautrin and a companion coming up the stairs in felt slippers, then the sound of money being counted in Vautrin's room—all this the more enigmatic because he knows the outside door was double bolted before Vautrin entered. This classic tale of ambition for riches, social position, and a beautiful woman that comes with both gets underway in darkness and mystery.

The enigma of Vautrin's identity is central to our experience of the novel, in which he becomes Rastignac's chief tutor in the ways of the Parisian world, and also his nearly diabolical tempter. He comes up with a quick fix for Rastignac's desire to transform his penniless studenthood into social dominance. It's simple: in the Pension Vauquer lodges also Victorine Taillefer, the repudiated daughter of the millionaire reprobate banker Frédéric Taillefer, and she is a sweet young thing who instinctively loves Rastignac. If Victorine's brother were to die, Taillefer would forget his doubts about Victorine's legitimacy and make her his sole legatee. Vautrin will arrange a duel: Colonel Franchessini (that beautiful young Italian whose crime of forgery Vautrin earlier took upon himself) will provoke young Taillefer, and Franchessini can be counted upon to win his duels. Rastignac reacts with horror to the plan, but Vautrin carries it forward anyway, one night when Rastignac has been drugged into oblivion—though Rastignac will then make it a point of high morality not to profit from the death of young Taillefer, but instead to become a kind of kept man of one of Goriot's exploitative daughters (think *King Lear*'s Goneril and Regan), Delphine de Nucingen.

"What kind of a man are you then?" Rastignac cries out. "You were born to torture me" (185). Faustian overtones: Vautrin as guide to a career in Paris society offers a diabolical pact. Nonetheless, the advice he gives Rastignac over the many pages of their recorded conversations is on target, and is also the most uncompromising moral lesson of the novel: "Virtue, my dear student, is not divisible: it either is or it isn't" (145). Rastignac won't heed that lesson—indeed, his whole career will be oriented to avoiding ethical absolutes, to finding instead the many paths of moral compromise that will allow him to use sentiment as a way to money. What kind of a man is Vautrin? The novel by its second half develops a plot by the police to answer this question in the kinds of terms the police understand. The police make use of two other lodgers, Mlle Michonneau and her sidekick Poiret, to drug Vaurin and then, while he is unconscious, slap him on the shoulder in order to see if the letters of *la marque* appear: the brand—*TF*, for *Travaux Forcés*, forced labor—that identifies Vautrin, forever, as the convict Jacques Collin. The ruse succeeds—the "fatal letters" appear under Mlle Michonneau's thwack, and the police move in to arrest Vautrin. A blow to his head knocks off his wig, revealing the brick red stubble underneath. He becomes an "infernal poem," a "fallen archangel who wants more warfare" (219) as he denounces the pitiful creatures who have betrayed him (for a mere 3,000-franc reward). "A convict in the mould of Collin, and here I am, is less of a coward than others, and he protests against the deep betrayals of the social contract, as it's called by Jean-Jacques whose pupil I proudly declare myself. What it comes to is that I am alone against the government, with its heap of courts, policemen, budgets, and I swindle them all" (220). So, a disciple of Rousseau whose perception that the social contract is dishonored by a corrupt and inegalitarian society provokes the commitment to wage war against its institutions, to undermine civil society as banker to a shadowy underground society of criminals.

That brand, la marque, that appears when Vautrin's shoulder is slapped hard will reappear at the most critical moment of the career of this personage who at that point—three-quarters of the way through *Splendeurs et misères*—is disguised as the Spanish priest Carlos Herrera but under interrogation by the magistrate Camusot, who suspects he may indeed be Jacques Collin but can't prove it. At that point, we shall see, the marque has been much more effectively erased by Collin's labors to reform his branded body. And here is an absolutely central nexus in the issue of identification. The practice of branding convicts was abolished by the French Assembly in 1832 on humanitarian grounds. Balzac was, then, writing at a time when la marque no longer existed, though about a period—the 1820s—when it did. His obsession with the brand, the efforts to read it—or to make it illegible—respond to the anxieties of an age in which the enforcers of society are searching for other means that would allow them to know, to track, to classify, to exercise surveillance over those identities judged dangerous to the social body as a whole, as I have tried to suggest in chapter 1.

At a climatic moment of *Le Père Goriot*, then, Vautrin is identified by the police as Jacques Collin—though he self-identifies as a kind of Byronic outlaw at war with society—and leaves the scene in handcuffs, escorted by police. Upon his leaving, the stool pigeon Michonneau falls prey to a collective suspicion and enmity, and is driven from the pension, though not before she has obliquely accused Rastignac of supporting Vautrin/Collin because of their homoerotic bond. Rastignac's reaction is to leap at her as if he wanted to strangle her. Her "venomous and interrogative look" at him in fact throws "a horrible light into his soul" (222). So now the novel gives explicit endorsement to a suspicion that the reader has for some time been entertaining: that Vautrin's bouts of avuncular advice to Rastignac, his willingness—even his ardent desire—to arrange the young man's future, seem to arise from more than simple affection or altruism. "A man is all or he is nothing. He is less than nothing when he is named Poiret: you can squash him like a bedbug, he's flat and he stinks. But a man is a god when he looks like you," he tells Rastignac. His devotion to his young protégé confirms Michonneau's surmise—though we never see him make a pass at Rastignac—and when he becomes the protector of Lucien de Rubempré, from the last episode of *Lost Illusions* (*Illusions perdues*), through to Lucien's suicide late in *Splendeurs et misères*, homosexuality becomes an explicit if discreet theme in Balzac's writing.

Vautrin/Collin is thus a marked man in a literal sense—though one intent upon effacing that mark—and also marked by society as sexually deviant, though, of course, he has effaced that orientation in his official social alibi. If there is in this and all of Balzac's novels a large deployment of the police, out to track crime and especially those criminals who have reintegrated themselves into society so that they look like ordinary folk, the figure who most fascinates the reader is not the policeman but his quarry. There is much of the detective story in Balzac's novels—especially in *Splendeurs et misères*, where several polices and counter-polices will carry on a grim and dubious battle in the shadows of society—in a kind of nearly simultaneous invention of the genre "invented," in most accounts, by Edgar Allan Poe's *The Murders in the Rue Morgue* in 1841. But Balzac's interest seems to lie less with the detective who must use his wits to solve the mystery—Poe's C. Auguste Dupin, Arthur Conan Doyle's Sherlock Holmes—than the outlaw who deploys extraordinary intelligence, energy, invention to keep out of the police's hands. Collin will himself become the detective at moments of *Splendeurs et misères*, in his efforts to stymie the plots that threaten his plans for his protégé's wealthy marriage, but he is nonetheless more often, or at the same time, the figure of the pursued, the object of police work. It's as if Balzac had intuitively understood the lure of a genre about to become highly characteristic of the time, and immensely popular, but also saw through to its ultimate implications, developed by many of the most self-conscious authors of detective fiction, including Conan Doyle from the moment he invents Sherlock Holmes's equal opposite, Professor Moriarty, the Napoleon of crime (an epithet attached to Collin as well): that the detective and the criminal are really alter egos whose contest is so engaging precisely because they understand each other. Each understands how the other's mind works, which makes their duel an exhilarating move and countermove.

All this is to say that the closer we get to knowing who Vautrin really is, the more that "really is" becomes complex. In fact, by the time of his arrest in *Le Père Goriot*, Vautrin has come so much to dominate the novel—and its discourse, since his populist criminal eloquence trumps all the other speech in the novel, even that of the adorable and pedigreed aristocrat Madame de Beauséant—that Balzac more or less has to make him disappear so that he can bring the other plots of the novel to their conclusion. Vautrin, now Collin, is hauled off to prison, and we assume we will never hear from him again, since his crimes are such as to keep him behind bars forever. The novel now is free to resolve Rastignac's conquest of society by way of Delphine de Nucingen, Madame de Beauséant's retreat from society following her lover's betrayal, and Old Goriot's death agony, in which his denunciation of a society where the cash nexus has come to dominate even blood relations strangely ratifies Vautrin's choice of war against society.

The next time Rastignac meets Vautrin—once again at liberty: he escapes from the prison at Rochefort almost immediately after being locked up there after his arrest at the Pension Vauquer in 1820, though we learn about this escape only much later—he is so deeply undercover that it takes a while for even the alert reader to discover his identity. He appears at the Opera Ball in 1824, masked—as are most of the patrons—and following, as a kind of bodyguard, the beautiful young man whom we discover to be Lucien de Rubempré, whose career we followed in *Illusions perdues* and now pick up again with this first installment of the sequel, *Splendeurs et misères des courtisanes*. The masked man will seize Rastignac by the shoulder with an iron hand, and lead him to the embrasure of a window where he will demand that Rastignac henceforth treat Lucien as a blood brother. "Silence and devotion," he dictates, "or I'll get into your game and knock over all your duckpins" (6:434). Rastignac is seized with vertigo; he feels as if he had fallen asleep in a forest and woken next to a lioness. " 'It could only be *him* to know. . . . and to dare. . ', he said to himself." Though this is given as an unspoken thought, the masked man replies to it, " 'Act as if it were *him*,' he said."

When the man in the mask finally—in the early morning hours—unmasks to Rastignac, it's to demonstrate that he is no longer recognizable as Vautrin. "The devil has allowed you to change everything about yourself—except the eyes, which no one could forget," Rastignac responds (6:446). Indeed, there is no point in calling the masked man Vautrin any more. That identity has been abandoned for another—at this moment itself temporarily effaced by the mask and the domino costume of the ball—which is that of the Reverend Father Carlos Herrera. To understand this identity, we have to double back from the first part of *Splendeurs et misères* to the fourth and final part of its predecessor, *Illusions perdues*. (We need not bother with the fact that the original version of part 1 of *Splendeurs et misères* actually appeared in periodical form before the last part of *Illusions perdues*, which in terms of the fictional chronologies precedes it.) By that last part of *Illusions perdues*, the career of Lucien Chardon, who wishes to call himself de Rubempré, annexing the more aristocratic moniker of his mother's family to the less glamorous family name of his pharmacist father, has come to its dead end. The poet who abandoned the muse for journalism in Paris, and then let his great talent be exploited by false friends and political sharpies, has returned to his native Angoulême disgraced and penniless, and then made things worse yet by luring his brother-in-law, David Séchard, out of his hiding place only to have him arrested for debt (caused by Lucien's Parisian extravagance, of course). Lucien writes a letter of supreme farewell to his sister and David, and goes off to drown himself in the river. He's in the process of looking for a remembered deep pool, where with his pockets full of stones he will sink to the bottom, when he appears, a bouquet of yellow flowers in hand, to Jacques Collin (now under the guise of Carlos Herrera).

Herrera, dressed in clerical black but smoking a cigar, slows his pace to allow Lucien to catch up with him. He is like a "hunter who comes upon a prey long sought in vain" (5:690). Marcel Proust wrote eloquently of this passage, which he then rewrote for himself in the meeting of the young Marcel with the Baron de Charlus, the dean of homosexuals, in *In Search of Lost Time* (*A la recherche du temps perdu*), the subject of Proust's meditations on the meaning of the world of Sodom, which in spite—or because—of the social malediction laid upon it is the realm of the most intense erotic passion. Lucien the poet—whose beauty is a kind of irrefutable given in all the social circles in which he moves—here on the brink of suicide represents a unique opportunity to Collin, the chance to succeed in the very fashioning of himself by way of another which he failed to achieve with Rastignac, both because Rastignac would never quite give in to him and because the police arrived at the Pension Vauquer a bit too soon for his schemes to mature. "You know what pleases me about you?" he says to Lucien. "It's that you have made a tabula rasa of yourself, so you can listen to a course in ethics preached nowhere . . ." (698). Herrera proposes to retrieve this blanked-out Lucien from suicide, to return him to Paris, indeed to make him a sultan in Paris society. In essence, Herrera/Collin will re-create himself through Lucien, in a kind of vicarious existence that explicitly evokes the *Arabian Nights*: "I gave you back your life, and you belong to me like a creature to his creator, as in fairy tales, like the Afrit to the genie, like the icoglan to the Sultan, like the body to the soul!" (703). He proceeds to lay out, more explicitly than ever he could in his conversations with Rastignac, his theory of vicarious pleasure— "*vie par procuration,*" the French says it, yet more strongly: life lived by a kind of surrogacy: "I want to love my creature, mould him, shape him to my use, in order to love him as a father loves his child. I will roll through Paris in your tilbury, my boy, I will know pleasure in all your successes with women, I'll say: This beautiful young man is myself! this marquis de Rubempré, I created him and put him in the world of the aristocracy; his grandeur is my work, he speaks or falls silent at my command, he consults me in everything" (708).

The protean malleability of identity in Collin/Vautrin/Herrera reaches here beyond the transformation of self into self-realization through another, through an explicitly homoerotic love that appears to find its satisfaction in being in and through another. Here John Keats's "negative capability" reaches its highest dimension, with a lived transformation of the "chameleon poet" into his creations. As Herrera puts it most simply, "I am the author, you will be the drama" (6:504).

This line comes from *Splendeurs et misères*, which picks up after Lucien has made his Faustian bargain with Herrera at the end of *Illusions perdues*, and recounts their life as an odd couple. Lucien lives on the ground floor of their elegant quarters, Herrera in the attic. Lucien lives out his ambitions for social prominence and for pleasure. It appears likely that the erotic bond of Herrera and Lucien never goes beyond the platonic—Herrera's most intense pleasure seems to come from his life in and through Lucien rather than in "possession" of Lucien in the more common erotic sense. He indeed allows Lucien to keep a secret mistress, Esther Gobseck, while he promotes Lucien's courtship of the aristocratic maiden Clotilde de Grandlieu, whose medieval sounding name suggests her descent from one of the grandest old families of the Faubourg Saint-Germain. She is thoroughly in love with Lucien—as all women are—but there are parental problems. Lucien's bounce back into society is a bit hard to explain, his source of income is enigmatic, there are rumors about him. He has managed—through Herrera's pulling of occult strings—to gain the right to wear his mother's name, Rubempré. Nonetheless, to make him respectable and a suitable husband for Clotilde, he needs to show that the name Rubempré means something, that he is truly landed gentry. He needs to buy back his mother's estate, long since alienated, and that will require a round million.

Here is the source of the infinitely baroque, and scabrous, plot that Herrera launches, and that animates *Splendeurs et misères*. In that initial scene at the masked Opera Ball, Lucien's mistress, Esther, has been unmasked by some of her old companions and lovers, who know her by her former nom de guerre as a high-class prostitute, "la Torpille"—the torpedo. She feels redeemed by her love for Lucien, and feels horror and despair at the return of her repressed past. She attempts suicide, lighting a charcoal brazier in a closed room (a common form of suicide among the Paris poor at the time). Herrera arrives in time to save her, and undertakes a program of "revirginization"—he believes in a kind of universal proteanism—placing her in a convent, promising her reunion with Lucien once she has been cleansed of her past. Released from the convent, she is made to live in the strictest seclusion—Lucien changes cabs several times when going to visit her—and allowed outdoor exercise only at night. It's when she is taking one of her moonlit strolls in the Bois de Boulogne that the banker Nucingen, returning from his country estate, spies her and is totally ravished by the spectacle. He falls hopelessly in love with her biblical beauty (there is indeed some ethnic predestination here, since both Nucingen and Esther are Jews), and activates an extensive network of spies and private police agents to find out who she is, and to get to her. Herrera at once understands the opportunity Nucingen's passion for Esther presents: he will sell her to the banker for the highest possible sum—in fact, for the million that Lucien needs to buy the Rubempré estates. Thus will Lucien become landed gentry more or less literally on the back of a prostitute.

Lucien puts up a feeble protest at selling Esther, but quickly concedes to Herrera's implacable logic. The greater problem comes from Esther, who considers herself genuinely redeemed from prostitution—Herrera's rehab plan has been that successful—and refuses to return to the life. As she plays a waiting game, Herrera manages to extract from Nucingen some 312,000 francs by creating false debts for Esther and bringing the bailiffs in just when Nucingen thinks he is on the verge of conquest. In the process of struggle between Herrera and his accessories—principally two ingenious and protean women: Europe, baptized Prudence Servien, aka Eugénie, over whom Herrera has absolute power since he liquidated the convict Durut against whom she turned state's evidence and who had sworn to kill her; and Asie, aka Madame de Saint-Estève and Madame Nourisson and, it turns out, "really" Collin's seventy-five-year-old aunt Jacqueline—and Nucingen's agents, mainly Peyrade and Corentin, much goes on in a murky underworld. Herrera/Collin himself takes on more disguises than we can quite keep up with. The plots and counterplots take a truly sinister turn when Peyrade's daughter Lydie is kidnapped by Herrera's agents, raped, and driven to madness. Meanwhile, Esther has decided to pay her "debt of dishonor" and take Nucingen as a lover—but only once; she commits suicide afterward. Alerted by Asie, Herrera writes a false will by which Esther makes Lucien her legatee—of a fortune that will turn out to be far greater than even Herrera knows since unbeknownst to her or almost anyone else she has just been made the legatee of the usurer Gobseck, perhaps the richest figure in the whole *Human Comedy*, whose lawyer is searching for her.

But this all transpires too late. By the end of part 2 of the novel, which bears the hard-boiled title "A combien l'amour revient aux vieillards" (How Much Love Costs Old Men)—ostensibly referring to Nucingen's tractations for Esther's favor, perhaps also to Herrera's love for Lucien—Herrera and Lucien are both apprehended by the police and taken to prison. The problem is that the servants Europe and Paccard have let the sight of the 7,500 francs left under her pillow by Esther as a legacy to Lucien overcome their loyalty to Herrera, and have decamped with it, making Nucingen suspect that Esther has been murdered for her money—and Collin and Lucien are assumed to be coconspirators in the crime. So as we move into the two final sections of *Splendeurs et misères*, we confront the climactic dramas of two exemplary careers of the *Human Comedy*: Lucien's and Collin's.

The *juge d'instruction*—a kind of one-man grand jury—takes over in the person of Camusot de Marville, an honest though not very clever magistrate whose career is driven by his highly ambitious wife. Camusot has received information from the police that the Abbé Carlos Herrera is almost certainly Jacques Collin, called Trompe-la-Mort, whose last arrest dates from 1819 at the Pension Vauquer. The chief of police has sent for Bibi-Lupin, head of the Sûreté, the state police, who made the 1819 arrest, in order to identify the suspect. Camusot interrogates Herrera first, without producing any admission or any sure indices of guilt. When asked about his relationship with Lucien, Herrera "confesses" that Lucien is his illegitimate son (nothing in the *Human Comedy* suggests confirmation of the assertion). This will prove Lucien's final undoing during his interrogation by Camusot: when the magistrate tells him that Herrera, in truth the escaped convict Collin—Lucien has had this confidence from Herrera already—claims to be his father, he responds uniquely to the disgrace involved, breaks down, confesses everything, to realize only too late that in betraying his benefactor he has revealed his own participation in the fortune-acquisition scheme. And Herrera's "infamous" claim of paternity (Freud's family romance in a reversal of generations?) also enlightens Lucien as to "a yet more infamous truth" that is not further specified but which clearly seems to be "the love that dare not speak its name." Lucien's reaction is to hang himself with his cravat from the bars of his cell. The farewell letter from Esther, proving that she has committed suicide and not been murdered, comes to Camusot's attention too late to save Lucien.

When Camusot first interrogates Herrera, he has him stripped to the waist and summons his bailiff to use an ebony bat—apparently a tried and true magistrate's accessory—to whack Herrera several times on the back of his shoulder. "Seventeen holes reappeared, all capriciously distributed; but despite the care with which they examined his back, they could not make out the shape of any letters. The bailiff did point out that the bar of a *T* was indicated by two holes separated by the distance between the serifs that would end the bar, and that another hole marked the foot of the letter. 'It's nonetheless very vague,' said Camusot . . .'" (6:751). So the *TF* that served for Collin's identification in 1819 has been largely effaced by 1830—not by natural process but because Collin has intentionally subjected himself to buckshot wounds in order to make la marque, if not invisible, at least the illegible buried palimpsest of his criminal identity. The story of his transformations seems to end with the triumphant affirmation of his nonidentity, his successful proteanism, his capacity to make himself wholly other.

Yet this is not the end. There is one more section of the novel left, and it is titled "Vautrin's Last Incarnation" ("La dernière incarnation de Vautrin"). Balzac in this manner revives at the last—when Collin is about to be definitively identified—the alias under which we first came to know him, while designating his return to his Collin identity as a final "incarnation." If this may appear slightly incoherent, it may be because the notion of a true identity for the figure has lost its meaning: the revelation of true identity is at the same time a new self-fashioning, a new incarnation. The moment is highly dramatic. Camusot has been whipsawed by contrary imperatives. Madame d'Espard, at the summit of Faubourg Saint-Germain society, has never pardoned Lucien's behavior toward her and her cousin Louise de Bargeton (Balzac might at this point insert, "see *Illusions perdues*") and wants him laid low, whereas two other grandes dames, Diane de Maufrigneuse and Hugret de Sérisy, as well as Clotilde de Grandlieu, not only still love the late Lucien passionately but might be compromised by their letters to him—which Collin, of course, holds. Thus they want Herrera to remain a Spanish priest, and for the whole affair to be covered up. These contradictory pressures on Camusot are conveyed by his scheming wife, who wants to see him in high administrative office, and by the Comte de Grandville, senior prosecutor of the royal court who connives as Madame de Sérisy throws the transcript of Lucien's interrogation into the fire.

Collin breaks through these dramatic doings by asking for an audience with Grandville. He enters the *procureur-général*'s office to announce, "Monsieur le comte, I am Jacques Collin, I surrender!" (6:895). What has happened? Grandville finds Collin on the last page of the novel somber and meditative, considering the "18th Brumaire" that he has carried out in his own life. The date—in the calendar invented by the French Revolution—refers to Napoléon Bonaparte's coup d'état in 1799 (the year Balzac was born). Collin has seized legitimate power—and we are told he will continue to exercise it for some fifteen years, until his retirement in 1845. "We were the game, now we are becoming the hunters, that's all," Collin explains to his aunt Jacqueline, who is stupefied by his change of allegiance (6:913). And that I think is the first lesson of Collin's passage from the ranks of crime to the ranks of what he calls "order and repression" (6:925): they are mutually dependent, and essentially interchangeable. One of John Le Carré's spies makes a similar point: "Hell, Jack, we're licensed crooks, that's all I'm saying. What's our racket? Know what our racket is? It is to place our larcenous natures at the service of the state."[16] Collin explains to Grandville that in holding the cold hand of Lucien's corpse during his nightlong vigil he decided to give up the "mad struggle against the whole of society that I have waged for twenty years" (6:922). He then launches into a denunciation of that society that goes beyond his ferocious words at the time of his arrest at the Pension Vauquer. He compares himself to Nucingen, who is merely a "Jacques Collin legally and in the world of money." Collin asserts that his own integrity and morality far exceeds that of Nucingen, who has made his fortune in the most dubious speculations and market maneuvers—and there is much in the *Human Comedy* that confirms the assertion. His stance of revolt against society recognizes the basic fraud of the social contract. He speaks particularly of the fate of the criminal who has done his time and is released back into society—but literally as a marked man, condemned to starvation or new crimes. In his own case, the only way to survive in his postcriminal career is to be at the very top of the criminal police.

The spectacular cops-and-robbers games of *Splendeurs et misères* thus end in a kind of victory of the cops, but with a sour recognition that they are not the moral winners but robbers under the mantle of the state. It also has a political dimension. In the last sections of the novel, there are several allusions to a coming attempt by King Charles X to reinstate a true monarchy in France—overriding the constitutionalism imposed after the fall of Napoleon in 1815. We are in the spring of 1830, and late in July the king indeed tried, in the Ordonnances de Juillet, to dissolve the elected assembly, to govern with ministers responsible only to the monarch, and to impose tight press censorship—which sparked the three-day July Revolution that sent the Bourbon monarchs into exile forever, and put the "citizen king" Louis-Philippe on the throne. To Balzac, the revolution of 1830 was merely further confirmation that the regime had become totally corrupt, selfish, governing only for the sake of the ruling elite and not for the good of the country. Not that the July Monarchy promised anything better: though it gave Balzac greater freedom to pursue his writing career, it merely demonstrated further that a government of principle was an illusion. The era opened up by the July Monarchy (which would last until the revolution of 1848) was one of rampant financial and electoral corruption, captured in the phrase of the prime minister, François Guizot, who famously (and perhaps apocryphally) told his compatriots, "Enrichissez-vous" (Get rich). And they did—except, of course, for the vast majority that was impoverished by the developing capitalist market economy.

I have skipped over many pages of detailed intrigue, both before and after Collin's 18th Brumaire. There are extraordinary prison scenes in which Collin, once more among his ilk, works to reestablish his authority among the prisoners and to establish the innocence of another beautiful young man, a Corsican, condemned to the guillotine. There is a baroque set of plots to recover, and hold for potential blackmail, the incriminating letters that the women of the Faubourg Saint-Germain had written to Lucien (Collin remarks that "grandes dames" write the way whores behave). And there is an exceptionally rich exploration of language, since it turns out that the argot of the criminal world is a highly metaphoric black-humored play on official language: a world in which the guillotine is known as *la veuve* (the widow—which it often creates), for instance, and the head that is severed there as *la sorbonne*, as the epitome of thought. Much of Balzac's information here comes from the memoirs of the historical personage who inspired the creation of Collin, Eugène François Vidocq, himself a sometime criminal mastermind who became a police informer, then a policeman—founder of the Sûreté, the state police agency that became the model for Scotland Yard and other bureaus of criminal investigation, in 1812—and later on head of a private bureau of investigation. Vidocq was perhaps the first systematic police official, intent on record-keeping, ballistics, and the study of criminology. He made the first plaster casts of shoe impressions, for instance. And he was an amateur anthropologist of the criminal world where, he insisted, his agents needed to work undercover—and they were originally mostly themselves ex-convicts. Vidocq's memoirs are so clearly a source of Balzac's work that returning from Balzac to Vidocq often gives the impression of redundancy—especially since a large part of the memoirs were apparently ghostwritten, and Balzac himself is reputed to have helped Vidocq with his later writing.

In the course of unraveling Collin's ultimate plot to save his own skin by redeeming the reputations of the illustrious women of the Faubourg Saint-Germain, which at the same time involves proving the innocence of the beautiful young Corsican Théodore Calvi, we learn, in a kind of narrator's homily, that theft is a "nearly natural emotion in man" (6:834). Thieves steal out of erotic passion, to make gifts to their girl (or boy) friends. The narrator goes on to generalize further: "The uncontrolled physical love displayed by these men would thus be, if one believes the School of Medicine, the origin of seventy percent of crime. The proof is moreover always found in striking, palpable form upon the autopsy of the executed criminal" (6:834). That palpable "proof" seems to be an outsized penis of these "monstrous lovers"—which is given as the basis of criminality, perhaps of the whole topsy-turvy world of unregulated desire which, in Collin's ultimate pronouncement, needs to be met by "order and repression" (6:925).

Yet order and repression, in Balzac's world as in Freud's, are only tenuous solutions, always threatened by the tumultuous passions that lie beneath. These are inchoate and also protean and metamorphic. As Collin explains to his aunt Jacqueline in justification of his impending cross-over to the ranks of the police, "'The estates that one creates in the world are only appearances; reality is the idea!' he added, striking his forehead" (6:912).

Collin/Vautrin/Herrera understands that "identity" is there for the taking. Like so many—one is tempted to say *all*—nineteenth-century novelists, Balzac appears to be fascinated by the question of identity, by the search to find bedrock in knowledge of who human beings are. And he comes curiously close to finding bedrock in anatomical sexual identity, very much in the manner of Freud, who notoriously identified "bedrock" in the human psyche as what he called "penis envy" in women and "the masculine protest" (against femininity) in men. But Balzac's answer also anticipates Freud's more sophisticated notion of the basic bisexuality of all human beings, and the price paid in policing oneself into becoming either man or woman. Above all, Balzac seems to respond to the question Who are you? with the answer Whoever you think you are.

That was Arnaud du Tilh's idea, and Ira Soper's. They were on one level simple con men, standing above their confrères in that genre only by their superior capacity to get away with it, and to leave confusion in their wake. But on another level they pose the most troubling questions about what we mean by identity. As Collin suggests, what we may most learn from the impostor is that we live amid multiple identities, those assumed for the world and those that we harbor in our heads. Their interaction in most cases does not seem to be all that problematic: most of us get through our lives in some compromise between the identities imposed by reality and those that we might choose to impose on reality. Yet in their intersection with the law, our imagined identities are channeled into rigid identifications. And ill-regulated passion, like that discovered in autopsies of the executed, can put all legal identities into question, can make identity into an enigma, and the search to know it the obsession of a society. The family romance, magnified to the scale of an entire society, becomes problematic, even sinister. If those who exercise the state's power are merely crooks in the guise of officials, the social contract is in danger. "My only ambition is to be an element of order and repression" (6:925): Collin's ultimate ambition chillingly suggests that the only answer to imposture, proteanism, and the as-if creation of self is the policing, social and psychic, that keeps identity relatively solid, usable, classifiable, unadventurous. Otherwise we might not know our proper places in the world.

# 4 | Discovering the Self in Self-Pleasuring

Much of the detection work that becomes so obsessive in the nine-teenth century has to do with identifying the individual responsible for whatever may be the case—indeed, the "case history" and the "case method" that become characteristic in medicine and law around 1900 are generally etiological explanations of present circumstances, and most often concern an individual case. The problem of detection cor-responds in part to a new recognition that individuals are just that: integers, whose privacy matters—and is recognized, as Justice William Douglas famously noted, in the "penumbra" of the Bill of Rights of the U.S. Constitution—yet constitutes a danger, the possibility of hiding from the eye of social regulation and normalization. Douglas formu-lated his doctrine of privacy in *Griswold v. Connecticut*, the Supreme Court decision that invalidated a state ban on contraceptives, with words expressing horror at the possible invasion of the privacy of the bedroom: "Would we allow the police to search the sacred precincts of marital bedrooms for telltale signs of the use of contraceptives? The very idea is repulsive to the notions of privacy surrounding the mar-riage relationship."[1] If the sexual was long considered the most private of realms (perhaps, as Michel Foucault has argued, in order to create the interminable discourse about it), within the sexual the most private has often been considered the sex that one has with oneself: masturbation. In turning from the public problem of identity to the private, masturbation may be a topic that rewards attention. It's probably no accident that it preoccupied those writers I keep returning to.

Jean-Jacques Rousseau and Marcel Proust both have a masturbation problem; Sigmund Freud may also, in his own way. If, as Thomas Laquer has argued in *Solitary Sex*, masturbation becomes a "problem"—rather than simply a fact of life, dating from infancy and openly discovered at puberty—with the advent of modernity (say, in the second half of the eighteenth century), this must have some bearing on the problem of individual identity, especially the sense of the individual as solitary, self-contained, a system complete in itself, a body responsive to itself. As Laquer writes, "Masturbation . . . came to prominence precisely when the imagination, solitude, and excess became newly important and newly worrisome. Private vice is the sin of an era that created the idea of society as the intermediary between the state and the individual and of an economy that depended on the desire for more and always more."[2] The "problem" of masturbation may derive from a sense that the world outside the self has become unnecessary: that the self has become entirely solipsistic and self-satisfying. This is, of course, dangerously unproductive in an age of nascent capitalism, where the imperative to productive work of all sorts includes the channeling of sexuality to disciplined reproduction. But even more disturbing, certainly to Rousseau, is the suspicion that autoerotic pleasure may be primary (an insight that will be confirmed by Freud), that the attachment of the libido to an object—a woman or a man—is a secondary formation, one that requires a certain discipline. Rousseau notes in his *Discourse on the Origin of Inequality* (*Discours sur l'origine de l'inégalité*) that "love," in the conventional sense of socially sanctioned mating, is artificial—"factice."[3] Rousseau discovers what Freud will call "primary narcissism."

A good deal of Rousseau's treatise on education, *Émile*, is about primary narcissism and how you break out of it, combat it with the positive human instinct to pity, have sympathy for the condition of others—what we would be most likely to call "empathy." Rousseau tends to call this primary narcissism "amour-propre": the great theme of the classical *moralistes*, such as François de la Rochefoucauld, to which Rousseau generally gives a somewhat more literal orientation. Self-love involves not just the ego but the body as well. Yet the bodily problem is for him most markedly a problem in the mind. And in fact, we discover over and over again in Rousseau that primary narcissism, at least in "civilized" humankind—post the state of nature—is a product of the imagination even before the body goes to work. When Émile reaches puberty—in what will prove the longest chapter of Rousseau's treatise—the problem turns out to be that the imagination has been there even before the body is ready to act on the fantasies produced in the head. For the individual growing up in society, nature has nothing more to teach him in making him a man: "He was already a man in his thought long before being a man in fact."[4] Nature alone works more slowly on the unsocialized, uninstructed individual: "he desires without knowing what: his blood boils in tumult; a superabundance of life seeks to extend itself outward" (502). Here is where the great teacher could lead his pupil away from the self toward the love of others: toward altruism, to plant in him "the first seeds of humanity."

We have this apparently paradoxical statement from the great apologist of individualism: "of all the enemies that can attack a young man, the most dangerous is himself" (662). Yet again, this self is dangerous only to the extent that it has succumbed to the blandishments of the imagination: "This enemy, however, is dangerous only through our own fault: for as I have said a thousand times, it is by the imagination alone that the senses become aroused" (662). So Émile must be under constant supervision, day and night. He can protect himself from outsiders, but you, as preceptor, have to protect him from himself. The worst thing he could discover is masturbation: "It would be very dangerous if [instinct] taught your pupil to cheat his senses and offer further means [suppléer] to satisfy them; if he once discovers this dangerous supplement, he is lost" (663). It would be better, if it is ab-solutely necessary to satisfy the needs he thinks he has, to take him to a woman: "whatever happens, I will snatch you back more easily from women than from yourself" (663). Rousseau senses the power of pri-mal narcissism, and the extremity of his denunciation of masturbation stands with his desire to link Émile to the rest of humanity.

But if this is the ideal proposed in *Émile*, it rarely seems to be the lot of the adolescent, and certainly not in Rousseau's own case. Rousseau's first account of masturbation in the *Confessions* is not of his own but that of another inmate of the hospice where he is undergoing conver-sion from Protestantism to Catholicism (a process he later reversed)—a hideous, tobacco-smelling bandit who tries to get the young Jean-Jacques into bed with him, then attempts to get him to touch his penis. When Rousseau recoils in horror, the bandit continues on his own and "I saw take off toward the fireplace and land on the ground something sticky and whitish that made me feel nauseous."[5] Masturbation is origi-nally placed under the sign of ugliness and nausea, somewhat in the manner that sensual arousal itself—as a child—has been placed under the sign of masochism: Émile's first experience of sexual pleasure comes from being spanked by his guardian Mlle Lambercier, in a famous sce-nario that, he tells us, determines his sexual tastes and even his charac-ter for the rest of his life. Yet the spanking arousal, though something shameful to confess, is clearly pure pleasure, in fact the very model of his idea of pleasure, one that he is going to spend much of the rest of his life trying to reproduce—for instance, in his "brief but lively" en-counters with one Mlle Goton, who deigns to play the schoolmistress to him, meting out the schoolboy's punishments.

The negative sign originally given to masturbation may be some sort of rhetorical compensation or self-punishment for the fact that once Rousseau learns to masturbate he evidently does so often and with pleasure. Here Rousseau presents himself as somewhere between the civilized young man, frequenter of society and of novels, who al-ready knows in his imagination before his body teaches him, and the solitary Émile, who must work through the processes of nature. The passage is worth quoting:

> I had come back from Italy, not quite as I had set out, but perhaps as no one of my age had ever returned. I had returned without my innocence but with my physical virginity. I had felt the progress of the years; my restless temperament had finally manifested itself, and its first eruption, completely involuntary, had given me anxieties about my health that depict better than anything else the innocence in which I had lived up till then. Soon reassured, I learned that dangerous method [ce dangereux supplément] that cheats nature, and saves young men of my disposition from many disorders at the price of their health, their vigor, and sometimes of their life. (108–9)

Here Rousseau picks up the antimasturbatory prejudice expressed—at about the time of the writing of the *Confessions*—by Dr. Samuel Auguste David Tissot in his famous and long-influential *L'onanisme* (1760), the remote cause of such Victorian inventions as penile rings designed to prevent nocturnal erections, and a host of other restraining devices for the masturbator. (Why Tissot's treatise was accepted so unhesitatingly and given such credence is a question that we may be able to work back to.) And we see that Émile must at all costs be prevented from finding this dangerous supplement. Yet Rousseau does not stop with the condemnation of masturbation, and what he goes on to say may come closer than the language about ruining one's health to the true problem he detects: "This vice that shame and timidity find so useful, has in addition a great attraction for lively imaginations: that is to dispose, so to speak, of the whole of the female sex, and to make the beauty that tempts them serve their pleasures without needing to obtain its consent" (109). Masturbation provides imaginary partners ready to do whatever provides the greatest pleasure, and thus promotes not only solitary sex but also a wholly solipsistic worldview. The "solution" to the problem, in Rousseau's own case, will be proposed by Madame de Warens, who takes him to bed with her (though she simultaneously has another lover, the groundskeeper Claude Anet). But it turns out that sex with Madame de Warens is not really what Rousseau wants. It doesn't "serve" his pleasures in the manner of the "dangerous supplement."

Masturbation is "supplement" because it adds a secondary level to the primary genital function, which to Rousseau is designed for reproduction. Yet this notion of supplementarity clearly is contradicted by Rousseau's discovery of primary narcissism, in the *Discourse on Inequality* and elsewhere. As Jacques Derrida has demonstrated, for somewhat different purposes, the logic of supplementarity may throw into question the autonomy of that which is supplemented for.[6] The supplement may be "dangerous" in part because it is primary. And its primacy depends not only on the "eruptions" of nature, but as well on those "lively imaginations." In fact, the language in which Rousseau describes his discovery of masturbation, in book 3 of the *Confessions*, echoes that in book 1, at the time of his misery as apprentice in the clock face engraving trade, when he becomes a devourer of books supplied by the ambulant lending library of La Tribu. He exhausts her meager supply in less than a year. What is he to do? "My senses, aroused for some time, called on me for a pleasuring of which I couldn't even imagine the object." In this peculiar situation, imagination takes over: "[M]y restless imagination took a step that saved me from myself and calmed my nascent sensuality: it nourished itself from the situations that had interested me in my readings, to recall them, to play variations on them, to combine them, to appropriate them to myself so much that I became one of the characters that I was imagining, that I always saw myself in the most agreeable positions according to my taste, finally that the fictive state I put myself into made me forget my real state which so distressed me" (41). He goes on to say that this love of "imaginary objects" became central to his character, which, full of passion yet disgusted by all that surrounded it, was forced to "feed on fictions."

Note that in the imagining of himself as a hero of the novels he has read, Rousseau "appropriates" fictional situations of pleasure to himself. That is the same term he uses to describe his masturbation fantasies, which "appropriate" women to his needs. If he "saves" himself from himself here, replacing sex by fantasy, fantasy leads right back to sex when he comes of age. We seem to be placed once again before the primacy of the imagination, of the fictional, in the very scenarios of self-pleasuring. The dangerous supplement in this manner takes us back nearly to the beginning of Rousseau's existence as he narrates it: from the time of his first readings, he tells us, he dates "without interruption the consciousness of myself" (8). The readings are largely novels, bequeathed by his mother (who died giving birth to him) and shared with his father. They take turns reading novels—sometimes until daybreak—and "I acquired, by this dangerous method, not only an extreme ease in reading and understanding, but a knowledge unique for my age of the passions." As a result, he received "bizarre and novelistic notions of human life, of which experience and reflection have never wholly cured me."

Once again, knowledge—always precocious, in Rousseau's account—is tied to a dangerous discovery of the real only by way of the fictional, and a fictional that is strongly marked by the erotic, and indeed is put to autoerotic ends. The appropriation or possession of the world comes about in fantasy, as in an act of masturbation. To pleasure the self is to enact its fictions, which are in turn one's entry into the "real" world. Freud would sketch the same scenario in his *Three Essays on the Theory of Sexuality* in 1905. For Rousseau—as to some extent for Freud also—the condemnation of a fantasmatic knowing of reality is juxtaposed to a claim that it is the knowledge most worth having—as when he talks of his plunge into the land of chimaeras, the only one worth inhabiting ("le pays des chimères, le seul digne d'être habité"). Here, in this primacy of the imagination—of fantasy, of fiction—in dealing with the sensual and especially the sensuous world, may lie both the glory and the dilemma of modern self-consciousness.[7]

Rousseau's youthful erotic life all takes place under the sign of fiction, of imaginary scenarios of fulfillment. Especially in books 2 and 3—the Turin episodes—he manages to fall in love with women from afar, and reach only imaginary outcomes. With Mme Basile, wife of the man to whom he is apprenticed, there is an extraordinary scene where he finds her alone in her room, seated knitting in a chair with her back to the doorway through which he enters, silently. Rousseau falls on his knees in ecstatic admiration on the threshold—only to have his presence revealed by a mirror hanging on the wall facing Mme Basile. She gestures him to her side, where he remains, his breast heaving with emotion—hers, too?—until the arrival of the shop foreman ends the moment without Rousseau's ever knowing what Mme Basile wants, and what might have been between them. Then there is Mlle de Breil, daughter of the House of Solar where Rousseau is now a valet, who is impressed by his philological prowess, in interpreting the family motto from Old French, and calls on him to pour her a glass of water—which he promptly spills over her plate and dress since his hand is trembling from emotion. She blushes. But then. "Here the novel ended" (Ici finit le roman) writes Rousseau, just as we were awaiting the denouement (96). There is none, there can be none, since realization takes place only in the imagination. Rousseau refers to this episode as one of the "too rare moments that put things back in their natural order." He always feels he is displaced—as a servant, for instance—and never in the place to which his imagination assigns him. But the moments of restoration are fleeting.

Many other episodes concur to the same end. In one of the most striking, Rousseau exposes his bare backside to servant girls drawing water from a fountain at the center of a courtyard in Turin. When one of them takes offense and comes up with a man to pursue him, he retreats into dark cellars leading from the courtyard—but eventually comes up against a blank wall. When confronted by his pursuers, he tells a story: he is a foreigner of high birth whose mind is deranged, and who has fled his father's house in order to avoid being locked up. Miraculously, the story works—the man lets him go. The fiction he invents here— what he calls an "expédient romanesque," which best translates as "novelistic invention"—is both false and obliquely true. He has fled his father's house in Geneva—managed to get himself locked out of Geneva after curfew—and his mind is certainly somewhat deranged, precisely by the fictions in which he tries to live, and he would like to think of himself (as in the typical Freudian "family romance") as of high birth, a kind of foundling who is always out of place. Rousseau spends much of his youth in some invented identity, as when he becomes aide to the "Archimandrite," the Orthodox priest who is traveling through Europe on a supposed mission to raise funds for the restoration of the Church of the Holy Sepulchre in Jerusalem. But he can't maintain his masks: when the French ambassador at Soleurre, in Switzerland, takes him aside for questioning, he spills out what he calls "ma petite histoire": the inner autobiography that is always just below the surface—and which is itself a mélange of the factual and the wishful.

It is interesting—and would merit much more comment—that what appears to be the one unproblematically happy sexual adventure in Rousseau's entire life occurs, while he is on a journey to Montpellier to consult with doctors, when he takes on a wholly false identity for his traveling companions. He renames himself "M. Dudding," an Englishman (though he admits he doesn't speak a word of English), and under this guise enters into a flirtation with Mme de Larnage that eventually (one has the impression she has to work hard for the result) lands him in her bed. Here, he "inebriates himself" during four or five days with sensual pleasures: "I enjoyed them pure, intense, without any admixture of trouble: they are the first and the only ones that I have thus enjoyed, and I can say that I owe it to Mme de Larnage not to have died without having known sexual pleasure" (253). But the liberating Dudding fiction cannot last. On his return trip from Montpellier, he has promised to come to visit Mme de Larnage at her home near Bourg-Saint-Andéol. The nearer his approach, the more he starts to worry. He knows she has a nubile daughter, and begins to imagine falling in love with the daughter, and causing pain and scandal for Mme de Larnage. This fictional scenario becomes so intense he decides simply to bypass Bourg-Saint-Andéol, and return directly to Madame de Warens— "Maman"—in Chambéry. The realization of desire through fictional self-reinvention can only take you so far. Since it is fictional, it returns you to fantasy, which then dictates your actions rather than reality.

These issues come to the fore again in a crucial way many years later—when Rousseau has reached his forties and leaves Paris for his rural retreat at the Hermitage. Though he has had a longtime mistress in his domestic servant Thérèse Levasseur, and the unsatisfactory companionship of Thérèse and her quarrelsome mother, he realizes that his life has gone by without his ever having experienced a true, reciprocated, passionate love. The scenario that now begins to unfold—it is recounted in book 9 of the *Confessions*—is brilliantly perverse. Thinking with regret of his lack of a true love, Rousseau begins to dream of one. It's June, he sits under fresh arbors and listens to the song of the nightingale. He falls back into the "too seductive softness for which I was born" and begins to call up in his memory the young women with whom he had fallen in love in younger years, including Mlle de Breil and Mme Basile, and two young women with whom he spent an idyllic afternoon picking cherries, and his music pupils—all those never possessed: "I saw myself surrounded by a harem of Houris from my old acquaintances, for whom the strongest affection wasn't a new emotion. My blood catches fire and simmers, my head spins despite hair already turning gray, and here is the grave Citizen of Geneva, here is the austere Jean-Jacques at nearly forty-five years of age suddenly become once again the extravagant pastoral shepherd" (427).

Yet he does not forget his age, and his resolution that love for him is a thing of the past, never to be realized in the present. What does he do? As he tells us, his reader will have guessed: "The impossibility of reaching real beings threw me into the land of chimaeras, and seeing nothing real that was worthy of my delirium, I nourished it in an ideal world that my creative imagination had soon peopled with beings according to my heart" (427). Here begins the composition of Rousseau's sole novel, *Julie, or the New Héloise* (*Julie, ou la Nouvelle Héloise*)—which, when published in 1762, would become the best-seller among all French eighteenth-century novels, creating in especial a readership that refused to believe its characters and their letters (it's an epistolary novel) could be anything but real. He invents his idealized characters—the beautiful, well-born, sexy Julie d'Etange; her tutor Saint-Preux (an idealized younger version of himself); her friend Claire d'Orbe—and starts writing letters from one to another, himself both the writer and the recipient, stimulating himself into an autoerotic frenzy as he mimics Saint-Preux's one night of lovemaking with Julie—the man in this version of the Eloise and Abelard story more the seduced than the seducer. It is a notable example of a novel created from within a masturbatory reverie (the only more explicit case I can think of is Jean Genet's *Notre Dame des Fleurs*, where the narrative overtly starts from an act of masturbation).

It is as Rousseau is about this process of self-pleasuring in the creation of fiction—he describes how he copies out his characters' letters on gilt-edged paper, using azure and silver blotting sand—that he receives a visit from Countess Sophie d'Houdetot, mistress of his acquaintance the poet Saint-Lambert, who has come to make sure he wants for nothing in his solitary retreat. Now, as if from out of his burst of fictional creativity, he falls in love with its realization in the person of Sophie d'Houdetot. Spring has fully arrived, to "redouble my tender delirium," and he has been composing the last letters of the novel "in erotic transports" when Sophie pays him a second visit, on horseback and in masculine dress: "She came, I saw her, I was drunk with love without an object, this inebriation fascinated my eyes, the object became fixed as her, I saw my Julie in Madame d'Houdetot, and soon I saw only Madame d'Houdetot, but embellished with all the perfections that I had given to the idol of my heart" (440). Love springs from a fictional matrix, the erotic from the autoerotic.

Though Rousseau considers this the only true love of his life, it cannot be erotically consummated. To be sure, Sophie d'Houdetot already has a lover—though Rousseau's adorations of her are such that one senses she might well yield to him nonetheless. Except that, in making the journey of a league from the Hermitage to Sophie's château in Eaubonne, Rousseau's imagination goes into overdrive again. He thinks of the kiss Sophie will give him upon his arrival, his head spins, he is dazzled into blindness—and he is never once able to make the trip "with impunity"—and he arrives "feeble, exhausted, spent"

(445). In other words, he must stop to masturbate along the way. And one gains the distinct impression that this is the way he prefers things to be. Love for Sophie is born from autoerotic fictions, and it must be satisfied through the autoerotic, in order, one might say, that it remain fiction. The whole episode with Sophie is placed under the sign of frustration, baffled desire, "continual irritation and privation that threw me into an exhaustion which it took me several years to climb out of, and which ended by giving me a hernia" (446). The erotic real turns back on him, provoking only the frustration both relieved and created by masturbation.

Rousseau's polemic against the theater, in his *Letter to d'Alembert*, responds to the same fear of the imaginary and the fictional. Since he believes that pity, or empathy, is a primal emotion in humans, he is sensitive to the effects that may be produced by playing on that emotion, by the staging of fictive affects. So when the *philosophe* d'Alembert in his article on Geneva in the *Encyclopédie*—the grand work of the French Enlightenment—proposes that Geneva would be improved by lifting its Calvinist ban on theater, Rousseau responds in a diatribe that argues the corrupting effect of the theater in its fictionalizing of emotion. The theater necessarily brings in its wake the corruption of the citizenry because it breeds artificial emotions. If it may be an inevitable institution in large, corrupt cities, Geneva should be protected from its effects. Rousseau picks up a long tradition of antitheatrical prejudice—represented notably by the church—in his own manner. What is an actor's talent? he asks. "The art of make-believe, of putting on another character than his own, of appearing different from what he is, of becoming aroused in cold blood, of saying something different from what one really thinks as if one really thought it, and, finally, to lose one's own place by taking that of another."[8] Here we recognize themes crucially central to Rousseau's thought: the fear of the fictional (allied, of course, to a particularly strong sense of fiction's power), the fear of dissimulation and imposture, the fear (surely allied again to the attraction) of losing one's assigned place in the world. The theater, like masturbation, becomes an arena in which one must be saved from oneself;

not so much from actors and actresses as from their effect on your own passions, which become aggrandized and artificial.

When Rousseau comes to publishing *La Nouvelle Héloise*, he faces the contradiction of offering the public a novel while castigating novels as fomenting the artificial life of the passions. He faces the paradox in the first lines of his preface: "Theatrical performances are necessary in large cities, and novels are necessary for corrupt peoples. I have witnessed the manners of my time, and I have published these letters. If only I had lived in a century when I would have had to throw them in the fire!"[9]

Here are all contrary impulses bundled into a perfectly contradictory but also coherent statement of the situation. Since we live in a fallen world (though Geneva is to be preserved as some prelapsarian ideal polity), we can send messages to one another only in corrupted genres. Indeed, no lesson preached by Rousseau could be received by the worldly French unless couched in a form that gives free play to the licentious fictional emotion. He is constrained to practice a form of communication, and forms of eros, that he reprobates. It's once again that "dangerous supplement" become necessity—become originary in the world we live in. Any purer form of existence belongs to a world imagined—as in the *Discourse on the Origin of Inequality*—before the coming of modern social order, before the institution of law, social rank, money—and all other forms of representation. Once within the world of representation, artifice, including the artificial stimulation of the passions, becomes inevitable.

Rousseau, though he can narrate from the standpoint of the ingénu, most often is aware of the "perversity" of both his argumentative positions and his erotic life. When Freud comes to write his first extensive study of sexuality, the *Three Essays on the Theory of Sexuality*, early in the twentieth century, he makes the interesting decision to begin by discussing "the perversions" in a strategy that I think is intended to demonstrate that all sexuality is in essence "perverse" in that it deviates from any simple aim, from the simply genital, and is always what he calls (precisely in relation to infantile sexuality) "psychosexuality," always bound up in fantasy, in fictions of satisfaction. Rousseau is in fact remarkably lucid on all this. It is not for nothing that he offers us early in book 1 of the *Confessions* a detailed account of his spanking by Mlle Lambercier, how it aroused him sexually, and how this first sexual experience then determined his sexual tastes, orientations, and indeed his whole character for the rest of his life. Freud in fact—in one of his rather rare tributes to this most important of his precursors—cites this episode in the *Three Essays*, in somewhat pompous manner, as an example to "educationalists" that spanking can cause the libido to flow into "collateral channels." Rousseau is constantly aware that he constitutes a case of the "collateral channel." The very premise of the *Confessions*, announced in its thunderclap of a first page, is his unlikeness to others: nature broke the mold in which she formed him.

Yet as Freud's references back to Rousseau indicate, the "perversities" displayed in the *Confessions* have more general reference, to the human condition as a whole. I noted earlier that Rousseau's claim that nature broke the mold in which he was cast self-consciously echoes a famous phrase from a precursor in introspection, Michel de Montaigne: "Each man bears the entire form, or impress, of the human condition" (Chaque homme porte la forme entière de l'humaine condition). The line takes us back to the original meaning of *character* as that which is engraved, as on a coin, or with a stylus. What Rousseau and Freud together suggest—and one then could call for confirmation on most of the modern writers who have dealt with sexuality, from Honoré de Balzac to Jacques Lacan, from James Joyce to Melanie Klein—is the extent to which psychosexuality and character are indistinguishable, and the extent to which both sexuality and character depend on fictional scenarios of fulfillment that may find their most characteristic or at least exacerbated form in solitary rather than reciprocal sex.

Here may be the moment to evoke Proust's contribution to the literary dramatization of masturbation, since the first volume of his very long novel contains one of the first explicit scenes of male masturbation in literature that doesn't otherwise fall into the category of pornography. As in the case of the Rousseau's *Confessions* and *Émile*, masturbation for Marcel—to give the protagonist of the novel the name he gives himself only once, and only hypothetically, in the course of some three thousand pages—is linked to imaginary, indeed highly fictional scenarios of erotic fulfillment. The topic, in fact, is broached in the fourth paragraph of the novel, during his liminary treatment of a self between sleeping and waking that is crucial (as we shall see later) to his exploration of self-understanding. Sometimes, like Eve born from Adam's rib, his sleep, his posture in bed gives birth to a woman. "Formed from the pleasure I was on the verge of enjoying, I imagined that it was she who offered it to me."[10] The imagination at work once again. The role of the imagination in self-pleasuring is more pronounced in the French, which makes of imagining in such an instance a reflexive verb: "je m'imaginais que c'était elle qui me l'offrait." The pleasure, in fact, is undecidably that of body and imagination.

The crucial and most explicit presentation of Marcel's masturbation comes later in "Combray"—the first part of the first novel (*Swann's Way*) in the complete structure *In Search of Lost Time* (*A la Recherche du temps perdu*). It is introduced by a long description of his autumnal walks, as an adolescent, in the direction of Roussainville and Montjouvain, which will eventually culminate in his account of how he witnessed, as a voyeur, the scene of eros and sadism enacted by Mlle Vinteuil and her female lover in the house that belonged to the composer (known in Combray as a humble piano teacher) Vinteuil. The scene witnessed at Montjouvain is, I think, crucial for the overall understanding of Proust's *Recherche* in its revelations not only of same-sex relations but, even more important, the complex relations of pain, humiliation, pleasure, morality—one might as well say, flat-footedly, the complex and nuanced relations of good and evil.

Roussainville/Montjouvain is coded, and will remain so throughout the novel, as the domain of erotic desire. During Marcel's walks, to the "exaltation brought by my solitude" is intermingled "the desire to see rise up before me a peasant girl whom I could press in my arms" (1:154). This new desire for a woman is so intermixed with all the other desires and exaltations set up by nature, his walks, the reflections in

the pond, the sun glinting off a wet tile roof, that he can't quite isolate it. The aesthetics of the natural landscape, the beauty of the books
he is reading, would all be contained in a kiss from this putative peasant girl. And as his imagination takes force from his sensuality, so his
sensuality expands "into all the domains of my imagination, my desire
had no more limits" (1:154). The passing girl evoked in his imagination
would be a necessary production of this very landscape, an erotic dryad
brought forth in response to his needs.

   Yet it is in vain that he implores the keep of the castle of Roussainville for "some child of the village," as if speaking to the sole confident
of "my earliest desires." The sentence continues, "when, from the top
storey of our house in Combray, in the small lilac-scented water closet,
I saw only its tower through the half-opened window, while with the
heroic hesitations of the traveler who sets out on a voyage of exploration or the desperation of a suicide, fainting, I opened in myself an
unknown path that I thought fatal, up to the moment when a natural
trace like that left by a snail came to rest on the wild current leaves
that hung down toward me" (1:156). I don't know that this is the first
explicit scene of male masturbation in the history of the novel, but like
the "exploration" of an unknown and possibly fatal path that it describes, the passage is itself daring, the infringement of a taboo, a self-
conscious choice to give a place to masturbation in this first volume of
a novel largely devoted to the emergence and formation of a self and its
identity. And while the sentence stresses the danger of an exploration
into an unknown within oneself, it ends with a "natural trace" of semen
on the leaf of the vine growing next the bathroom window, as if in a
reminder that this vertiginous new experience, after all, also belongs to
the natural world.

   By the time the long paragraph in which this description occurs
is finished, masturbation has become the very model of desire and its
frustrated satisfaction. "In vain"—the phrase becomes a leitmotif—
does he search for the woman who would respond to his aching desire.
When he understands that no peasant girl will emerge from behind
the trees in the Roussainville wood, he resigns himself to turning back

toward Combray. And he asks himself whether, had such a girl in fact appeared, he would have dared speak to her. She would doubtless have considered him a madman: "I ceased to believe that the desires I formed during these walks and which never came to realization were shared by other beings, were true outside myself. They came to appear to me only as purely subjective creations of my temperament, in themselves impotent, illusory" (156–57).[11] It is not insignificant that the very next paragraph will begin the narrative of the scene witnessed between Mlle Vinteuil and her lover through the window at Montjouvain—bringing "an impression, obscure at the time, from which later on emerged the notion I was to form of sadism." The sadism of Mlle Vinteuil, it develops from a long analysis, does not derive from her finding pain and evil pleasurable but from the opposite: that pleasure itself seems to her evil, illicit, and thus to be enjoyed only in a theatrical, melodramatic form. In a sense, sadism in the narrator's analysis of the Montjouvain episode is not so much the opposite of masochism as the opposite of narcissism, its frustrated twin.

The point to stress, I think, is that Proust, like Rousseau before him, understands masturbation as a key act and a key metaphor in the understanding of the self's desires. It is a form of self-love, to be sure, yet an unsatisfactory one in that the self would really wish recognition from and gratification by another—Rousseau's women from "novels" read or self-created, Marcel's imagined peasant girl from Roussainville—and accepts the narcissism of masturbation only reluctantly. Yet simultaneously with an affirmation that it expresses the nature of human desire more accurately than other forms of sexual desire, or perhaps more precisely, that other forms of sexual gratification are modeled on, and founded on, the autoerotic. Freud is in agreement on this point. As he succinctly puts it in the *Three Essays*, "In childhood, therefore, the sexual instinct is not unified and is at first without an object, that is, auto-erotic" (*SE* 7:233). And when Jacques Lacan writes, "What is desired? It is the desirer in the other" (Qu'est-ce qui est desiré? C'est le désirant dans l'autre[12]) he is, in his bleak way, making the same point: I want to be wanted by you in the same way that I want myself.

In saying that Freud has his own kind of problem with masturbation, I mean to point out that his attitude toward masturbation seems
to be ambivalent and shifting. While he has no problem in identifying
infantile autoeroticism as foundational to later erotic investments of
all types, he at times suggests that the habit of masturbation can (as in
Dora's case) produce undesirable secondary symptoms or even (as with
the Rat Man) indicate a kind of weakness of disposition. While he is
capable of recommending masturbation as at least a temporary relief
from sexual tension, he seems unable to free himself entirely from Victorian prejudices on the subject. Masturbation isn't the real thing, it
is a distraction—in the manner of fetishism—from the goal of genital
intercourse. Yet his own theorizing of human psychosexuality is too
wise and sophisticated to be content with the latent Victorianism of
his attitudes. (It was left to one of Freud's disciples, Wilhelm Stekel,
to write what might be considered the first "modern" psychoanalytic
study of masturbation, *Auto-Eroticism*, first published in English translation in 1940.)

Freud's "problem" with masturbation is suggested in a sentence
from his "Concluding Remarks" to the long discussion of the subject
by the Vienna Psychoanalytic Society in 1911–12: "Masturbation corresponds essentially to infantile sexual activity and to its subsequent
retention at a more mature age."[13] Adolescent and adult masturbation
is really a revival of what interests him more: infantile masturbation.
And the infantilism of masturbation may replicate a situation in which
there "is no necessity for trying to alter the external world in order to
satisfy a great need." Thus, masturbation can represent "a persistence of
psychical infantilism." It corresponds to "a carrying into effect of phan-
tasy—that half-way region interpolated between life in accordance
with the pleasure principle and life in accordance with the reality principle" (252). This, you might say, brings us back exactly to Rousseau's
problem: the masturbator loses a clear insight into the distinction
between fantasy and reality, the *pays des chimères* becomes as real to
him as any other. The question may then be why Freud, like Rousseau,
attaches pathogenic significance to such a surrender to a fantasmatic

version of the pleasure principle when so much in the thought of both of them tends to show both that the rejection of the reality principle can have its benefits—for the reality principle includes too much aggression, as Freud points out a few lines later—and that in any case the fantasmatic is in some large measure constitutive of the self. As Freud will suggest in his forays into art and literature—as in "The Moses of Michelangelo" or "Creative Writers and Daydreaming"—everyone is a potential poet or artist, and at the core of artistic activity is a kind of regression into infantile narcissism, which only the great poet can make acceptable to others. Freud's description of artistic activity is in fact not all that different from Rousseau's account of the composition of his novel: a self-pleasuring activity working toward the satisfaction of "His Majesty the Ego," and bribing us into compliance through the incentive of forepleasure and foreplay.[14] Jacques Lacan will bring to this understanding of everyman-as-poet a more sophisticated rhetorical and grammatical analysis, in his identification of basic psychic operations with fundamental literary tropes.

Freud's suspicion directed to fantasy, which he nonetheless sees as constitutive of the self, bears some affinities to his literary tastes, which on the whole fall within the realist tradition (though certainly he speaks with appreciation of fairy tales and of the tales of E.T.A. Hoffmann), and it's not clear that he entirely approves of the intimate confessional manner of a Rousseau: one senses that like many other readers he finds Rousseau a bit too "unmanly." It's not clear what he would have said about Proust, whom he might have found too ready to allow primary narcissism to become terminal solipsism. The last pages of Proust's novel record a decision to turn from the world and real people toward a life devoted to the creation of fiction. His book will be like a cemetery in that real people, family and friends, will die in order that the fiction live. The final model for the *Recherche* is *The Thousand and One Nights*: Scheherazade's nightly creation of fictions in order to stay alive by keeping the Sultan's desire alive, where desire includes both sexual and novelistic curiosity. Freud may confirm such a view of art but doesn't always seem consciously to subscribe to it.

In Freud's work on individual cases—that is, those case histories he wrote up and published—masturbation probably plays the most important role in the life of the "Rat Man" (in *Notes upon a Case of Obsessional Neurosis*, 1909). This may interest us because Freud here makes a strong case for obsessional neurosis as the typical form of mental illness afflicting intellectuals, those given to introspection and self-analysis. What happens in an extreme case of obsessional neurosis—that of the Rat Man and also, with very different results, that of Leonardo da Vinci—is that the drive toward knowledge—the "epistemophilic instinct," in James Strachey's lovely transposition of Freud's term *Wisstrieb*—leads to a brooding intellectualism. Freud writes, "Where the epistemophilic instinct is a preponderant feature in the constitution of an obsessional patient, brooding becomes the principal symptom of the neurosis. The thought-process itself becomes sexualized, for the sexual pleasure which is normally attached to the content of thought becomes shifted on to the act of thinking itself, and the satisfaction derived from reaching the conclusion of a line of thought is experienced as a *sexual* satisfaction."[15] Conjugated with what we have learned from Rousseau, from Proust, and from Freud himself, this suggests that intense intellectual activity—of the questing, brooding, Faustian sort—can become an act of self-pleasuring equivalent to masturbation, with both its satisfactions and its frustrations. If, as Walter Benjamin has argued, the modern novel is the realm of the solitary individual who, himself uncounseled, seeks the forever foreclosed meaning of life as a kind of wisdom to transmit to others, that solitude includes, mimics, finds at least an analogy in solitary sex. And isn't the figure of the detective, from Dupin to Holmes, also an instance of eroticized thought process? Holmes, in between the stimulation of the cases he is given to work on, falls into the lethargic stupor supposed to characterize the postorgasmic state of the masturbator.

It is interesting to find Freud returning to the question of masturbation in one of his very late notes—one found on the sheet he labeled "Findings, Ideas, Problems," dated from London on June 16, 1938—the day after his arrival there following his last-minute escape from the

Nazi takeover of Austria. On August 3, he added two notes, the first beginning, "A sense of guilt also originates from unsatisfied love. Like hate. In fact, we have been obliged to derive every conceivable thing from that material: like economically self-sufficient states with their *Ersatz* [substitute] products" (*SE* 23:300). It may be his reflecting on unsatisfied love that produced the second note jotted down later that same day:

> The ultimate ground of all intellectual inhibitions and all inhibitions of work seems to be the inhibition of masturbation in childhood. But perhaps it goes deeper; perhaps it is not its inhibition by external influences but its unsatisfying nature in itself. There is always something lacking for complete discharge and satisfaction—en attendant toujours quelquechose qui ne venait point—[always waiting for something that never came] and this missing part, the reaction of orgasm, manifests itself in equivalents in other spheres, in *absences*, outbreaks of laughing, weeping [Xy], and perhaps other ways. —Once again infantile sexuality has fixed a model in this. (*SE* 23:300)

So masturbation returns, just about a year before Freud's death, as an image of sexual incompletion and the very unsatisfactoriness of sexual satisfaction—a kind of Schopenhauerian or Faustian view of sexuality as inherently never satisfiable, always on the outlook for a coming that never is fulfilled. It's a bit like the Jews and the Messiah, in the manuscript of *Moses and Monotheism* that he was working on contemporaneously with these notes. It also, of course, expresses a basic pessimism about the possibility of human desire reaching any finally satisfactory end (and condemned to the final end of death). Masturbation at the last for Freud is the very emblem of that "quelquechose" that eludes human contentment, that spoils the work of the pleasure principle.

The formation of the modern self, in which, as Charles Taylor puts it in *Sources of the Self*, "self-completion through art" becomes a possible replacement for an earlier adherence to religious belief, seems to me to be bound up with the somewhat obsessional discourse on masturbation that takes shape in early modern Europe—in the manuals used for the training of confessors after annual confession was made an obligation for Christians at the Fourth Lateran Council in 1215, for instance, then in the anonymous *Onania* published around 1712, then in Tissot's *L'onanisme* in 1760, and its extraordinary Victorian and post-Victorian legacy, in whose wake Freud still stands, and which was still echoing in sex-education manuals as late as the 1950s.[16] It was perhaps only through Alfred Kinsey's report on sexuality in the human male, in 1948—with its claim that 92% of men and 62% of women masturbated—that the way was prepared for a positive valuation of masturbation, such as Shere Hite's report on sexuality in women in 1976. In the world of literary fiction, no doubt Philip Roth's *Portnoy's Complaint*, published in 1969, completed the descriptions undertaken by Rousseau and Proust—and Joyce, in Leopold Bloom's self-induced orgasm while watching Gerty McDowell on the beach—in a fictional frame that has Portnoy talking to the psychoanalyst Dr. Zeitbloom.

These accounts are by men, though certainly Freud has a good deal to say about masturbation by women, especially in the case history of Dora (in *Fragments from the Analysis of a Case of Hysteria*, 1905). And a number of depictions of women masturbating are also by men—for instance, in John Cleland's *Memoirs of a Woman of Pleasure*—since women masturbating, alone or with one another, becomes a topos of male eroticism, a turn-on regularly exploited in literary and cinematic pornography. Here, as in so many other domains, the woman's firsthand account seems to have been smuggled away by men, though more recent fiction, especially in France, has offered some compensation in the work of such novelists as Catherine Breillat, Catherine Millet, Elizabeth Barillé, and Catherine Cusset. While there were plenty of Victorian devices designed to prevent girls as well as boys from masturbating, the panic reaction to masturbation seems to have focused largely on males. The clue may lie in Proust's "natural trace" on the wild current leaf: the loss of semen, of a vital bodily fluid, was branded—

from Tissot onward—as debilitating, the destruction of virile strength, the undoing of manhood. If England's wars of Empire were won on the playing fields of Eaton and Rugby, that kind of play was designed in some measure to counteract and substitute for playing with oneself. Empire and industry needed a measure of sexual frustration ready to be sublimated into conquest and the accumulation of wealth, as well as into well-regulated familial and dynastic reproduction.

From Rousseau to Roth, by way of the Victorian doctors who invented the sadistic devices to prevent masturbation, one detects a suspicion that the solitary, self-regarding, self-pleasuring individual is dangerous if fully unleashed. That person requires discipline, socialization, surveillance. Hands need to be tied (often literally, to the bed rails) in order to prevent one from getting at oneself, as if the discovery of the self-sufficiency of self-pleasuring would undermine reproductive sex and, even more important—here we are back with Rousseau in *Émile*—destroy the sociosexual connections on which human civilization is based. A masturbator, in Rousseau's view, is not a good citizen. Those who in the wake of Tissot claimed masturbation would drive you blind or mad or kill you perhaps were recognizing, in dim and perverse ways, that getting at yourself in this way would be counterproductive, the promotion of reckless expenditure—and "to spend" in British slang has long had the meaning of "to come"—rather than thrift. It would be a version of the countereconomy envisioned by Georges Bataille in *The Accursed Share* (*La part maudite*), an economy of wasteful, useless expenditure rather than hoarding and capitalization.[17] As Michel Foucault has suggested, aristocratic marriage in traditional societies assured purity of descent, of the patrilineal bloodline: the antiquity and the glory of alliances created, the clear tracing of inheritance rights (no adultery allowed to women) defined your identity. The advent of the bourgeoisie in modern times tends to increase the importance of sexuality in marriage: instead of the bloodline, what counts is the projection of self, family, and property into the future, through one's descendants:

sperm rather than blood. Marriage becomes the guarantee of future descendants, of a kind of symbolic immortality through passing on of one's genetic material and one's cultural identity. Hence the emphasis on bodily health, on the protection of sperm (no masturbation) and the anxiety of venereal disease as seen in its hereditary consequences, a theme in a number of nineteenth-century novels.[18]

But one might also say—and here we turn to Georg Lukács and Walter Benjamin, and the notion of the modern novel as the realm of the solitary individual—that masturbation as a solitary act, getting at yourself as both subject and object of pleasure, may offer as well an encounter with an abyss. Those who claimed the horribly deleterious effects of masturbation might have been recognizing something else as well: the inherent unsatisfactoriness of human desire and fulfillment. As Freud recognized in his note of August 1938, desire never quite satisfies demand, which, in the Lacanian gloss on Freud, is always absolute, unconditional, modeled on the infant's demand for its mother's recognition. "Civilized sexual morality," Freud recognized, could never be fully satisfactory. There is an urge to return to the polymorphous pleasures of infancy, to touching and self-touching. It may be that in exploring masturbation as an instance of the modernity of the modern self we encounter a problem similar to that Freud explored in his essay on the "derealization of the self," which we will explore in chapter 6: the self at its fullest, most engaged, most aroused, continues to sense some hollowness in itself or to itself. Is this one more instance of the death drive showing its latent omnipresence?

In any event, the "great fear" unleashed by the "problem" of masturbation must be related to the intimacy of masturbation with the exploration of self-identity. In an age—our own—where talk about sexuality seems to be omnipresent and largely free of censorship, masturbation remains the most private of topics, referred to largely in nervous humor.[19] That, I think, is because it touches so closely the enigma of identity: the enigma of the self and desire, and the relation of enduring, ineradicable fantasy to the finite body. As William Butler Yeats fa-

mously writes of the self in "Sailing to Byzantium," addressing himself
to the "Sages" of Byzantine icons,

> Consume my heart away; sick with desire
> And fastened to a dying animal
> It knows not what it is; and gather me
> Into the artifice of eternity.

The "artifice of eternity" sets an achieved and static work of art—as hi-
eratic, Byzantine icon, for instance—against the desiring, and decaying,
body and the self "fastened" to it. In Yeats's poem, the artifice of eternity
represents explicitly the wish of an old man. One should not take it as
his only or final word, even on old men and desire. For there is also the
call to "frenzy," to a continuing eros in the exploration of self. "Why
Should Not Old Men Be Mad?" asks a title of a late Yeats poem that
becomes an affirmation of the kind of creation of fiction from eros that
Rousseau so carefully described in book 9 of his *Confessions*. And in another late poem, "An Acre of Grass," which I will discuss in chapter 7:

> Grant me an old man's frenzy.
> Myself must I remake
> Till I am Timon and Lear
> Or that William Blake
> Who beat against the wall
> Till Truth obeyed his call;

One senses such an inward erotic turn in the late work of a number
of great artists who lived long lives: in late Titian painting, in the late
quartets of Ludwig von Beethoven, in Paul Cézanne's final years of
painting in Provence. The old man's frenzy insists on the persistence
of desire in relation to the self in the face of impending decay and extinction of the body. The enigma of identity is never done with the
complex relations of desire to the self.

# 5 | "Inevitable Discovery": Searches, Narrative, Identity

In the law as in detective fiction, finding and determining someone's identity often entails a search. It's a problem not only of identity but of identification. In American law, searches and seizures are governed by a set of fairly elaborate (though confusing and contested) rules derived from the Fourth Amendment, which states, "The right of the people to be secure in their persons, houses, papers, and effects, against unreasonable searches and seizures, shall not be violated, and no Warrants shall issue, but upon probable cause, supported by Oath or affirmation, and particularly describing the place to be searched, and the persons or things to be seized." So that the legal search would seem to depend upon the probability of finding what one is looking for, detailed in a search warrant sworn before a judge. Things are, of course, not so simple: the very problem at issue—the search to know—dictates complications of "probable cause"—and effect.

What you might call here the "identificatory paradigm"—the process of finding out and pinning down identity—is in fact marked by a double impulsion, toward protection and violation. And there may be a strange logic in our thinking about knowledge of identity at work here, one in which the means used may be justified by the ends reached, but only if you can make it look as if the process moves in the reverse direction: that the means are in themselves untainted, and necessarily produce the end. To reach the moment of identification you must, in the theory of the law, at least, be able to establish that you have good grounds for knowing you can make that identification stick.

It would be interesting to write a whole book about the Fourth Amendment (this isn't that book) since it implicates so much of the modern sense of finding and knowing, from the most traditional kinds of sleuthing to the problems posed by contemporary technologies. The "search engines" of computers align with the question of privacy. We believe we have a constitutional protection against the police battering down our front door. What about against software that detects our buying habits, our addiction to certain websites, for instance? Does heat-imaging technology that can detect lights used to grow marijuana through the walls of house, from a van parked in the street, constitute a search?[1] The notion of privacy arises, historically, precisely in relation to threats to its invasion. The rise of the novel, for instance, can be read as both a fascination with private life—very much including sexual life—and a kind of invasion of that very privacy it values. To the extent that individual identity is bound up with the notion of privacy—of an autonomous self that has both physical and psychological boundaries that should not be breached without permission—the issue of searches and seizures very much reflects central tenets of modern identity.

In an English case well known to the framers of the U.S. Constitution, *Entick v. Carrington*, Lord Camden ruled in 1765, in an opinion summarized and enshrined by Justice Joseph P. Bradley of the U.S. Supreme Court in 1896: "It is not the breaking of his doors, and the rummaging of his drawers, that constitutes the essence of the offense; but it is the invasion of his indefeasible right of personal security, personal liberty, and private property, where that right has never been forfeited by his conviction of some public offense,—it is the invasion of this sacred right which underlies and constitutes the essence of Lord Camden's judgment."[2] Camden's and Bradley's words are echoed in

Justice William O. Douglas's famous opinion in *Griswold v. Connecticut*, which overturned laws banning the use of contraceptives: "Would we allow the police to search the sacred precincts of marital bedrooms for telltale signs of the use of contraceptives? The very idea is repulsive to the notions of privacy surrounding the marriage relationship. We deal with a right of privacy older than the Bill of Rights—older than our political parties, older than our school system."[3] And eventually, Douglas's "sacred precincts" would be expanded to include not only marital bedrooms but any space where human beings, of any sexual orientation, were engaged in what are now generally recognized to be private acts when performed by consenting adults.[4]

The understanding of the home as an inviolable private space reaches far back into history. It was famously summarized by Sir Edward Coke in *Semanyne's Case* (1604): "The house of every one is to him as his castle and fortress, as well for his defence against injury and violence as for his repose."[5] Searches in colonial America on the general warrant known as a "writ of assistance" were considered so abusive that Massachusetts and Virginia sought to outlaw the writ—leading to the confrontation led by James Otis that is often considered to be one of the sparks of the American Revolution. Those "sacred precincts" that Douglas sees as protected by a right of privacy remind us that domestic architecture itself reflects and enables modern notions of privacy. A medieval household, even of some affluence, might have provided privacy only in the form of a curtained bed in a general-use room. By the eighteenth century, houses begin to multiply small rooms and "cabinets," the kinds of spaces in which Samuel Richardson's heroines, Pamela and Clarissa, seek solitude to read and write letters— spaces threatened by invasion of the male seducer. The legislation of the French Revolution made domestic space inviolable to search and seizure between nightfall and sunrise, imaging a time and space in which the state was supposed to stay out of the individual's way. The front door remains a symbolic as well as a real barrier: police must still (in U.S. constitutional theory) knock and identify themselves before entering. Automobiles may be searched for what lies in "plain view," but opening a car trunk normally requires a demonstration of probable cause. Lines are uncertain and shifting in Fourth Amendment doctrine, but there is an underlying sense that somewhere lies a space, real and psychological, that the state cannot enter absent a showing of cause and its sanction by a warrant.

The extrapolation from the Fourth Amendment's protection of persons and places from unreasonable search and seizure to the notion that a basic right of personhood is at stake is often identified with Justice Louis Brandeis, who in 1890 wrote that the principle involved is "not the principle of private property, but that of an inviolate personality."[6] Then, in a famous dissent from the Supreme Court's refusal to extend Fourth Amendment protections to telephone conversations in *Olmstead v. United States* in 1928, he declared,

> The makers of our Constitution undertook to secure conditions favorable to the pursuit of happiness. They recognized the significance of man's spiritual nature, of his feelings and of his intellect. They knew that only a part of the pain, pleasure and satisfactions of life are to be found in material things. They sought to protect Americans in their beliefs, their thoughts, their emotions and their sensations. They conferred, as against the Government, the right to be let alone—the most comprehensive of rights and the right most valued by civilized men. To protect that right, every unjustifiable intrusion by the Government upon the privacy of the individual, whatever the means employed, must be deemed a violation of the Fourth Amendment.[7]

Brandeis postulates (though many a legal scholar would disagree with him) the large principle underlying the prohibitions of the Fourth Amendment: that the security against intrusion it promises really reposes on the notion that there is an area of individual privacy and personality that—like those "sacred precincts" of the marital bedroom—cannot be invaded by the state.[8] In this sense, the Fourth Amendment parallels the Fifth, which says the state cannot compel someone to be a witness against himself. There must be rules laid down to protect the individual's inner sense of identity against the state's need to know, classify, inventory that identity. If courts often interpret this as a balancing act, attempting to draw lines and establish rules about where and what can be searched and seized and in what manner, fundamentally it represents a conflict and a clash, in which the internal sense of "inviolate personality," in Brandeis's phrase, and the state's external need to know persons are at a standoff. I have argued the interdependence of the inner and the outer senses of identity—even in their very opposition— just as I see the understanding of privacy, including individuality, as interdependent with its invasion. Searches and seizures as adjudicated in the law (and in detective fiction) may offer some insight into our sense of identity, how we seek it out, establish it, protect and violate it. And the story told in many a case of search and seizure may tell us something about the very logic of narrative in the modern understanding of who we are.

## Searching for Pamela Powers's Body

The case of *Brewer v. Williams*, decided by the Supreme Court in 1977, turns on a fateful ride in a police cruiser over the "snowy and slippery miles" between Davenport and Des Moines, Iowa, on December 26, 1968. In the police cruiser, Detective Leaming delivered what became known as "the Christian Burial Speech" to the man he had in custody, Robert Williams, suspected of murdering ten-year-old Pamela Powers. Addressing Williams, whom he knew to be a deeply religious person, as "Reverend," Leaming evoked the weather conditions, the forecast of several inches of snow, the likelihood that the young girl's body would be buried and unlocatable. Since, Leaming claimed, Williams surely knew where the body was he could take the police officers to it—and then her parents could give her a decent Christian burial. "I want to give you something to think about while we're traveling down the road," Leaming said. And then:

> "They are predicting several inches of snow for tonight, and I feel that you yourself are the only person that knows where this little girl's body is, that you yourself have only been there once, and if you get a snow on top of it you yourself may be unable to find it. And, since we will be going right past the area on the way into Des Moines, I feel that we could stop and locate the body, that the parents of this little girl should be entitled to a Christian burial for the little girl who was snatched away from them on Christmas [E]ve and murdered. . . . I do not want you to answer me. I don't want to discuss it any further. Just think about it as we're riding down the road."[9]

Williams eventually directed the police to a service station, where he claimed to have left the girl's shoes, then to a rest area where he claimed to have left a blanket in which the body was wrapped; finally he led them to the body itself.

The problem is that the Davenport attorney representing Williams had obtained a promise from the police that his client would not be questioned during the ride (from which the attorney had been excluded) and that promise had been confirmed in a phone call to Williams's attorney in Des Moines. Thus the information about the location of the body elicited by the "Christian Burial Speech" was obtained through a violation of Williams's Sixth Amendment right to the assistance of counsel and, by the Supreme Court's 5–4 decision in *Brewer v. Williams*, should not have been allowed as evidence. The court remanded the case for retrial, noting that at retrial evidence of the body's location and condition "might well be admissible on the theory that the body would have been discovered in any event, even had incriminating statements not been obtained from Williams" (407, n. 12). That discovery "in any event" would then be the issue at contest when the case of Robert Williams—convicted of first degree murder at his second trial, and sentenced to life imprisonment—returned to the Supreme Court in 1984 as *Nix v. Williams*.

Back to December 26, 1968. While Detective Leaming and Robert Williams were shut in the police cruiser making its way west on Interstate 80, a search party of some two hundred volunteers directed by Agent Ruxlow of the Iowa Bureau of Criminal Investigation was searching for the body of Pamela Powers. The search party set off at 10:00 a.m., moving westward through Poweshiek County into Jasper County. Ruxlow had marked highway maps of the two counties as grids, and assigned teams of four to six persons to search each grid. The searchers were instructed to "check all the roads, the ditches, any culverts. . . . If they came upon any abandoned farm buildings, they were instructed to go onto the property and search those abandoned farm buildings or any places where a small child could be secreted."[10] The search party did not find the body: at about 3:00 p.m., Leaming sent word to Ruxlow that Williams would lead him to the body, and the search was called off. At this point, searchers were some two and a half miles from where the body lay, near a culvert in Polk County. The map of Polk County had not yet been sectioned into grids for searching, but Ruxlow testified that he had that county map, and would have marked it off for the search party had it been necessary for the search to continue. The body was found in the easternmost part of Polk County. Another three to five hours of searching should have been sufficient to discover it.

On the basis of this record, the Supreme Court in *Nix v. Williams*, in an opinion written by Chief Justice Warren Burger, accepted the notion that the so-called exclusionary rule—excluding evidence illegally seized—allows of an exception for "inevitable discovery."[11] This was the conclusion of the trial court when Williams was retried and convicted. As summarized and underlined by Burger,

> The trial court concluded that the State had proved by a
> preponderance of the evidence that, if the search had not been
> suspended and Williams had not led the police to the victim,
> her body would have been discovered *"within a short time"* in

essentially the same condition as it was actually found. The trial court also ruled that if the police had not located the body, "the search would clearly have been taken up again where it left off, given the extreme circumstances of this case and the body would [have] been found *in short order*."

In finding that the body would have been discovered in essentially the same condition as it was actually found, the court noted that freezing temperatures had prevailed and tissue deterioration would have been suspended. (437–38; emphasis in the original)

In other words, the inevitable discovery exception to the exclusionary rule—accepted in a large majority of courts, state and federal, but not explicitly by the Supreme Court before the present case—appears to depend on a factual narrative, one that can precisely prove, or at least forcefully suggest, true inevitability. The search party had proceeded methodically across those grids in Poweshiek and Jasper Counties; it was about to enter Polk County, which was about to be grid-lined as well; it was only two and a half miles from the site. As the court case tells us, "The child's body was found next to a culvert in a ditch beside a gravel road in Polk County, about two miles south of Interstate 80, and essentially within the area to be searched" (436). Like "the place where the three roads meet" in Sophocles' *Oedipus Tyrannos*—where Oedipus meets and slays his unknown father—the place of Pamela Powers's body is designated as a place of fatal and inevitable convergence. The body was there—and preserved by the freezing weather—waiting to be discovered.[12]

Yet counsel for Williams makes an ingenious attempt to rebut the doctrine of inevitable discovery, arguing that it is "only the 'post-hoc rationalization' that the search efforts would have proceeded two and one-half miles into Polk county where Williams had led the police to the body" (448). The point may be well taken. The doctrine of inevitable discovery clearly starts from the end of the trail of the search—at the dead body—and then traces the path, be it inevitable or merely probable, that would have led to it. "Inevitable discovery" implicitly suggests that narratives work back from their ends, which are the real determinants of their vectors, the direction and intention of their plotting. A number of theorists of narrative have argued that such is the logic of narrative: that a large part of its coherence derives from the knowledge that an end lies in wait, to complete and elucidate whatever is put in motion at the start.[13] Narratives tend to make their endings appear inevitable, since that is part and parcel of their meaning-making function. If, as Aristotle claims in his *Poetics*, stories have a beginning, a middle, and an end, it would be the poor (or particularly challenging) story in which there appeared to be no relation between beginning and end. And in this sense, Williams's lawyer's effort to contest "inevitable discovery" may be on target: inevitable discovery perhaps has less to do with the way things happen in the world than with our narrative expectations. The body was there, waiting for the search party to discover it. Just as, in a famous example from Anton Chekhov, the gun hung on the wall in act 1 of the play is waiting to be discharged at someone's head in act 3.[14] To call discovery inevitable is to view the story from the perspective of the end, and to subscribe to a possibly mechanistic notion that plots grind on to their logical outcome, in a version of Jean Cocteau's "infernal machine."

Justice William Brennan—joined by Justice Thurgood Marshall— dissents in *Nix v. Williams* precisely on a version of this point. Brennan accuses the court, "in its zealous efforts to emasculate the exclusionary rule," of losing sight of the "the crucial difference between the 'inevitable discovery' doctrine and the 'independent source' exception from which it is derived" (459). The "independent source" exception allows the use of evidence found by an independent and lawful investigation even when there has been a constitutional violation elsewhere in the search. "Inevitable discovery" similarly requires an independent and lawful investigation, but "it differs in one key respect from its next of kin: specifically, the evidence sought to be introduced at trial has not actually been obtained from an independent source, but rather would have been discovered as a matter of course if independent investigations were allowed to proceed. . . . The inevitable discovery exception necessarily implicates a hypothetical finding that differs in kind from the factual finding that precedes application of the independent source rule." Brennan finds, then, that inevitable discovery contains a measure of the hypothetical—what Williams's lawyer calls a "post-hoc rationalization"—and therefore concludes that it requires a higher standard of proof than the "preponderance of the evidence" test accepted by the majority. Instead, says Brennan, the court should insist upon "clear and convincing" evidence when the inevitable discovery exception is invoked. That is, since inevitable discovery, unlike independent source evidence, depends on a hypothetical narrative, it requires a heightened burden of proof, which the lower courts failed to insist on.

The distinction between evidence in fact discovered by an independent investigation and that which "inevitably" would have been seems more crucial than the majority in *Nix v. Williams* allows. The hypothetical "would have been discovered," operating post-hoc, may be more determined by the narrative logic of retrospectivity than the court sees or admits. In the case of Pamela Powers's body there was an actual search party on course to reach the object of the search with high probability, if not true inevitability. In some subsequent cases, the inevitable discovery doctrine has been given far more dubious uses. For instance, cocaine found in a person's baggage in a search not incident to his arrest, a search only held later without apparent probable cause, was allowed as evidence on the grounds that the cocaine would inevitably have been discovered since there would have routinely been an "inventory search" of the suspect's possessions.[15] This doubles the "would haves." Even more dubiously, courts have held that evidence found in an illegal warrantless search was admissible because a search warrant could have and would have been obtained if the police had sought it.[16] On this logic, the exclusionary rule could become a dead letter whenever one could plausibly argue that evidence would have been legally discovered—if the police had discovered it by legal means.

Standing at the vantage point of the end of the story, the proof that the suspect was in fact guilty of illegal activity, the post-hoc logic of the inevitable discovery doctrine can be used to justify practically

anything—because it is the very logic of narrative, which makes sense
by way of its end. Note that application for a search warrant, as required by the Fourth Amendment, itself involves telling the story of
what you expect to find in the search—an expectation that then will
be confirmed or falsified by the search itself. When you elide the difference between the standpoint from which you state what you expect
will be the outcome, and the standpoint of the outcome from which
you state that this was what you expected all along, you begin to efface
the difference between the probable—the hypothetical fiction—and
the actual. You confuse the logic of the telling of the story with the
putative logic of the events the story tells.

I shall return to the logic of narrative in a moment. First, I want
to explore a bit more the hypothetical search versus the real search. In
an Eighth Circuit Court of Appeals case in 1988, *Feldhacker v. United
States*, Julia Lynn Feldhacker and Mark David Critz claimed that the
government obtained the names of five witnesses (purchasers of drugs
from Feldhacker) through statements of the defendants subsequently
ruled to have been illegally obtained, whereas the prosecution responded that the identities of the purchasers-witnesses would inevitably have been discovered because it legally discovered two address
books containing the names of the purchasers. To which the defense
responded that the prior "tainted knowledge" permitted the prosecution to pick out the relevant names from the lists of addresses, which
were fragmentary and vague. The Court of Appeals ruled in the government's favor, but conceded in a footnote,

> There are reasonable limits to the scope that courts will impute
> to the hypothetical untainted investigation. An investigation
> conducted over an infinite time with infinite thoroughness
> will, of course, "ultimately or inevitably" turn up any and all
> pieces of evidence in the world. Prosecutors may not justify
> unlawful extractions of information post hoc where lawful
> methods present only a theoretical possibility of discovery.
> While hypothetical discovery by lawful means need not be

reached as rapidly as that actually reached by unlawful means, the lawful discovery must be inevitable through means that would actually have been employed. Cf. Williams. . . . [17]

This comment opens the dizzying perspective of a kind of narrative utopia where an infinitely extended search of infinite thoroughness would inevitably discover everything in the world. It registers a breathtaking confidence in the legibility of the world, and the capacity of human intelligence to decipher it. Or is the court being ironic, simply offering a reductio ad absurdum of search doctrine? Whatever the intended tone here, the comment stands with the premises of the classic detective story—in the tales of Sherlock Holmes, for instance—or such as Wilkie Collins's *The Moonstone*, in which Sergeant Cuff believes that if you search the detritus of civilization long enough, the needed clues will come to light.[18] But it also figures a kind of eventual impasse of narrative as discovery in the infinitely protracted search for all the evidence in the world—something that might figure in a story by Jorge Luis Borges. In fact, Borges's "Funes the Memorious" instances the narrative problem created when someone has infinite powers of memory, which result in the re-creation of a past in every detail, which means that going over that past will take as much time as the past itself.[19] The doctrine of "infinite discovery," as one might call it, may return us in disquieting ways to the hypothetical narratives of "inevitable discovery," which depend—as narrative always does—on a selection of what is considered to be relevant, thus on the creation of that sense of the inevitable. Do we traffic also in "inevitable identities" in our search for malefactors?

## Searching on Dartmoor, and the Hunter's Wisdom

"'You reasoned it out beautifully,' I exclaimed in unfeigned admiration. 'It is so long a chain, and yet every link rings true.'"[20] Thus Dr. Watson to Sherlock Holmes, at the end of "The Red-headed League." Similar statements can be found at the conclusion of many of the Holmes stories: they image a process of narrative reasoning that brings the detective to his discovery. In a variant: " 'Wonderful!' cried the colonel. 'Wonderful! You might have been there!' "[21] Discovery is so acute that it mimics eyewitness. This line comes at the end of "Silver Blaze," a case in which Holmes is faced with the disappearance of the famous race horse only a week before the running of the Wessex Cup in which he is the favorite, and the apparent murder of his trainer, John Straker, found bludgeoned to death in a hollow on Dartmoor.

Holmes's discoveries in "Silver Blaze" occur because he is looking for them, he expects to find them. For instance, at the scene of the crime:

> "Hullo!" said he suddenly. "What's this?" It was a wax vesta, half burned, which was so coated with mud that it looked at first like a little chip of wood.
>
> "I cannot think how I came to overlook it," said the inspector with an expression of annoyance.
>
> "It was invisible, buried in the mud. I only saw it because I was looking for it."
>
> "What! you expected to find it?"
>
> "I thought it not unlikely." (1:534)

That which is hidden reveals itself when you know it must be there, when you have postulated its discovery as inevitable. The "wax vesta" match had to be there since Straker would have had to strike a light in order to perform the delicate operation—nicking Silver Blaze's tendon—that Holmes now knows Straker must have planned. Similarly, since "The horse is a very gregarious creature," Silver Blaze cannot be running wild on the moor; he must have gone to a stable—if not his own, King's Pyland, then the nearby rival, Mapleton: "He is not at King's Pyland. Therefore he is at Mapleton. Let us take that as a working hypothesis and see what it leads to. This part of the moor, as the inspector remarked, is very hard and dry. But it falls away towards Mapleton, and you can see from here that there is a long hollow over yonder, which must have been very wet on Monday night. If our supposition is correct, then the horse must have crossed that, and there is the point where we should look for his tracks" (1:535). So it is that the finding of the very tracks to be followed is determined by what Holmes calls his "working hypothesis," a prediction of what is to be discovered. He and Watson find the tracks, then lose them for half a mile, then pick them up again close to Mapleton stables—and now a man's footprints appear next to the horse's. Tracks of horse and man now make a sharp turn back toward King's Pyland—but Watson quickly perceives that the same prints reappear parallel to the first track, now returning toward Mapleton. In other words—as Holmes reconstructs the scene—Mapleton's trainer, Silas Brown (who has heavy stakes on Silver Blaze's rival) encountered the horse wandering on the moor early in the morning, recognized him, and in a first impulse thought to return him to King's Pyland—but then changed his mind, led him to Mapleton, and there painted over his silver blaze to disguise him.

Holmes need now only confront Silas Brown:

> "He has the horse, then?"
> "He tried to bluster out of it, but I described to him so exactly what his actions had been upon that morning that he is convinced that I was watching him." (1:538)

The clues, the tracks, are so exactly followed that Holmes "might have been there."[22] Even when found, Silver Blaze, his blaze concealed, is not detected by his owner, Colonel Ross, and it is only after the horse has won the Wessex Cup that Holmes dramatically discloses his discovery to the others: the identity of the horse, and the horse's identity as the murderer—in self-defense—of John Straker.

The most memorable exchange in "Silver Blaze" concerns the dog in the night. Inspector Gregory asks Holmes,

> "Is there any point to which you would wish to draw my attention?"
> "To the curious incident of the dog in the night-time."

"The dog did nothing in the night-time."

"That was the curious incident," remarked Sherlock
Holmes. (1:540)

That the dog did nothing during the night—while Silver Blaze was being abducted from the stable—indicates to Holmes that the abductor
must have been familiar to the dog, who would otherwise have barked.
So what sounds like a Monty Python routine is one more indication of
how the chain of discovery gives significance to each incident that constitutes one of its links, even that incident which is a nonhappening.

The chain of discovery offers one example of what narrative theo-
rist Gérard Genette calls "the determination of means by ends . . . of
causes by effects." Genette states further, "This is that paradoxical logic
of fiction which requires us to define every element, every unit of the
narrative by its functional character, that is to say among other things
by its correlation with another unit, and to account for the first (in
the order of narrative temporality) by the second, and so on. . . ."[23]
The linking of events means that their enchainment is determined by
the post-hoc reasoning of the discoverer, then laid out as a plot leading from beginning to discovery. The discourse of narrative "motivation"—as in Chekhov's example of the gun hung on the wall—plots
the story from end to beginning, then recounts it from beginning to
end. The continuing popularity of detective fiction may in part derive
from its dramatizing so evidently—perhaps too facilely—the very process of narrative plotting.

"Discovery" in "Silver Blaze" is not inevitable—indeed, all the
would-be discoverers are stumped until Holmes comes on the scene.
But it is part of Holmes's prestige and continuing appeal to make discovery *appear* inevitable. The Holmes stories postulate a knowable
world, a universe governed by laws that are ultimately discoverable to
the percipient and patient investigator—like that world imaged in the
strange footnote to *Feldhacker*. Crime is an aberrancy in the world, the
introduction of the menace of chaos. Think of Holmes's baffled meditation at the end of "The Cardboard Box." But discovery through rea-

son shows that the chaos is only apparent. Holmes's discovery sounds as a victory of law over chance, reason over aberrancy, and restores a world of perfect order.

In an ambitious argument that touches on Sherlock Holmes, on Sigmund Freud, and on the prototype of a kind of discovery procedure used by both that was devised by the art historian Giovanni Morelli—whose premise was that in order to authenticate a painting one should look to minute details such as ear lobes and fingernails, where an artist's unique characteristics would be better revealed than in the ensemble—historian Carlo Ginzburg undertakes to isolate and define a special form of cognition by way of clues.[24] Knowing by way of clues—following the traces left by one's quarry—is, of course, the detective's method. It doesn't work by deduction from a general law (though it may call upon fragments of general wisdom, such as "the horse is a gregarious animal"), nor does it quite work inductively from part to whole. It is rather a science of the concrete and particular that achieves its discoveries through putting particulars together in a narrative chain. Ginzburg identifies this science with the huntsman's lore, noting, "Man has been a hunter for thousands of years. In the course of countless pursuits he learned to reconstruct the shapes and movements of his invisible prey from tracks in the mud, broken branches, droppings of excrement, tufts of hair, entangled feathers, stagnating odors. He learned to sniff out, record, interpret, and classify such infinitesimal traces as trails of spittle. He learned how to execute complex mental operations with lightning speed, in the depth of a forest or in a prairie with its hidden dangers" ("Spie," 166/"Clues," 102). Even in a posthunting society, searches reach their discoveries by such tracking of details, making them into a chain of meaning, uncovering their connections. Ginzburg speculates that this kind of knowing may in fact lie at the inception of narrative itself: "This knowledge is characterized by the ability to move from apparently insignificant experiential data to a complex reality that cannot be experienced directly. And the data is always arranged by the observer in such a way as to produce a narrative sequence, which could be expressed most simply as 'someone passed this way.' Perhaps the very idea of narrative (as distinct from the incantation, exorcism, or invocation) was born in a hunting society, from the experience of deciphering tracks" ("Spie," 166/"Clues," 103).

On Ginzburg's hypothesis, narrative would be a cognitive instrument of a specific type, one "invented" for the decipherment of details of the real that only take on their meaning when linked in a series, enchained in a manner that allows one to detect that "someone passed this way." This is what Sherlock Holmes's searches—for a wax vesta, for hoofprints in the muddy hollows of the moor—are all about. And the "huntsman's paradigm" may indicate in more general terms the use value of narrative as a form of speech and cognition: it is the instrument we use when the putting together of particulars into a meaningful sequence seems to be the only way to track down our quarry, whatever it may be. Working from Ginzburg's suggestions, Terence Cave argues that the huntsman's paradigm or "cynegetic paradigm" points us toward that most basic and enduring and useful of plots: the story that leads to anagnorisis or recognition. "The sign of recognition in drama and narrative fiction belongs," writes Cave, "to the same mode of knowledge as the signature, the clue, the fingerprint or footprint and all the other tracks and traces that enable an individual to be identified, a criminal to be caught, a hidden event or state of affairs to be reconstructed."[25] Signs of recognition in literature reach back to antiquity and forward to modernity: see the scar on Odysseus's thigh that enables his old nurse Eurykleia to recognize him by touch; see the hidden birthmark of William Shakespeare's Cymbeline; see the notorious *la croix de ma mère* of nineteenth-century melodrama, the token that at the denouement allows the orphan to be recognized, true identities established. It is easy to recognize that the law, particularly when dealing with issues of evidence, must make use of the huntsman's paradigm, seeking to show how finding signs and deciphering tracks will lead to the apprehension of what passed that way.

Ginzburg further specifies the relation of the huntsman's paradigm to law in his discussion of the arcane subject of divination, as in the Mesopotamian tradition, based on the minute investigation of seemingly trivial details: "animals' innards, drops of oil on the water, stars, involuntary movements of the body." According to Ginzburg, Mesopotamian jurisprudence was similarly oriented toward the interpretation of particulars: "Mesopotamian legal texts themselves did not consist of collections of laws or statutes but of discussions of concrete examples" (168–69; 104). So the same paradigm can be found in the divinatory and jurisprudential texts, with this difference that the former are directed to the future, the latter to the past. Ginzburg then further stretches his hypothesis to suggest that narrative modes of knowing (such as archaeology, paleontology, geology) all make what he calls "retrospective prophecies" (183; 117), which he sees as the key to the popularity of detective fiction.

The "case method" of American legal study—introduced by C. C. Langdell at Harvard Law School shortly before Arthur Conan Doyle began his Sherlock Holmes tales—resembles the Mesopotamian approach in its insistence that argument be worked up from concrete particulars.[26] And here, too, the concept of "retrospective prophecy" is relevant: that which is plotted forward from the initial situation to the predictable outcome can be so ordered because one in fact stands at the point of the outcome. The point of the exercise, in a pedagogical and cognitive sense, is to retrace how that outcome was inevitable from the "facts of the case." And if we enjoy the mental processes activated by detective fiction and legal argument, it must be in part because of the satisfaction derived from the demonstration of inevitability: it had to be this way, and no other way.

Searches for evidence may always include a "retrospective prophecy" factor. As I mentioned earlier, application for a search warrant must contain a prediction of what is to be found. The warrant application sets forth the evidence that the police believe they (inevitably) will find if given permission to search. Warrants must be based on "probable cause" that what is sought will be found. In this sense, searches for evidence always involve a prior story, a hypothetical story that the search intends to confirm.[27] But the doctrine of "inevitable discovery" offers a particularly clear instance of "retrospective prophecy." It makes the claim that a trail to the quarry exists, and that the (hypothetical) following of the traces and tracks making up this trail would (certainly) lead to the quarry. In other words, it takes the logic of the huntsman's paradigm—the logic of narrative knowing—and, in its hypothetical application of the paradigm, to a case in which the quarry was not but would have been found, exposes the logic of discovery as a narrative process. In the doctrine of inevitable discovery, we know that the quarry is there, at the end of the trail. The question is whether following the trail would inevitably have led to it. When you decide—as in *Nix v. Williams*—that it would have, you sign on to the logic of narrative discovery in a particularly telling way, accepting that the huntsman's lore is infallible, and infallibly cognitive. When as a legal decision maker you so decide, you may be simply affirming the nature of the law as discipline: affirming its belief in evidence as the meaningful entailment of tracks and traces.

The inevitable discovery doctrine, pushed to its limits, can indeed result in some (limited) version of the "all pieces of evidence in the world" becoming admissible in some putative search of "infinite thoroughness." For instance, as I noted earlier, in cases where police claim that a passenger's luggage or the trunk of a car would inevitably have been subject to an "inventory search," the fruits of an illegal search have sometimes been admitted on grounds that they would have inevitably been discovered by the later routine search.[28] Yet more dubiously, the doctrine has been used to admit evidence found in an illegal warrantless search on the grounds that a warrant could have and would have been obtained, and thus the evidence would have been inevitably discovered.[29] Both these instances further lay bare the device, and further suggest how assumptions about the narrative outcome shape the story and confer, precisely, the sense of inevitability on the unfolding of its plot.

The huntsman's lore may be said to intersect in modern societies with an identity problem. As I tried to suggest in chapter 1, the era in which the classic detective story came into being and flourished was one in which emergent bourgeois society became increasingly anxious about signs of identity of its criminal elements. Cities were growing rapidly, especially from an influx of the poor from the provinces, looking for work. The laboring classes, as Louis Chevalier so well demonstrated, came to appear dangerous classes.[30] The increasingly undifferentiated mass of city dwellers called for positive identification of its malefactors and marginals. Prostitutes in Paris, for instance, were required to register with the police, to carry a card if streetwalkers, to be assigned a number if in a brothel. When *la marque*—the practice of branding convicts' bodies with letters signifying their sentence—was abolished on humanitarian grounds in France in 1832, a new anxiety developed concerning the identification of recidivists. Honoré de Balzac's protean figure of Jacques Collin offers, as we saw, a striking dramatization of the anxiety.

The hypothesis of identification by way of the apparently insignificant detail proposed by Morelli for art historical authentification belongs to the same movement that produced Alphonse Bertillon and his systematic measurements, and Cesare Lombroso and his study of criminal "types." Freud later found confirmation in Morelli for his own methods in his study of revealing "parapraxes" and details in obscure corners of dreams. (Freud also found inspiration in Sherlock Holmes.) The coming of fingerprinting at the dawn of the twentieth century appeared to offer a definitive solution, especially to the problem of identifying recidivists. Now we knew that each individual carried on his fingerprints a sure and recordable mark of his or her identity. Judge Pollak's decision in *United States v. Llera-Plaza* reassigned fingerprinting to some version of the huntsman's lore—and, of course, set off a seismic reaction within the forensics community. Freud's sense of identity is more complex and problematic, but the problem of saying who you are remains crucial in psychoanalysis.

Narrative Retrospect

All the practices of identification by way of signs interpreted as clues in the narrative of what happened, who passed by, involve a "retrospective prophecy," a construction of the story of the past by way of its outcome, what it was leading to. It is in the peculiar nature of narrative as a sense-making system that clues are revealing, that prior events are prior, and causes are causal only retrospectively, in a reading back from the end. As Genette argues, narrative offers "the determination of means by ends . . . of causes by effects." If the narrative goes nowhere—never becomes a complete story—there would be no decisive enchainment of its incidents, no sense of inevitable discovery; the units of the narrative would cease to be functional. Such, Jean-Paul Sartre has argued, is the difference between living and telling. To tell is to conceive life as adventure, in the etymological sense of the *ad-venire*, that which is to come, and by its coming to structure what leads up to it. It is worth quoting at some length the reflections of Sartre's fictional spokesman, Antoine Roquentin of *Nausea*, on the problem. When you begin to tell a story, you appear to start at the beginning. But, says Roquentin,

> In reality you have started at the end. It is there, invisible and present, it is what gives these few words the pomp and value of a beginning: "I was out walking, I had left the town without realizing, I was thinking about my money troubles." This sentence, taken simply for what it is, means that the guy was absorbed, morose, a hundred miles from an adventure, exactly in a mood to let things happen without noticing them. But the end is there, transforming everything. For us, the guy is already the hero of the story. His moroseness, his money troubles are much more precious than ours, they are all gilded by the light of future passions. And the story goes on in the reverse: instants have stopped piling themselves up in a haphazard way one on another, they are caught up by the end of the story which draws them and each one in its turn draws the instant preceding it: "It was night, the street was deserted." The sentence is thrown out negligently, it seems superfluous; but we don't let ourselves be duped, we put it aside: this is a piece of information whose value we will understand later on. And we feel that the hero has

lived all the details of this night as annunciations, as promises, or even that he lived only those that were promises, blind and deaf to all that did not herald adventure. We forget that the future wasn't yet there; the guy was walking in a night without premonitions, which offered him in disorderly fashion its monotonous riches, and he did not choose.[31]

On this statement, any narrative telling presupposes an end that will transform its apparently random details "as annunciations, as promises" of what is to come, and that what is to come transforms because it gives meaning to, makes significant the details as leading to the end. Carlos Fuentes has provided an appropriate commentary and confirmation in a short story called *Aura*, where the plot works precisely backward, from death to birth.

Roland Barthes once suggested that narrative may be built on a generalization of the philosophical error of *post hoc, ergo propter hoc*: narrative plotting makes it seem that if *b* follows *a* it is because *b* is somehow logically entailed by *a*.[32] And certainly it is part of the "logic" of narrative to make it appear that temporal connection is also causal connection. This indeed may be one of the uses of narrative: we need to be able to discover connections in life, to have it make sense, to rescue passing time from meaningless succession. One of the projects of complex narratives—such as novels—has often been to question such connections, to ask about the possible randomness of existence. If we associate the random and arbitrary with modernist questionings of traditional plotting—see, for instance, the inconclusive wanderings of such a film as Michelangelo Antonioni's *L'Avventura*, or the last line of Albert Camus's *The Stranger*, where Meursault gives himself up to the "tender indifference" of the universe—the nineteenth-century novel often suggests through its multiple plots the contingencies that attend upon the ways things turn out. Novels often appear to stage a struggle between chaos and meaning. But their very existence as novels, as writing about life rather than life itself, must generally assure that they conclude, however tenuously, in favor of meaning.

In the inevitable discovery doctrine, the law comes down firmly on the side of meaning, conjuring away the specter of meaninglessness, a chaotic universe in which searches would not necessarily lead to anything. It is in this context that the footnote of *Feldhacker* appears so portentous: it images law's belief that an infinitely long and infinitely thorough search would inevitably lead to "any and all pieces of evidence in the world." This remarkable comment presupposes an infinitely knowable world, one laid out in tracks and traces—recall the gridlines marked off by Agent Ruxlow in *Nix*—waiting to be deciphered. If this may be a contestable picture of the world, it is an accurate picture of the law, which assumes that its quarry exists, and that its discovery procedures, if patient and thorough enough, will find it. In the doctrine of inevitable discovery, then, the law is merely affirming—in fairly spectacular form—its own nature. And inevitable discovery allows us to see that its nature is that of the "retrospective prophecy," of the narrative put together from tracks and traces into a coherent plot that gains meaning from its end, from what it leads to. Inevitable discovery is in this sense what the Russian formalists might have called a "laying-bare of the device": one of those moments that images the procedures and the very nature of the text in question.

When we speak of "the narrative construction of reality"—in Jerome Bruner's terms, how narrative "operates as an instrument of mind in the construction of reality"—we must mean, among other things, the ways in which narrative sequence, plot, and intelligibility are used by humans to make sense of their lives and their world.[33] It was precisely Sartre's reflection on the workings of narrative structure in the creation of intelligibility and meaning in human action—a reflection continued in his autobiography, *The Words* (*Le Mots*)—that led him eventually to renounce the novel as genre, since it came to appear to him a violation of existential freedom, a misrepresentation of the open-endedness of becoming. Yet one might respond that the renunciation of narrative is not an option, since narrative construction of reality is a basic human operation, learned in infancy, and culturally omnipresent. Juries could not reach decisions without the capacity to construct narratives of identity. For better or worse, we are stuck with narrative and its ways of making sense.

Bruner notes that the way the human mind processes knowledge as story "has been grossly neglected by students of mind raised either in the rationalist or in the empiricist traditions" (8). One can add that it has been neglected as well by students of the law. Certainly where Fourth Amendment jurisprudence is concerned—when we are talking about searches and seizures and how we understand their workings in relation to constitutional "rules"—the narrative construction of the reality is the reality, and how it is constructed makes all the difference in the defendant's story.

There is, I believe, only one case in which the U.S. Supreme Court, in the person of Justice David H. Souter, explicitly acknowledges the importance of narrative in legal argument. The case is interesting because it has to do precisely with our understanding of a person's character and identity. In *Old Chief v. United States*, decided in 1997, the question at issue was whether a defendant with a prior conviction on his record should be allowed to "stipulate" to the prior conviction, thus disallowing the prosecution from presenting the facts of the earlier felony in making the case against him for his new alleged crime.[34] Defendant Johnny Lynn Old Chief knew he had to admit to a prior crime and conviction—on an assault charge—but didn't want the prosecutor to be able to detail the prior crime, for fear that it would aggravate his sentence on the new crime (which in fact was quite similar to the prior one). The prosecutor refused to accept the stipulation, and the district court judge ruled in his favor: the full story of the prior crime and conviction was offered as evidence. Old Chief was found guilty on all counts of the new charges of assault, possession, and violence with a firearm. He appealed. His conviction was upheld by the Ninth Circuit, which essentially restated the traditional position that the prosecution is free to make its case as it sees fit. When the case reached the Supreme Court, Justice Sandra Day O'Connor, in a dissenting opinion joined by Chief Justice William H. Rehnquist and Justices Antonin Scalia and Clarence Thomas, endorsed that traditional position (192–201).

Yet this claim was rejected by the majority (consisting of Justices Souter, John Paul Stevens, Anthony M. Kennedy, Ruth Bader Ginsburg, and Stephen G. Breyer) in an opinion written by Souter that argues that introduction of the full story of the past crime could be unfairly prejudicial; it could lead the jury to convict on grounds of the defendant's "bad character" rather than on the specific facts of the new crime. The story of the past crime might "lure the factfinder into declaring guilt on a ground different from proof specific to the offense charged" (180). The story of the past crime must be excluded, not because it is irrelevant, but because it may appear overly relevant: "it is said to weigh too much with the jury and to so overpersuade them as to prejudge one with a bad general record and deny him a fair opportunity to defend against a particular charge" (181). The story of Old Chief's past crime must be excluded because it risks creating too many narrative connections between past and present. It risks establishing a powerful perspective that ends up creating that inference—one we regularly derive from narratives—that goes under the name "character," hence authorizing the jury to convict on the basis of identifying Old Chief as a "bad character" rather than the specifics of the present story.

Justice Souter in this manner orders the exclusion of the past story, reverses Old Chief's conviction, and remands the case for further proceedings. But the most interesting moment of his opinion comes in his discussion of the dissenters' point of view, their argument that the prosecution needs to be able to present all the evidence, including the story of past crime and conviction, in its specificity. He concedes the need for "evidentiary richness and narrative integrity in presenting a case," and goes on to say that "making a case with testimony and tangible things . . . tells a colorful story with descriptive richness." He continues, "Evidence thus has force beyond any linear scheme of reasoning, and as its pieces come together a narrative gains momentum, with power not only to support conclusions but to sustain the willingness of jurors to draw the inferences, whatever they may be, necessary to reach an honest verdict. This persuasive power of the concrete and particular is often essential to the capacity of jurors to satisfy the obligations that the law places on them" (187). It is almost as if Souter has been reading literary narratology and been persuaded by the argument that narrative is a different kind of organization and presentation of experience, a different kind of "language" for speaking the world. In the conclusion to this section of his opinion, he writes, "A syllogism is not a story, and a naked proposition in a courtroom may be no match for the robust evidence that would be used to prove it. People who hear stories interrupted by gaps of abstraction may be puzzled at the missing chapters. . . . A convincing tale can be told with economy, but when economy becomes a break in the natural sequence of narrative evidence, an assurance that the missing link is really there is never more than second best" (189). Here Souter turns back to the case of Old Chief, to argue that the prosecution's claim of the need to tell the story of the earlier crime is unwarranted because it is *another* story; it is "entirely outside the natural sequence of what the defendant is charged with thinking and doing to commit the current offense." Old Chief's stipulation does not result in a "gap" in the story, it does not displace "a chapter from a continuous sequence" (191).

Souter hence rules out the prosecution's longer, fuller narrative as the wrong story, something that should not be part of the present narrative sequence. It is interesting that in so doing he feels the need to speak at some length of the place and power of narrative in the presentation of legal evidence: its "richness," its "momentum," its "persuasive power." "A syllogism is not a story": in this phrase, Souter appears to recognize what a few scholars within and without the legal academy have argued, that the law's general assumption that it solves cases with legal tools of reason and analysis that have no need for a narrative analysis could be mistaken. Souter thus breeches the bar over what you might call an element of the repressed unconscious of the law, bringing to light a narrative content and form that traditionally go unrecognized. Yet curiously, or perhaps predictably, he does it by way of an argument that in the present case the lower courts failed to guard against the irrelevant and illegitimate power of narrative, admitting into evidence story elements—the story of Old Chief's prior crime—that should not be considered part of the "natural sequence" of the present crime. The past story would give too much credence to the present story that the prosecution must prove. It is in defending *against* the power of storytelling that Souter admits its force. And his riff on narrative has not been cited in any subsequent Supreme Court opinions.

Nonetheless, *Old Chief* points to the nexus of identity, character, narrative, and the law. In trying to distinguish between Old Chief's actions—his punishable crimes—and the sum of his actions that constitute his "character," Souter makes a strong legal and ethical case for limiting the jury's attention to the specifics of the case at hand. Yet he also, in his discussion of "narrative integrity," points to our need to assemble all the specifics—the clues to someone's overall identity that we call "character"—into a whole, into something like a biography that says: here is what the person is like. Recall Jean-Jacques Rousseau's statement on page one of the *Confessions*: "Here is what I did, what I thought, what I was (Voilà ce que j'ai fait, ce que j'ai pensé, ce que je fus).The law does not necessarily or always want that. It can be interested only in the "what I did." Yet at other times—in "character evidence," in victim impact statements and sentencing hearings that weigh mitigating or aggravating factors in the crime committed—the biographical person is relevant. And to the extent that criminal law is interested in motives for the crime, and in criminal intent—the establishment of *mens rea* or a crime-intending mind—the need to use a narrative evidentiary trail to establish someone's "true identity" is crucial.

If *Old Chief* points to preoccupations of our modernity—as, in its own way, does *Nix v. Williams* in its reflections on "inevitable discovery"—one can also say that the matrix of identity here is both modern and ancient. It is all laid out—as Freud the detective would recognize—in Sophocles' retelling of the story of Oedipus. That it is a retelling of a story—a myth—already known to Sophocles' audience is important. This audience witnesses Oedipus going over again terrain that is well known. It is a detective story where the outcome is known to the spectators. Yet it is nonetheless gripping for that. In fact, the dramatic tension of *Oedipus* may derive in large part from the dramatic irony: every statement of the protagonist has a double edge, since he is both the detective and the criminal, as we know and he doesn't. Oedipus's self-confidence in his identity as the riddle-solver—"He solved the riddle of the sphinx, and became a man most mighty," the line Freud's disciples engraved on a medal presented to him on his fiftieth birthday—is undermined when Tiresias asks him, "Do you know who your parents are?" The detective does not know where he stands, does not know the essentials of his identity.

Oedipus leads a double inquest: to identify the killer of Laius and then, following the Corinthian messenger's announcement that he was never the biological son of Polybus and Merope, rulers of Corinth, to know his parentage. The two lines of inquest converge at "the place where three roads meet": the point of junction of routes leading to and from Corinth and Thebes, presumably, at which Oedipus meets and slays Laius, king of Thebes, and his father—though he "knows" none of this, although the Delphic oracle knew it all from the beginning (so that Oedipus is repeating not only what the audience knows but what the gods know as well). That "place where the three roads meet" becomes a site of detection where Oedipus's identity is both defined and doomed. He returns to this site in his final *kommos*, or lament:

> O triple roads—it all comes back, the secret
> dark ravine, and the oaks closing in
> where the three roads join . . .
> you drank my father's blood, my own blood
> spilled by my own hands—you still remember me?[35]

In a translation of *Oedipus* long out of print, Thomas Gould provides a notable running commentary on the play, in which he argues that "this vivid picture of entering (or rather, reentering) the narrow, wooded glen—coming as it does immediately after the mention of the parents and then climaxing with the cry 'Oh marriages! Marriages . . .'—must be a return, at one and the same time, to the place where he assaulted his father and to the place—that is, the part of the body—where he 'assaulted' his mother."[36] The "dark ravine . . . where three roads join" becomes the place of origin, the woman's genitals in a kind of crude sketch, and doubly the place of crime. That would, of course, make perfect sense: it is in Jocasta's (his mother and his wife's) genitals that Oedipus finds and loses his identity. I say "finds and loses" because the discovery of identity, in this most profound of detective stories, brings only the wisdom of suffering. When you find out who you are, you discover you are nothing but confusion, incoherence, the set of contradictory relationships that Oedipus names at the end: "he fathered you where his own seed was plowed," and so on. The outcome of "discovery" here is that the knower himself is an insoluble problem.

Stories tend toward discovery, toward what Aristotle—whose prime example was *Oedipus*—called recognition, and strive to make this discovery or recognition inevitable. That is in a sense what the rhetoric of narrative is all about. When we start probing the interesting piece of Fourth Amendment doctrine known as "inevitable discovery" we find implicated within in it a larger problem of legal narrative, which is in turn a problem of narrative as a human function and cognitive instrument in the establishment of identity. As the stories of searching for Pamela Powers's corpse, and the proper framework for judging Old Chief's crimes, and Oedipus's search to know his origins all demonstrate, narrative—as a language in which we speak the world, and in so doing give it shape and meaning—itself becomes an event in the world that in turn determines our understanding of identity. Searches, seizures, identifications: these are crucial to legal culture, and they reach beyond the law, to our core understandings of how we know who we are.

If Justice Brandeis found the core principle of the Fourth Amendment to lie in the protection of "an inviolate personality" and in that "most comprehensive of rights"—the "right to be let alone"—we can see in *Oedipus* the countervailing need to violate that right in the individual's own search to know his identity. If we can try to make rules to keep the state out of our private precincts, we find it hard to ignore the oracles that present us with the enigma of our own identity. Knowing the self can be a frightening though necessary violation of all the protections constitutional law seeks to give us. Like Oedipus, like Freud, we can't simply remain content with the knowledge of our identity that lies to hand. We want to know more. And in that search for knowledge we may uncover what we wish we had never sought to know. Yet when the old shepherd—who knows before his king what the truth is—says to Oedipus: "No—/god's sake master, no more questions!" Oedipus responds, "You're a dead man if I have to ask again." (ll. 1280–81). Thus the shepherd, "I'm right at the edge, the horrible truth—I've got to say it!" and Oedipus, "And I'm at the edge of hearing horrors, yes, but I must hear!" Here is the matrix of the identificatory paradigm: the rejection of the possibility of not knowing, the assertion that to know who the self is crucially matters.

What we have not had to decipher, to elucidate by our own efforts, what was clear before we looked at it, is not ours. From ourselves comes only that which we drag forth from the obscurity which lies within us, that which to others is unknown.

—Marcel Proust, *In Search of Lost Time*

# 6 | The Derealization of Self

A curious late text of Sigmund Freud's—from 1936—is the letter he sent to French novelist Romain Rolland on the occasion of Rolland's seventieth birthday. It bears the title *A Disturbance of Memory on the Acropolis*. But *Disturbance*—the German is *Erinnerungsstörung*—seems an overstatement. The story Freud tells is of a planned trip to Corfu with his younger brother, Alexander (in 1904), and their discovery during their stopover in Trieste that it would make more sense for them to give up Corfu—much too hot in early September—and take the Lloyd steamer to Athens that afternoon instead. Disappointed, the two brothers wander about Trieste in "a discontented and irresolute frame of mind," then go to the Lloyd office and, without ever discussing their options and their choice, unhesitatingly book their passage to Athens. When, the following afternoon, they at last stand on the Acropolis, Freud's first reaction is, "So all this really *does* exist, just as we learnt at school!"[1] He feels himself divided, he says, in the manner of someone walking on the shores of Loch Ness who suddenly glimpsed the monster, and was forced to admit, "So it really *does* exist"—while the other half of himself is astonished that the reality of the Acropolis could ever have been in doubt.

As he begins to analyze the experience, the depression in Trieste occasioned by the directive to go to Athens rather than Corfu becomes something like what happens to those people who are "wrecked by success," who cannot deal with the realization of what are in fact deepest wishes, and arrange for them not to happen—a result of the workings of a punishing superego. Going to Athens is "too good to be true" (as Freud puts it, in English). Then, when faced with the reality of the Acropolis, his thought process is subjected to a double distortion. First, doubt about the real existence of the Acropolis is displaced into the past (he never really believed what they taught him in school) and second, the issue of his relation to the Acropolis is displaced onto the question of the very existence of the Acropolis. Unpacking the displacements leads to the notion that at the time of the experience "I had (or might have had) a momentary feeling: '*What I see here is not real.*' Such a feeling is known as a 'feeling of derealization' [Entfremdungsgefühl]. I made an attempt to ward that feeling off, and I succeeded, at the cost of making a false pronouncement about the past" (244). He goes on to say that such "derealizations are remarkable phenomena" that come in two forms: "the subject feels either that a piece of reality or that a piece of his own self is strange to him." They are more or less the negative opposites of "déjà vu" phenomena. They aim at keeping something away from the ego by disavowing it. There is a reaction against a certain burden of guilt in having—upon reaching the Acropolis as the symbol of the cradle of Western culture—gone beyond his businessman father.

It all seems much ado about very little. Though as is so often the case in Freud's essays, the final paragraph turns the screw one more turn. After remarking that it was "a feeling of *filial piety*" that interfered with his enjoyment of the trip to Athens, he concludes, "And now you will no longer wonder that the recollection of this incident on the Acropolis should have troubled me so often since I myself have grown old and stand in need of forbearance and can travel no longer" (248). At the last, we are brought home to Freud's immobility, his standing in the place of the father, on the threshold of extinction. The "derealization" of a piece of reality seems to overlap derealization of a piece of self—Freud the traveler and tourist, the walker and hiker, for whom all of Europe during summer vacation time was a potential playground—before the murderous drives unleashed by the First World War, and the yet darker forces of 1936. What appears to insinuate itself into the recollection of the disturbance of memory is the disturbing presence of the death drive.

The strange workings of derealization strike me as potentially helpful in understanding some of the writers who undertake to explore the enigma of identity in its peculiarly modern forms—such writers as Jean-Jacques Rousseau, William Wordsworth, Marcel Proust, Virginia Woolf, Robert Musil, Italo Svevo, and, of course, Freud himself. These writers all tend to come upon moments at which introspection, or inquest into the formation of the self, encounters a dissolution or estrangement of self that is somehow key to its understanding. Wordsworth in fact offers up praise for what seem to be similar moments:

> Fallings from us, vanishings;
> Blank misgivings of a Creature
> Moving about in worlds not realized.

It's as if the subject seeking self-knowledge had to encounter its complicity with nescience, with non-knowing, with the extinction of self. The death drive—which Freud does not mention explicitly in *A Disturbance of Memory on the Acropolis* but which surely peeps out at the end, as it does in so many of his late essays—seems to inhabit the project of narrating the self.

It is, of course, part of Freudian dogma that we can never really imagine our own deaths—that when we do so we are present in a corner of the tableau, as witness to the self (a bit like Huck Finn attending his own funeral in Mark Twain's novel). "It is indeed impossible to imagine our own death; and whenever we attempt to do so we can perceive that we are in fact still present as spectators," as Freud puts it in *Thoughts for the Time on War and Death*, an essay of 1915, written some six months after the outbreak of the murderous world war that would force him to revise the place he gave to death in his thinking—leading, by the end of the war, to *Beyond the Pleasure Principle* and the postulation of a death drive working silently but with even more force than the pleasure principle (*Standard Edition* 14:289). In the 1915 essay, Freud claims that "in the unconscious every one of us is convinced of his own immortality." If that is so, there is no place to stand from which we can view our own lives. The mention of his immobility at the end of *A Disturbance of Memory on the Acropolis* may have to do with this problem of standing, made literal in the problem of the walker who can travel no more, who stands in need of forbearance. If he has outstripped his father ("den Vater übertreffen"), nonetheless it is at the last to find himself in a place where he can no longer travel ("nicht mehr reisen kann"). The master story of self-knowledge in Freud's canon, Sophocles' *Oedipus*, seems to have to do in some measure with the problem of standing—of being *Homo erectus* as a kind of act of hubris as well as the stance of the knower in nature. All the names in Oedipus's extended family, the Labdicae, have to do with trouble in standing or walking, according to Claude Lévi-Strauss.[2] The strange entry of the immobilized Freud at the end of the letter to Rolland may quietly introduce the silent workings of the death drive as providing—but unrecognized as such—the place of self-narration.

More to come on this, but I need further examples. The first, almost inevitably, comes from Rousseau. It, too, implicates the problem of walking and standing. As Rousseau tells the story, on October 24, 1776, he was returning on foot from a day of botanizing, thinking about the impending winter, comparing it to his own old age, when he spied a Great Dane, rushing toward him at full tilt. Now the screen goes blank. Then he describes at length what follows as he regains consciousness:

> Night was coming on. I saw the sky, a few stars, and a bit of greenery. This first sensation was a moment of delight. That is all that I felt. I was being born in this instant to life, and it seemed to me that I filled with my frail existence everything

that surrounded me. Completely in the present moment, I
remembered nothing; I had no distinct notion of my self as
a person, and no idea of what had just happened; I didn't
know who I was or where I was; I didn't feel pain, nor fear
nor anxiety. I saw my blood flowing as I would have watched a
stream, without even thinking that this blood belonged to me
in any way. I felt in my whole being a ravishing calm to which
I have never been able to find anything comparable in all the
pleasures we engage in.[3]

Rousseau goes on to say that he can't tell those who succor him what
his name is or where he lives. He has momentarily lost his identity. The
moment is one of delight, of infantile bliss prior to any realization of an
identity separate from the maternal body.[4]

This state of bliss soon will be superseded by a realization of the extent of his injuries—his wife screams at his appearance when he arrives
home—and then by the sinister report soon circulating in Paris that
he has died in the accident. To the by now nearly clinically paranoid
Rousseau, the incident provides an excuse for his enemies to circulate
a defamatory obituary and reveals the existence of a plot to attribute
fabricated writings to him after his death. The haunting anxiety that
his enemies will obliterate the truth of his character and present a disfigured portrait of him to posterity pervades Rousseau's late autobiographical work: the so-called Geneva Manuscript of his *Confessions*
is prefaced by an undated paragraph in which he implores whoever
comes in possession of his manuscript—be it one of his "implacable
enemies"—not to destroy this "sole portrait of a man, painted exactly
from nature and in all its truth, that exists and probably will ever exist."
And when he finished the manuscript of the later *Dialogues*, he tried to
carry it to the Cathedral of Notre Dame in Paris, to place it on the high
altar for safekeeping (with a church in which he did not believe)—only
to find the choir was locked for the night.

The incident of being felled by the Great Dane implicates Rousseau's whole autobiographical project. Like Freud—though yet more

consciously—Rousseau worries repeatedly about his standing in narrating the self. That narration is crucial: he is obsessed with what he sees as the need to get his truthful portrait through to the future. Knocked down, and out, by the dog, he is given a momentary respite from the burden of that task—indeed, the whole burden of selfhood is suspended in a moment of pure existence without knowledge of his identity. It is a moment of delight in being without the anxious weight of self-consciousness. It's a condition that Rousseau has consciously attempted to cultivate in the state of reverie described in the Fifth of *The Reveries of a Solitary Walker* (*Les Rêveries du promeneur solitaire*), when he lies in the bottom of his rowboat while drifting aimlessly on the Lac de Bienne, looking up at the sky, letting the rhythms of the water take the place of those of his consciousness; or else spends the evening reposing on the lakeshore: "The ebb and flow of the water, its unvaried sound occasionally swelling louder, striking continually my ears and eyes, took the place of the inward movements that reverie extinguished in me, and sufficed to make me feel my existence with pleasure, without taking the trouble to think."[5] He continues in his reflection, "In what does one take pleasure in such a situation? In nothing outside oneself, in nothing other than oneself and one's own existence, as long as this state lasts one is sufficient to oneself like God."[6] The experience is self-contained, but now the self has ceased to be the self-conscious ego, has become instead an organism responsive to the sensations of existence. It is, I suppose, comparable to states of exstasis, of out-of-self experience sought for in zen or psychedelic drugs. But what the dog gives Rousseau is more radical and authentic, a true loss of identity to self. It's a moment of what Geoffrey Hartman characterizes as "Romantic anti-selfconsciousness," a moment at which the largely ego-expanding project of the Romantics seeks the lifting of "the burden of the mystery" in the shedding of self.[7] As usual, Rousseau is not only the first but also the most extreme in his claim that happiness can come only in the loss of ego and the loss of any sense of self-identity within temporality.

This wish for the loss of self may strike us as dissonant with Rousseau's whole project of self-narration, which makes the related claims that he is unique, and thus alone empowered to tell us who he is—and to pass judgment on himself—and that his project of knowing and making known who he is must of necessity be narrative, the story of a temporal unfolding, at once a story of change (often through suffering) and of essential immutability: his character has never been altered from what it became during childhood. As I have noted in chapter 1, in the Tenth of the *Rêveries*—almost the last page he wrote before his death—Rousseau asserts that he is the same person he was fifty years earlier, on the day he first met Madame de Warens, who "fixed" his mobile character forever. And in the *Confessions* he tell us that he wants to make himself "transparent to the reader's eye," which means that he must not let the reader lose sight of him at any moment of his life; he must be continuously visible: "I have only one thing to fear in this enterprise: that is not saying too much or speaking untruths; it is rather not saying everything, and silencing truths" (175).

Transparency and the need to "say everything" can produce paroxysms of self-display, as when he exposes his naked backside to young women in Turin—which leads him, when caught in the act, to the invention of a false identity. But transparency also encounters moments of loss, dropping out, falling from consciousness, as with the Great Dane. This is a strange moment of nescience in an autobiographical project that seems to be all about self-consciousness. But moments of loss, falling from consciousness—and literally falling on the ground—perhaps are necessary to the very project of self-knowledge and self-narration; or better: self-narration as the way to self-knowledge. Loss is for Rousseau connected with the pleasure of the fantasmatic and the fictional, as in his moments of false identity, following the self-exposure in Turin, for instance, when he tells his captor that he is a foreign prince whose mind is deranged, or when he becomes the pretend Englishman "M. Dudding" and has the one satisfactory sexual adventure of his life, or in his frequent masturbatory reveries, or the very similar moments in which he writes the amorous letters of his epistolary novel, from himself and to himself. Self-knowledge in Rousseau leads to moments of madness, of extravagance and ecstatic self-denial, of a sort that later on the Great Dane more perfectly provides. It is, I think, a kind of madness that belongs to the project of introspection itself, since that project depends on a kind of self-alienation or derealization, an Entfremdungsgefühl. The standing point turns out to be the falling point. And that falling, that self-estrangement, seems to uncover the silent workings of the death drive in the knowledge of the self.

Consider an incident from book 1 of the *Confessions*, in which Rousseau as a young apprentice to a master he detests takes to stealing apples from a storeroom to allay his constant hunger. (The passage is striking in part because it must be a self-conscious evocation of Saint Augustine's famous stealing of pears, in his own *Confessions*.) The apples are held in a bin surrounded by a louvered blind. Rousseau tries to reach them with a spit. When this is too short, he attaches an additional spit to the first one. But then upon raising the impaled apple to the blind, he finds it's too big to pass through the slots. So now he has to find a long knife to split the apple while holding the spit in place with a lathe. He is just about to succeed in his ingenious theft when "[s]uddenly the door to the storeroom opens; my master emerges, crosses his arms, gazes at me and says: Bravo! . . . . . . the pen falls from my hand" (la plume me tombe des mains; 34). Notice how the scene of discovery by his master, recounted in the dramatic present tense (easier to do in French than in English), suddenly flashes forward from the scene of the crime, the narrated moment, to the scene of writing, the moment of narration. It's not "the spit falls from my hand" that Rousseau writes, but "the pen falls from my hand." One could imagine a visual representation of this shift—in an awkward History Channel–type film—in which the scene of apple stealing does a quick fade into the scene of writing.

Why does Rousseau, who wants to make us intimate with his childhood affects—never more so when talking about his education in dissimulation and thievery at the hands of his bad master—suddenly break the illusion in a kind of "metalepsis of the author," a dramatic intrusion of the act of composition of the scene? There are a few other examples in the *Confessions*: for instance, writing about his unmerited punishment for breaking a comb—a depredation from which he re-declares his innocence so many decades later—he tells us, "My pulse still races" and that these moments "will always be present should I live for be a hundred thousand years" (20). One needs to take the pres-entness of such incidents seriously: they become of the present mo-ment in the autobiographical act. Such moments all point us to the same issue: Rousseau's discovery that the writing self cannot evoke the written-about self, the subject of the narration, without encountering precisely the narrating self, the Rousseau who, at his desk pen in hand, is trying to evoke and revivify his past self. There is no knowledge of the self independent of the process of trying to know that self, some-thing we noted in Stendhal's and Rousseau's self-conscious declarations of the enunciative positions from which they speak their truths. Self-knowledge, to the extent that it might imply a knowing self distinct from that to be known, turns out to be contaminated at its source. To know and write about the self is to come face-to-face with the knower as the writer, to learn that all we can know about ourselves is what our selves tell us is there. It is a deathly mirroring in which the self escapes from the structurations—present and past, knower and known, narra-tor and narrated—that we have attempted to impose upon it. The self doing the understanding cannot wholly distinguish any other version of the self from itself, which leads to vertigo, loss, a kind of embarrassed self-consciousness or else a fall from consciousness. Thus it is that the incident with the Great Dane fulfills as it literalizes the moment of loss inherent in self-exploration, the discovery of the death of the self as part and parcel of self-knowing.

Much of the art of the generally "realist" tradition, in the century following Rousseau, will be about finding ways to efface the presence of the narrator, to let the story apparently "tell itself," as in free indirect discourse. It's as if the dramatized loss foregrounded from time to time in Rousseauian self-narration is too self-indulgent, or too threatening, to furnish the major tradition of narrative fiction—though it will be revived on a number of occasions in the twentieth century, precisely as a provocation to realism, a putting into play of the agency of narration.

I am on my way to Proust here, but I want to pause again, briefly, over Freud, this time not talking about his own self-knowledge but that of his patient, the "Wolf Man." What I particularly have in mind in this case history (*From the History of an Infantile Neurosis*) is the "screen memory."

Freud learns early in his treatment of Sergei Pankejeff, better known as the Wolf Man, that his patient, along with his panic fear of wolves, can recall running after a beautiful tiger swallowtail butterfly, then, when it settled on a flower, suddenly being seized with a terrible fear of the insect, and, giving up the chase, screaming.[8] The memory recurs during the analysis, and Freud postulates that it is a "screen memory," that is a detail that has held its enduring place in memory because it represents something more important with which it is connected. A screen memory is in this manner a form of representation of one's personal past that both reveals and conceals, that misrepresents (and derealizes) in order to get at some crucial and uncomfortable piece of truth. In the case of the Wolf Man, understanding the screen memory becomes possible only late in the analysis, after elucidation of the traumatic wolf dream and its evocation of the real or fantasized "primal scene" of parental coitus. The screen memory indeed takes us once again into material from the "primal period" in the patient's life. The tiger swallowtail butterfly sets up a complex chain of verbal and visual associative links.

One day, writes Freud, his patient tells him that a butterfly in Russian is called *Babushka*, "Granny," and this tentatively initiates a series of evocations of women—though not, as Freud first intuits, through an association of the yellow-striped butterfly with a woman's dress. That idea goes nowhere. Rather, Sergei later tells him that the butterfly on the flower opening and closing its wings looked like a woman opening her legs, and the shape of the *V* evoked the hour of five o'clock when his depressions set in. Now things begin to follow a more complex course, which I won't rehearse in full detail. The butterfly leads to Sergei's recollection of a yellow-striped pear called *Grusha*, which then turns out to be the name of his nursemaid. In what way might she be the source of anxiety associated with the butterfly? Now a scene begins to emerge from behind the screen memory: Grusha kneeling on hands and knees, beside her a pail and a broom made of a bundle of twigs, scolding the two-and-a-half year-old child. "The missing elements," Freud now informs us, "could easily be supplied from other directions" (*SE* 17:91). There is Sergei's later uncontrollable sexual attraction to peasant girls kneeling in the same position, and his fascination with the bundles of twigs used to burn John Huss at the stake—Huss being the "hero" of those who suffer from enuresis, uncontrolled urination. These details allow the analyst to "complete" the Grusha scene with the young Sergei urinating and Grusha replying with a joking threat of castration.

Take it on faith, if you can, that the scene represented in hidden form under the screen memory connects back to the "primal scene" and forward to Sergei's erotic obsession with peasant girls. To confirm Freud's interpretive adventure here, his patient now obligingly produces the "particularly ingenious dream" of tearing off the wings of an *Espe*. What's an *Espe*? asks Freud. Why, says Sergei, it's "that insect with yellow stripes on its body, that stings." Oh, says Freud, you mean a *Wespe*, a wasp. Sergei Pankejeff's verbal production, the *Espe*, is, he now recognizes, himself: S. P. "The *Espe*," Freud continues, "was of course a mutilated *Wespe*," a castrated version of self. Self-knowledge encounters this punning version of loss, of self-destruction.

Freud notes, "It was easy to understand how the patient's later comprehension of castration had retrospectively brought out the anxiety in the scene with Grusha" (*SE* 17:96). Accurate or not, such an interpretation represents one of Freud's truly crucial contributions to the narration of the self: the understanding that the affect and the meaning of an event can be produced retrospectively, by retroaction. Freud's theory of trauma hinges on the possibility of such retroaction, since it is often a later occurrence—postpuberty—that retrospectively sexualizes a childhood event. The double structure of trauma is about knowledge catching up with experience and in the process rendering it radioactive. No surprise here, since this is the very structure of Freud's master text, Sophocles' *Oedipus*, where wisdom consists in discovering the utterly self-annihilating meaning of the personal experience that lays waste to everything around you—father, mother, children—and yet is also encoded in your name as "wounded-foot." It's not what Oedipus did that counts most in Sophocles' play (and the audience knows what he did before the play begins); it's his discovery of what he did, his act of detection and its catastrophic result, precisely knowledge catching up with experience (and the audience, though knowing the outcome, still finds following the detection absolutely compelling).

As I mentioned, anthropologist Lévi-Strauss has suggested that the Oedipus story has something to do with difficulty in walking, and with standing erect as a hubristic act in the world—one that invites the gods' thunderbolts.[9] Standing erect, with the brain and the eyes elevated, does, of course, implicate other Freudian scenarios, especially that of *Civilization and Its Discontents*, where the moment when humankind assumes the erect posture becomes responsible for more or less everything: the exposure of the genitals to visual inspection; the suppression of the sense of smell in favor of vision; the transformation of estrus into menstruation; the man's need to control the woman's sexuality (thus the creation of the family unit), and the beginnings of *Kultur* itself. In the Oedipus context, the hubris of the riddle-solver who becomes King of Thebes is precisely to think he knows where he stands, as knower, and that he can swear out a search warrant calling for the identification and banishment of the homicide identified by the Delphic oracle in full confidence of his own exemption from the inquest he has initiated. What I want to see as a key process in Rousseau—the necessary loss, fall from consciousness of the knower in search of self-knowledge, the uncovering of death in the place of the self—is already dramatized by Sophocles as the very condition of self-knowledge and indeed identity. As Tiresias says to Oedipus early in the play, Do you really know who you are? Can any act of self-knowing tell you?

This, then, is the starting point of psychoanalysis. It is not that Freud gives an answer that is any more negative than Rousseau's—they share an ultimate or at least ideal goal of transparency—but that he makes more explicit the stark problematics of the project. In that late

essay where he names psychoanalysis an "impossible" profession—
*Analysis Terminable and Interminable*—Freud rediscovers Empedocles
of Agrigentum as confirmation of his conclusion that psychoanalysis,
like life itself, turns on the struggle of Eros and Thanatos. This makes
any understanding gained through psychoanalytic process tentative,
incomplete and, even more important, makes the role of the analyst
incomplete and unstable. "It would not be surprising," writes Freud,
"if the effect of a constant preoccupation with all the repressed material which struggles for freedom in the human mind were to stir up in
the analyst as well all the instinctual demands which he is otherwise
able to keep under suppression."[10] Hence the need for the analyst's own
self-analysis to continue interminably. Not only the known but also
the knower and the knowing are subject to an unending uncertainty, a
processual movement.

One needs also to take into account that the formation of a self-
knowing self may be bound up in the possibility of concealment of the
self. Oedipus's concealments are unwitting: as he flees from what he
conceives to be his prophesied destiny, assuming the identity of the
riddle-answer and the *tyrannos* of Thebes, he is playing into the trap
of his identity. Rousseau, I have suggested, despite his project of total
transparency falls into moments of nescience that are necessary to his
project of self-knowing. Perhaps the most explicit account of how nescience and self-concealment can become necessary to selfhood comes
in Henry James's challenging novel, *What Maisie Knew* (1897), which
attempts to track the consciousness of a young girl subjected to the contrary pressures of two angry parents, and their succession of partners
and lovers, following a divorce. After discovering that her reports from
one estranged parent to the other are being used as ammunition in the
custody war—and as a sign of her own "stupidity"—she discovers the
benefits of appearing not to know, of forgetting everything, of cultivat-
ing "the seeds of secrecy" and finding pleasure in being called "a little
idiot." In the key phrase of this passage, "She had a new feeling, the feeling of danger; on which a new remedy rose to meet it, the idea of an inner self or, in other words, of concealment."[11] What is breathtaking here

is James's "or, in other words": the postulation, as in a matter of course, that the idea of an inner self is consubstantial with the idea of concealment. In some manner, all of *What Maisie Knew* is about the uses of not knowing, about nescience as a kind of necessary position in which to protect the self from the inquisitions of others. And if the self truly is bound up with concealment and not knowing, or appearing not to know so that others won't know you, we have another version of the loss or fall or death of the self on which self-knowing seems to depend.

My final example, perhaps the most obvious, is Proust. To begin with a seemingly pedantic point: there has been much debate over the years about whether and when one should call the speaker in the text (of the text?) "the narrator" or "Marcel" (assuming that the basically unnamed protagonist does bear this name, which he only hypothetically assigns to himself in a moment of *The Captive* [*La Prisonnière*]). It would be an assumption of any rhetoric of fiction that in a retrospective first-person narrative one can and generally needs to distinguish narrator from protagonist and to be able to mark the gap that separates the contemporary experience of the one (as a child, say) from the retrospective understanding of the other (as the narrator of his childhood, for instance). And this distinction often is possible in *In Search of Lost Time* (*A la Recherche du Temps Perdu*), which is indeed often concerned to distinguish the contemporary understanding (or more often lack of understanding) of an event from the meaning one can later find in it. In this sense, Proust's novel bears some resemblance to the title Jane Austen originally gave to *Pride and Prejudice*: "First Impressions." Initial impressions, in Proust as in Austen, are generally erroneous (though in Proust their error can hold a superior kind of truth) and need later correction. Particularly with the protagonist's discovery of the vast world of sexual "inversion," as he calls it, at the start of *Sodom and Gomorrah*, he undergoes a tectonic revision of his views of society and sexuality.

Yet the correction of erroneous first impressions is only part of the story. There are many pages where Proust's text refuses to allow us to make a clear distinction between the person living the experience and the person reflecting back on it, suspending us between error and correction. The whole opening movement of the novel is set in an indistinct time zone, first suggested by the grammatically disorienting opening, "Longtemps, je me suis couché de bonne heure," which uses the *passé composé*—past participle plus present auxiliary—where one would expect the imperfect of the habitual action ("I used to go to bed"), to give a very difficult to translate suspension between present and past, the punctual and the continuing ("For an extended period of time, I have gone to bed early"—which is not intended to be an acceptable translation). The opening movement of the novel takes place in bed, as a place of both suffering (the asthmatic insomniac) and pleasure (even to orgasm), but especially the place of the time travels of the man (protagonist or narrator?) attempting to sleep in unfamiliar surroundings. It seems to be all about the looping and indeed loopy effect of self-narration. Sleep, the self, and self-knowledge in narrating, in writing, are explicitly dramatized here, just a few pages into the novel: "A sleeping man holds in a circle around him the thread of the hours, the order of the years and worlds. He consults them instinctively as he wakes, and reads in a second the point on the earth that he occupies, the time that has elapsed before his waking; but their orders can be mixed up, broken apart."[12] The narration goes on to describe the kinds of disorientation produced by falling asleep while reading a book, or falling asleep in a chair that turns into a "magic armchair that will make him travel full speed ahead in time and in space, and at the moment when he opens his eyelids, he will believe himself to have gone to bed a few months earlier, in another country." Then leaving the generality of the "homme qui dort" the narrator tells us that a deep sleep will make his own mind lose the map of the place where he fell asleep:

> [A]nd when I woke up in the middle of the night, since I
> didn't know where I was, I didn't even in the first moment
> know who I was; I had only in its original simplicity the
> feeling of existence [le sentiment de l'existence] as it may
> quiver in the depths of an animal; I was more destitute than

a caveman; but then memory—not yet of the place where I
was, but of some of those where I had lived and where I might
have been—would come to me like help from on high to pull
me from the nothingness from which I couldn't have got out
on my own; I crossed centuries of civilization in one second,
and the half-glimpsed images of oil lamps, then of wing-collar
shirts, gradually recomposed the original features of my self."
(1:5–6/1:5–6)

Freud's sense of derealization on the Acropolis, Rousseau's experience
of loss of self when felled by the Great Dane, here in Proust becomes
an habitual experience of the sleeper, and an analogue of the narrator seeking to orient himself in relation to the self to be told. In both
Rousseau and Proust *le sentiment de l'existence* (the words are precisely
the same in the two writers) can be experienced, momentarily, before
finding the plotted coordinates of one's identity, and that moment of
floating incertitude is for both of them the precondition of an orientation that requires a narratorial fidelity to both past and present selves
and, perhaps most of all, to their interaction.[13]

   That this intersection of past and present selves is the basic model
of the experience of art—analogous to the model of Freudian trauma—
finds repeated demonstrations over the long arc of the *Recherche*. The
simplest instance may be Swann listening to the *petite phrase* of Vinteuil's sonata at Mme de Sainte-Euverte's soirée, which produces a doubling of himself: one self reliving his time of happiness with Odette,
the other condemned to the knowledge that the doors to that world
are closed: "And he perceived, motionless in presence of this happiness
relived, a wretch who inspired him to pity since he didn't at once recognize him, so that he had to lower his eyes so that people wouldn't see
they were full of tears. It was himself" (1:341/1:360). Marcel, to whom
Swann is always a cautionary figure—the dilettante too unenterprising
to push his fine perceptions through to the creation of art—must at the
moment of his "vocation" assume this doubled self as the very principle
of creation.

What is most often emphasized, in the moment of revelation that comes in *Time Regained* (*Le Temps retrouvé*), is the discovery, through the experiences provided by "involuntary memory," of the possibility of an essence of things freed from time, and thus of a self out of time. Through the double structure of a past experience revived in the present, "the permanent and habitually hidden essence of things is freed, and our true self which seemed, sometimes for long periods, to be dead but wasn't entirely so, wakes up, takes on new life in receiving the heavenly sustenance brought to it" (4:451/6:264–65).[14] It is the temporal doubling of certain key sensations that gives them transcendent meaning, as in the double structure of trauma analyzed by Freud.

Yet these moments when one appears to step out of time are a "*trompe l'oeil*," says the text. The optical illusion of timelessness is evanescent. What's needed is a disciplined process comparable to the temporal and perceptual disorientation of the man waking from sleep—a process modeled in Vinteuil's sonata and septet as architectures of signification within temporality. It's "as if our finest ideas were like tunes which, as it were, come back to us although we have never heard them before, and which we must force ourselves to listen to and transcribe" (4:456–57/6:272). Freud, I think, would have been pleased at this definition, since he claims that the finding of the object—of love, for instance—is always a refinding. So by the end it is not simply a matter of finding, but of refinding, in order to read that "book of figural characters, not written by us, that is our only book" (4:458/6:275). And here we reach the statement that I set as epigraph to this chapter: "What we have not had to decipher, to elucidate by our own efforts, what was clear before we looked at it, is not ours. From ourselves comes only that which we drag forth from the obscurity which lies within us, that which to others is unknown" (4:459/6:276). That dragging forth from obscurity well figures the kind of psychic work proposed by Freud, and before him by Rousseau in his pursuit of self. It is work that proceeds without any certainty in the place of the knower or the place of knowledge, which lies in obscurity and demands a work of decipherment. And as the revelation, to himself, of Marcel's vocation continues to unfold, we find that the work of decipherment depends on—or really is—a work of creation, creating a book that must have "the shape . . . that normally remains invisible to us, that of Time" (4:622/6:526).

Marcel's discovery of his vocation resonates with a kind of triumphant joy: he undertakes introspection and self-narration with less anguish, it seems, than Rousseau and Freud. Yet the triumphalism of *Time Regained* should not deafen us to what makes possible the transmutation of life into understanding, and its cost. Human life is mowed down by death—Marcel quotes Victor Hugo's bitter line, in his elegy for his drowned daughter: "Grass must grow and children must die"(Il faut que l'herbe pousse et que les enfants meurent; 4:615/6:516). But it is scythed also by the writer, in a frighteningly self-absorbed gesture: "a book is a huge cemetery in which on the majority of the tombs the names are effaced and can no longer be read" (4:484/6:310). Art becomes indifferent to life; it is the transformation of the pains of living into idea: "Ideas come to us as the substitutes [succédanés] for griefs, and griefs, at the moment when they change into ideas, lose some part of their power to injure our heart; the transformation itself, even, for an instant, releases suddenly a little joy" (4:485/6:315). The word *succédanés* means both "substitutes" and "successors," and the next sentence of the text makes clear that the temporality of the transformation is crucial. What's at issue is a process of "getting over" pain in order to get into art. It is a process of overcoming that only partly abolishes suffering, and brings only a temporary and small joy.

There is indeed in these pages a great deal on suffering as the precondition of a knowledge that incorporates pain, sorrow, and even death as necessary conditions of creation. The key passage (though only one among many) comes a few pages later: "Sorrows are servants, obscure and detested, against whom one struggles, beneath whose dominion one more and more completely falls, dire and dreadful servants whom it is impossible to replace and who by subterranean paths lead us towards truth and death. Happy those who have first come face to face with truth, those for whom, near though the one may be to the other, the hour of truth has struck before the hour of death!" (4:488–

89/6:320). The record of life—the object of the autobiographical project—reveals a suffering animal whose sufferings are not replaceable.
But the sufferings do lead us forward, by underground ways, to the
undecidable outcome in death and truth.

By the end of the revelation scene, the "idea of death" comes to keep
Marcel company "as ceaselessly as the idea of the self" (4:620/6:523).
The narration of the self is threatened by death—after so much time
wasted, will there be time enough to create? By that very fact, the idea
of the self and the idea of death become close companions, in an effect
of derealization that cuts to the heart of reality. The idea of self depends
on the idea of death, as Rousseau foresaw. The production of Marcel's
novel finds at the last its analogue in *The Thousand and One Nights*: the
would-be narrator of the self is Scheherazade, telling her tale—as it can
only be told—under sentence of death.

Marcel's discovery of vocation is not about finding a stable position from which to see, to know, and to narrate. It's much more about
rediscovering that original position of the sleeper and the dreamer. The
self that would know and tell its story must experience derealization, an
imaginary doubling in time, which, upon analysis, seems to be produced
by the incursion of the death drive. The death drive—habitually silent
and invisible—is revealed to inhabit within the self. Marcel notes here
that his fascination with dreaming may derive from the "formidable
game that it plays with Time" (4:490/6:323). And that "jeu formidable"
played with time describes the whole manner, technique, and goal of
Proust's *Recherche*.[15] His sentences seek to hold different temporal moments together in one intellectual and emotional fluid medium. The
syntax of the *Recherche* does not repudiate time—language, like mortality, forbids that—but instead seeks to pervert it, to bend it to nonlinear
ends. There is no defeat of time or liberation from time but instead a
usage of time. And in this process, the agency of narration in relation to
the agent narrated can only be ambiguous. Perhaps in a future book of
revealed truth—the book Marcel might be able to write following the
end of this one—there could be a place for a disambiguated autobiographical narrator, freed from time, delivered to a place beyond death,

a true analyst, a "subject supposed to know." But for now, he, too, is like the dreamer enabled only to play a slippery game with time.

Walter Benjamin, in his essay "The Storyteller," makes the cryptic and profound remark, "Death is the sanction of everything that the storyteller can tell. He has borrowed his authority from death."[16] Since the knowledge of our own death, and the meaning it would retrospectively give to our life, is not delivered to us we seek in the telling of the lives of others that wisdom that comes in knowing a life from death to birth, as an obituary, as a meaningful utterance that has reached its end-stop. It is something like this that Benjamin means when he calls death in fiction the "flame" at which we warm our own "shivering life" (101). The arresting image of life as "shivering" has to do with the forlorn condition of the contemporary individual for whom the meaning of life lies lost in the forward movement of irredeemable time. It can be found only in the struggle with time, the effort to wrest meaning from ongoing temporality—an effort doomed in any larger sense, since we will not be around to comprehend the ultimate meaning, if there is any such thing. Once upon a time, an eschatological sense of meaning—of time reaching the fulfillment of a promised end—held out, to some, the hope of a reinscription of life in an eventual redemptive timelessness. John Milton's angel Michael, in the last book of *Paradise Lost*, presents a future vision of time redeemed in the second coming of Christ, and his listener Adam responds,

> He ended; and thus ADAM last reply'd.
> How soon hath thy prediction, Seer blest,
> Measur'd this transient World, the Race of time,
> Till time stand fixt: beyond is all abyss,
> Eternitie, whose end no eye can reach.[17]

Those modern writers for whom the narrative enterprise is explicitly about finding a place for self-understanding—such as Rousseau, Freud, Proust, and a host of other creators of our modernity—can never find a moment where time "stands fixt." So they can never find consolation in that "meditation on the happy end" that Milton's Adam is offered at the close of *Paradise Lost*. They can as a consequence never find any stable point from which to offer a retrospective narration of the self's becoming what it is. What they all seem to discover, each in his own way, is some frightening if also possibly alluring immanence of Benjamin's authoritative death, in the lurking presence of the death drive within the eros of literary creation itself. To undertake an enterprise of self-understanding is to enter a state where lines drawn between present and past selves tend to blur, where self-consciousness unburdens itself in nescience, where the search to posit moments withdrawn from time encounters the sentence of death. To understand the self may be at the same time to acquiesce to its dissolution.

If Rousseau, Freud, and Proust all appear to be dedicated to the retrieval of the past, particularly the retrieval of the truth of a past self, the story they tell of the past self constantly is held hostage to the present self, in an undertaking that cannot but lay bare the complicity of the narration of self with death. The agency charged with narrating the self encounters the death drive as a condition of its knowing and telling. If I have read the ending of Freud's *Disturbance of Memory* correctly, the terminal melancholy of the last paragraph has to do not so much with the moment of derealization on the Acropolis itself as with the recollection of this derealization, and its repressed drama of filial-paternal conflict, at the later moment when the self stands face-to-face with its extinction. The derealized self is an analogue of the self removed from time, and from life. The problematic in Rousseau is slightly different but functionally similar. His goal of making his soul transparent to the reader's gaze cannot result in an unmediated narrative of his childhood and young manhood since it inevitably runs up against the obstacle of the knower, discovering the writing hand rather than the stabbing hand of his youth, butting his head against a kind of mirror. He claims a kind of oxymoronic innocence, a claim that is predicated on his fall from innocence, hence with the death of what he would eternalize. As Proust writes, as if in commentary on Rousseau's *Confessions*, "The true paradises are those that we have lost" (4:449/6:261). Paradise is coterminous, for us, with knowledge that it is lost.

For Marcel at the very end of the *Recherche* it is crucial that he still be able hear the peal of the bell—"resilient, ferruginous, interminable, fresh and shrill" (rebondissant, ferrugineux, intarissable, criard et frais; 4:623/6:529)—of the garden gate in Combray announcing the departure of Swann and his mother's imminent arrival with a goodnight kiss. It proves that the lost childhood self can be retrieved. The peal of the bell has always been within him; he has only to block his ears to current sounds, the conversation around him, to hear it again. Yet the peal of the bell reheard is also terrifying, since it proves the unalterabilty of the past, and its irredeemable pastness. This moment in fact *echoes* (a word almost not literal enough) one early in the *Recherche* in which Marcel growing old reflects on his moment of childhood trauma in the "drame du coucher"—the moment of his mother's withheld kiss. Now that his mother and his father are dead,

> Never again will such moments be possible for me. But of late I have been increasingly able to catch, if I listen attentively, the sound of the sobs which I had the strength to control in my father's presence, and which broke out only when I found myself alone with Mama. In reality their echo has never ceased; and it is only because life is now growing more and more silent around me that I hear them again, like those convent bells which are so effectively drowned during the day by the noises of the street that one would suppose them to have stopped, until they ring out again through the silent evening air. (1:36–37/1:49)

As Rousseau discovers in the Tenth of his *Rêveries*, there has been "no break in the continuity of the self" (that's quoting Proust; Rousseau's words are almost identical). But this identity in time is, of course, linked to death—bodily death—that effaces even memory; for at death, "Time withdraws from the body." The paragraph that contains this curious sentence (the next-to-last paragraph of the novel) ends with the evocation of Albertine, the woman whom he made a prisoner but could never fully possess except when she lay sleeping. "Deep

Albertine [profonde Albertine]—whom I saw sleeping and who was dead" (4:624/6:530).

Depth—depth of knowledge of depth, one might say, of what lies beneath the sleeping form—cohabits with death. Recall that when Marcel evokes those "subterranean paths" that lead us "towards truth and death" he adds, "Happy those who encounter the first before the second, and for whom, near though they must be one to another, the hour of truth has struck before the hour of death!" (4:488–89/6:320). Near though they must be to one another, and dependent one on the other.

So, to conclude, the experience of "derealization" evoked by Freud in his recollection of a disturbance of memory is about a doubling of self, indeed a self-estrangement, which is the condition of a kind of self-knowledge that comes with, or takes the form of, a narrative of the self, where the agency of narration discovers that it cannot maintain a proper distance from the narrated agent, discovers rather its interference and complicity in what it would narrate. And in this manner, in this kind of mirroring, it discovers the complicity of the eros of self-knowing with death. When you finally catch up with the self, you have run out of time

# 7 | The Madness of Art

There have over the ages been artists in all sorts of media who have had the capacity for self-renewal late in their careers, almost a capacity for self reinvention—often involving a whole new manner, a "late style" that is often their principal claim to greatness in the eyes of posterity. I am thinking, for instance, of William Butler Yeats's late poetry, explicitly a poetry of old age and the resistance to it ("Why Should Not Old Men Be Mad?"); of Victor Hugo's astonishing last novel, on the French Revolution, *Ninety-three* (*Quatrevingt-treize*); of Paul Cézanne's final works in Provence, from around 1901–6; of Henri Matisse's late cutouts, done when he was crippled, often unable to stand and to manipulate a paintbrush; of Titian's late nudes; and of the late quartets of Ludwig van Beethoven, among the most challenging music ever written, or Richard Wagner's *Parsifal*. Jean-Jacques Rousseau's *Reveries of a Solitary Walker* (*Les Rêveries du promeneur solitaire*), and much of Marcel Proust—what was written under the shadow of impending death—fit this class, and so do Sigmund Freud's late essays, among the most radical and disturbing texts he wrote.

As I began to think about these self-reinventors, I found myself wondering about the relation of self-reinvention to self-dissolution: Is that the alternative, or perhaps a moment in a dialectic that produces, in reaction, the affirmation of a self that will not "go gentle"? By "dissolution" I mean both the moments of nescience, loss of self, and the intrusion of the death drive that I discussed in chapter 6, and the encounter with this loss writ large in the impending reality of death. Both senses of dissolution are captured in classical form at the end of the final story of James Joyce's *Dubliners*, "The Dead"—in Gabriel Conroy's meditation unto death on all that his love for his wife Gretta has not meant, and on the insubstantiality of his entire experience of life:

The air of the room chilled his shoulders. He stretched himself cautiously along under the sheets and lay down beside his wife. One by one, they were all becoming shades. Better pass boldly into that other world, in the full glory of some passion, than fade and wither dismally with age. He thought of how she who lay beside him had locked in her heart for so many years that image of her lover's eyes when he had told her that he did not wish to live.

Generous tears filled Gabriel's eyes. He had never felt like that himself towards any woman, but he knew that such a feeling must be love. The tears gathered more thickly in his eyes and in the partial darkness he imagined he saw the form of a young man standing under a dripping tree. Other forms were near. His soul had approached that region where dwell the vast hosts of the dead. He was conscious of, but could not apprehend, their wayward and flickering existence. His own identity was fading out into a grey impalpable world: the solid world itself, which these dead had one time reared and lived in, was dissolving and dwindling.

A few light taps upon the pane made him turn to the window. It had begun to snow again. He watched sleepily the flakes, silver and dark, falling obliquely against the lamplight. The time had come for him to set out on his journey westward. Yes, the newspapers were right: snow was general all over Ireland. It was falling on every part of the dark central plain, on the treeless hills, falling softly upon the Bog of Allen and, farther westward, softly falling into the dark mutinous Shannon waves. It was falling, too, upon every part of the lonely churchyard on the hill where Michael Furey lay buried. It lay thickly drifted on the crooked crosses and headstones, on the spears of the little gate, on the barren thorns. His soul swooned slowly as he heard the snow falling faintly through the universe and faintly falling, like the descent of their last end, upon all the living and the dead.[1]

And so it ends. It recalls Joyce's master Flaubert, who in the last lines of his late novella *A Simple Heart* (*Un Coeur simple*) takes us nearly across the threshold of death to the servant Félicité's final vision, in which her stuffed parrot becomes the Holy Ghost, as she leaves life: "Her heartbeats slowed one by one, more uncertain each time, softer, like a fountain growing dry, like an echo fading; and, when she exhaled her last breath, she thought she saw, in the opening heavens, a gigantic parrot, soaring over her head."[2] Joyce moves us into a realm of last ends where the self can no longer cohere, and where Gabriel's evocation of Michael Furey, who died from love for Gretta, leads to a general gathering of shades as in Hades: "His own identity was fading out into a grey impalpable world." So it is when identity no longer seems affirmable.

It's against this grayness and impalpability that one hears Yeats, for instance, protesting, as in "An Acre of Grass" (1938). Its first two stanzas give us the anguished impasse of old age, in the (highly contrived) simplicity that may evoke the children's book ("where nothing stirs but a mouse"):

Picture and book remain,
An acre of green grass

For air and exercise,
Now strength of body goes;
Midnight, an old house
Where nothing stirs but a mouse.

My temptation is quiet
Here at life's end
Neither loose imagination
Nor the mill of the mind
Consuming its rag and bone,
Can make the truth known.

The "rag and bone" chewed over in the mill of the mind cross-references a poem to come a year later, "The Circus Animals' Desertion," which recapitulates the poet's search for a theme, and more particularly his enamorment of a theme's symbolic representation:

Players and painted stage took all my love,
And not those things that they were symbols of.

But at the end, the poet is forced back to the sordid material from which his "masterful images" derived. And the poem ends,

Now that my ladder's gone,
I must lie down where all the ladders start,
In the foul rag-and-bone shop of the heart.

But "An Acre of Grass" does not end with the poet lying down. Following the first two stanzas comes the revolt against the accepted interpretation of old age:

Grant me an old man's frenzy,
Myself must I remake
Till I am Timon and Lear
Or that William Blake
Who beat upon the wall
Till Truth obeyed his call;

Though this rousing challenge to persist until truth be made patent may be tempered a bit by the fourth and final stanza:

> A mind Michael Angelo knew
> That can pierce the clouds,
> Or inspired by frenzy
> Shake the dead in their shrouds;
> Forgotten else by mankind,
> An old man's eagle mind.

It's hard to evaluate the precise dosage of optimism and pessimism in the concluding lines. The old man's eagle mind needs an outlet in artistic "frenzy." Just what one can expect from the frenzy seems unclear to me; is the truth Blake made come to his call always available? The poem may be most of all an affirmation of resistance, of the refusal to yield to the decay of mind and body, and the accompanying loss of the self. It is less the completed work of art that is envisioned, perhaps, than simply the capacity to go on working at art, to go on making.

We are somewhere near the edges of King Lear's heath, with its experience of old age as the betrayal of everything life has meant. The famous words of wisdom spoken by Edgar in William Shakespeare's play

> Men must endure
> Their coming hither even as their going hence.
> Ripeness is all.[3]

don't quite seem adequate to the old man's rage, the need to keep beating at the wall. In the limiting circumstances of that enduring, at life's candle-end, come such phenomena as Beethoven's late quartets—which in his by then total deafness he could not hear—or Matisse's late cutouts, these a kind of return to the art and techne of childhood at a point where he could no longer wield the paintbrush, in which one can find the brilliant invention of a new "period" in his work and far more than that: the invention of a form of art never done before, a soaring invention in response to necessity. Nearer to us, one finds a parallel self-reinvention in the work of the artist Chuck Close following a neurological illness that made it impossible for him to use the paintbrush as he once had done.

Then there is the case, more mysterious in its causes, of Cézanne. Some have attributed his late, notational style—I am thinking mainly of the work done in Provence in 1901–6, his final years—to disturbances of vision that made him unable to see landscape "normally." A painting such as *The Garden at Les Lauves* (1906), in the Phillips Collection in Washington, D.C., resolves the world into a patterned set of paintbrush patches, at the same time strikingly nonrepresentational, on their way to abstract expressionism, yet utterly lucid and readable (see frontispiece). One often finds this painting labeled as "unfinished." Yes, if by "finished" one means the polished patina of academic art, or even the completely filled-in canvas of most of Cézanne's work to this point. But surely the blanks of the composition are part of its whole style and message. Art is taking place in the interstices of "art." The eye is being retrained, called upon to learn anew to picture landscape as a production of the mind. As Cézanne wrote to Émile Bernard a month before his death in 1906, "I am still studying nature, and sometimes I think I make slow progress."[4]

Biographers and critics have suggested that Cézanne's eyesight may have been failing by this time, possibly from the advancing effects of his diabetes. In a letter to Bernard in 1905, Cézanne wrote, "Now, being old, nearly seventy years, the sensations of color, which give the light, are for me the reason for the abstractions, which do not allow me to cover my canvas entirely, nor to pursue the delimitation of the objects, where their points of contact are fine or delicate, from which it results that my depiction in the painting is incomplete."[5] To which Philip Conisbee, who cites the letter, adds, "the aging artist had almost literally reverted to that state of infantile vision, which had been his rhetorical aspiration years before—if not quite intended on these terms—'to see like a newborn child.'"[6] In this sense, the move toward abstraction, simplification, and the foregrounding of the patchy work of the paintbrush itself resembles a return to the vision and even the art of childhood through the most audacious artistic innovation, whatever its source in body or mind. If this late style is caused by infirmity, it also uses that infirmity to spectacular ends. And it summons forth much of the twentieth-century art to follow; it will be learned by subsequent artists, incorporated into their very knowledge of their task.

As Gabriel Conroy's fading away leads to—justifies, one might say—the utter sureness and simplicity of Joyce's prose, a prose that can almost (and later will) unfold without punctuation because it is syntactically and rhythmically so perfect, so lucid, so also do Cézanne's late "abstractions," colors given in themselves and not in their points of contact with one another. Yeats, too, achieves something of the childhood of art in much of his late poetry, in the simplicity of line and language, in the rough vulgarity of theme and vernacular—as, notably, in all the "Crazy Jane" poems (renewing a tradition from William Wordsworth's simpletons), or, to stay with the *Last Poems* (1938–39), something like "John Kinsella's Lament for Mrs. Mary Moore," a kind of rough elegy on the death of an old whore. The final stanza:

> The priests have got a book that says
> > But for Adam's sin
> Eden's Garden would be there
> > And I there within.
> No expectation fails there,
> > No pleasing habit ends,
> No man grows old, no girl grows cold,
> > But friends walk by friends.
> Who quarrels over halfpennies
> > That plucks the trees for bread?
> *What shall I do for pretty girls*
> > *Now my old bawd is dead?*

Though he would not have approved of either the matter or the tone, this, as much as Cézanne's later painting, would fit T. S. Eliot's description, in "Little Gidding" (the last of his *Four Quartets*),

> A condition of complete simplicity
> (Costing not less than everything)

Since we are quoting analogues here, it would seem a shame not to bring to bear a famous (overquoted) passage from Henry James's tale *The Middle Years*, about a dying writer, Dencombe, who doubts the worth of everything he's done. When Doctor Hugh tells him that's he's "a great success," then, "Dencombe lay taking this in; then he gathered strength to speak once more. 'A second chance—*that's* the delusion. There never was to be but one. We work in the dark—we do what we can—we give what we have. Our doubt is our passion and our passion is our task. The rest is the madness of art.'"[7] The "madness of art" in old age is in some sense a response to Dencombe's disabused realization that there are no second chances. Under the shadow of death, living on borrowed time, like Proust's Marcel, who compares himself to Scheherazade, Yeats and Cézanne do seem to find in the madness of their late work a second chance, an opportunity to reinvent the self.

Rousseau—to return for a moment to him—is a special case. His final work, *The Reveries of a Solitary Walker* (*Les Rêveries du promeneur solitaire*), "finished" only by his death, are also in their way a remarkable achievement, though one ostensibly founded—as the title implies—on the disillusioned renunciation of the attempt to write *for* anyone but himself. "Here I am then alone upon the earth" (Me voici donc seul sur la terre) begins the first of the *Reveries*, claiming he no longer has any brother, any neighbor, any friend, any society but himself.[8] In a blend of paranoia and lucidity typical of his late work, Rousseau recognizes the isolation created about him—if not fully his own contribution to it. "Everything external to me is henceforth foreign to me." He has no more *semblables*, no more fellow men—those to whom he addressed his challenge on the opening page of the *Confessions*. So if he picks up the "severe and sincere" examination begun in the *Confessions*, it no longer has the same goal. *Confession* implies an interlocutor, and he now has none. Rather, he will apply daily "a barometer to his soul," and report the results without order or method. Now the implicit comparison to Michel de Montaigne in that "broken mould" at the start of the *Confessions* becomes explicit: "I undertake the same enterprise as Montaigne, but with a completely opposite goal to his: for he only wrote his Essays for others, and I write my reveries only for myself."

So what is this writing for, to whom is it addressed? Here Rousseau ingeniously goes beyond the "dear diary" formulation. He understands the implicit dialogue of any writing project—that the claim to disavow any readership whatsoever can't be taken literally. Instead, he proposes himself—grown older still—as the reader: "If in my older age, near the time of my departure, I remain as I hope to be in the same disposition as I am at present, reading [the *Reveries*] will recall to me the sweetness that I taste in writing them and, reviving for me past time, will so to speak double my existence." This is pre-Proust, in a sense, in its postulation that it is the revival, the reliving in writing, of *le temps passé* that holds the key to joy: a "doubling" of existence, which is similar to what Marcel experiences in the revelatory experiences of *Time Regained*. And the *Reveries* are indeed all about redoubling: not only the anticipation of future pleasure in rereading, but the pleasures of reviving in the act of writing pleasures experienced, be they the pleasures of nirvanic loss of self in the rowboat on the Lac de Bienne. He has found an excuse for telling even in the absolute silence of solitude. No longer is he tormented by the future fate of his pages, as he was with the *Confessions* and the *Dialogues*; he's now indifferent to the fate of these "monuments to his innocence": "Let them spy on what I am doing, let them worry about these pages, let them take possession of them, suppress them, falsify them, none of that matters to me any more. I neither hide them nor show them" (1:195).

To neither hide nor show his writings: there may be a kind of striptease going on here, a challenge to come read that which is not written for you, but for the writer—doubling himself—alone. Again, it is not so very different from Proust's reducing all of his acquaintance to a "vast cemetery" in order to write his book. If Rousseau were slightly less belligerent in his paranoia, he might agree with Marcel's insight that a book exists to make a reader "the reader of himself," since already reading the self is postulated as the goal of writing the *Reveries*. If you want to ferret out and steal his pages, Rousseau is not going to stop you—though he's not inviting you, either. You will be, as it were, overhearing a dialogue between self and self. And that seems to me an honest assessment of any writing project, and a point of some wisdom achieved with he coming of age and the continued dedication to the madness of art.

Freud's late work is all quite odd, at once self-deprecating and audacious in its claims, deeply pessimistic about the nature and the future of humanity while resolute in its confrontation of death as absolute extinction—yet with a concurrent claim to intellectual immortality that lets him compare himself to Charles Darwin. It is in the next-to-last of his completed essays, *Analysis Terminable and Interminable*, that he famously declares psychoanalysis to be an "impossible" profession. But surely the most curious of his last works, and the one that in its composition displays most clearly the characteristics of lateness and lastness, is *Moses and Monotheism*, composed over a four-year period, 1934–38, during which Freud in Vienna witnessed the rise of the National Socialist Party in Germany—and escaped to England just in time to avoid perishing in the Nazi *Anschluss* that swept through his native land in March 1938. The book presents a compositional structure so strange that one wonders why he didn't revise it. We are given three essays of differing length, the last of which recapitulates everything that has been said earlier, along with two prefaces, both at the start of the third essay, then another "preface" halfway through that essay, and a host of repetitions along with apparent non sequiturs that really trace the central argument. It's as if Freud wished to preserve and publish a certain roughness of organization that corresponds both to the subject of the book and to the circumstances of its publication. One is put in mind of late Cézanne.

Much is explained in the implicit pathos of the two prefaces to essay 3, the first dated from Vienna, before March 1938, where he announces his decision to break his "well-grounded intention" of not adding to the two essays—previously published in *Imago*—what he calls "the final portion which I have held back," and yet not to publish the book (*Standard Edition* 23:54). The withholding has to do not only with "the weakening of creative powers which goes along with old age" but also, more forcefully, with the political moment. Freud sees Austria as "under the protection" of the Catholic Church, and he does not want to publish anything that would arouse the hostility of the church—as surely *Moses and Monotheism* would, as his writing already had. So, very much in the manner of Rousseau in his *Reveries*—where Rousseau claims to be writing only to himself—Freud declares, "I do not only think but I *know* that I shall let myself be deterred by this second obstacle, by the external danger, from publishing the last portion of my study on Moses" (*SE* 23:55). He continues, very much in the spirit of Rousseau: "I shall not give this work to the public. But that need not prevent my writing it." He will write it—and conceal it, in a gesture that in fact mimes the story of murder and its concealment that he will have to tell in the book.

The first preface is then followed by "Prefatory Note II," dated from London in June 1938. Briefly he records that the wished-for protection of Austria by the church had proved a "broken reed," and that, certain that he would be persecuted "not only for my line of thought but also for my 'race'—accompanied by many of my friends, I left the city which, from my early childhood, had been my home for seventy-eight years" (*SE* 23:57). But to these external circumstances inflecting the composition Freud adds his sense of the internal difficulties posed by his book: "No less than before, I feel uncertain in the face of my own work; I lack the consciousness of unity and of belonging together which should exist between an author and his work" (*SE* 23:58). The uncertainty doesn't arise from any doubt about the truth of his argument, of which he has been convinced from the time of *Totem and Taboo* in 1912, but from doubt about whether he has made the case about Jewish monotheism: "To my critical sense this book, which takes its start from the man Moses, appears like a dancer balancing on the tip of one toe." So here is the product of Freud's "old man's frenzy": a delicate balletic balancing act of a man more than eighty years old.

The argument of *Moses and Monotheism*—originally subtitled "an historical novel"—is not easily summarized, given the layered and tortuous composition of the book. Yet the kernel is clear enough, and shocking enough to make the doubts about publication expressed by Freud (and some of his friends) seem warranted. Moses was an Egyptian who adopted the monotheism of the Pharaoh Akhnaton. His leadership of his followers out of Egypt ended in his murder—itself a kind of repetition of the murder of the "primal father" hypothesized in *Totem and Taboo*, and with similar consequences: guilt, and the institution of the law. The killing of this "outstanding father-figure" was "a case of 'acting out' instead of remembering, as happens so often with neurotics during the work of analysis" (*SE* 23:89). Then, whereas the Jews continued to deny knowledge of the killing of the father, the Christians incorporated it into their religion by way of a displacement: the sacrifice of the son.

The crucial figure here is Paul—originally Saul—a Roman Jew from Tarsus, who "seized upon this sense of guilt and traced it back correctly to its original source." Paul's ingenious solution is to turn the murder of the primal father into the source of "good news":

> He called this the "original sin"; it was a crime against God
> and could only be atoned for by death. With the original sin
> death came into the world. In fact this crime deserving death
> had been the murder of the primal father who was later dei-
> fied. But the murder was not remembered: instead of it there
> was a phantasy of its atonement, and for that reason this phan-
> tasy could be hailed as a message of redemption (*evangelium*).
> A son of God had allowed himself to be killed without guilt
> and had thus taken on himself the guilt of all men. It had to be
> a son, since it had been the murder of a father. (*SE* 23:86)

The Christian ceremony of communion in this interpretation repeats the totemic meal, ingesting the father. If originally Christianity wishes to propitiate the father, it in fact dethrones him in favor of Jesus: "Judaism had been the religion of the father; Christianity became a religion of the son" (*SE* 23:88). In the process, Christianity takes on various symbolic rituals and divine figures from neighboring religions—including the mother goddess—and "superstitious, magical and mystical elements," which inhibit its intellectual development: "The Christian religion did not maintain the high level in things of the mind to which Judaism had soared" (*SE* 23:88). On the other hand, "The poor Jewish people, who with their habitual stubbornness continued to disavow the father's murder, atoned heavily for it in the course of time" (*SE* 23:90).

Freud has in this manner completed not only *Totem and Taboo* but also *The Future of an Illusion* in "demonstrating" the origins of religion in a sense of guilt, tracing that guilt back to murder of the primal father (universalizing the oedipal myth), then showing up the peculiarities of the responses to guilt displayed by Judaism and Christianity. His argument—however unfounded: the notion that Moses was murdered, which he took from a book by Ernst Sellin published in 1922, seems to have no substantiation—effectively declares a pox on both the major houses of religion of his time, and at a time when the Nazis represented a kind of revival of a vicious know-nothing paganism. The destructive arrogance of *Moses and Monotheism* is striking. What is less clear is why Freud, with such a negative view of religion of all sorts, feels the need to write about Moses at all.

The answer may have occurred to any reader who has had the patience to read through *Moses and Monotheism*: Freud has thoroughly identified himself with the man Moses, the Egyptian destined to lead the people of Israel out of captivity, to teach them the law—and then to be murdered for it. On the Mosaic model, his teachings will return only in the manner of the return of the repressed.[9] One captures an allusion to this sense of his future importance when, looking for an analogy to the delayed effect of Mosaic law—originally rejected, later permanently established—he mentions Darwin's theory of evolution, originally violently disputed and largely rejected, but within a generation recognized "as a great step forward towards truth." And here he adds, "Darwin himself achieved the honour of a grave or cenotaph in Westminster Abbey." To the future of an illusion one can, wishfully, juxtapose the future of a truth.

In the second essay of *Moses and Monotheism*, Freud has noted "the evidence afforded by circumcision, which has repeatedly been of help to us, like, as it were, a key-fossil" (*SE* 23:39). The cut penis as key fossil: the full explanation is given us only many pages later: "Circumcision is the symbolic substitute for the castration which the primal father once inflicted upon his sons in the plenitude of his absolute power, and whoever accepted that symbol was showing by it that he was prepared to submit to the father's will, even if it imposed the most painful sacrifice on him" (*SE* 23:122). The assertion is sufficiently outlandish that we may want in some measure to accept its symbolic, if not its literal, truth. It's in any case interesting that the penis marked by the substitute for castration appears to Freud as the key fossil in his exploration. It is the cut of the law, imposing itself on God's chosen people in an act of violence that will in the future be characteristic of the legal word.[10]

The circumcised penis returns him, as we move toward the conclusion to *Moses and Monotheism*, to the ethical attainments of the Jewish people, the second great achievement of their religion (monotheism being the first), which, based on the guilt of father murder, in a kind of extreme version of the scenario of *Civilization and Its Discontents*, imposed more and more "meticulous and even trivial" commandments on themselves, increasing "instinctual renunciations" responding to a kind of "moral asceticism." He writes, "In a fresh rapture of moral asceticism they imposed more and more new instinctual renunciations on themselves and in that way reached—in doctrine and precept, at least—ethical heights which had remained inaccessible to the other peoples of antiquity" (*SE* 23:134). Yet the "ethical ideas" cultivated by Judaism cannot "disavow their origin from the sense of guilt felt on account of a suppressed hostility to God. They possess the characteristic—uncompleted and incapable of completion—of obsessional neurotic reaction-formations; we can guess, too, that they serve the secret purposes of punishment" (*SE* 23:134–35). The Jewish religion sounds in this manner like a continuing psychoanalytic therapy as described in Freud's contemporaneous essay, *Analysis Terminable and Interminable*. For the Christianity of Paul, on the contrary, the killing of God is over-

laid by the sacrifice of his son, and the notion of redemption. This offers a more powerful distortion of "what happened" than in Judaism:
"The unnameable crime was replaced by the hypothesis of what must
be described as a shadowy 'original sin'" (*SE* 23:135). And yet the Jews
remained burdened by the failure to admit—as Christians indirectly
do—that they murdered God: "In a certain sense they have in that way
taken a tragic load of guilt on themselves; they have been made to pay
heavy penance for it" (*SE* 23:136).

And so Freud rather abruptly—and unexpectedly—brings his
book to a close in a final paragraph that begins, "Our investigation may
perhaps have thrown a little light on the question of how the Jewish
people have acquired the characteristics which distinguish them. Less
light has been thrown on the problem of how it is that they have been
able to retain their individuality till the present day" (*SE* 23: 136–37).
We didn't know that illuminating the characteristics distinctive of the
Jewish people was the aim of *Moses and Monotheism*—it was never its
announced purpose. But to conclude in this manner, of course, enables
us to see better how Freud has cast himself in the Mosaic role. To conclude in this manner in the summer of 1938, following discussion of the
"tragic load of guilt" that Jews have taken on themselves and the "heavy
penance" they have paid for it, induces a certain chill. Freud was acutely
aware of the Nazi aggressions that had made his flight from Vienna
necessary, and the purges of Jews from all positions of professional authority in Austria that followed the Anschluss. What he could not yet
know was the coming plan for a "Final Solution" to the "problem" of
the Jewish people. And yet, on the threshold of his own extinction, he
seems to foretell a vaster murder of the bearers of ethical consciousness.

"Late Freud" is notable not only for its disabused humanism—where
the aggressive and destructive drives of human beings more and more
demand confrontation—but also for its self-critique of psychoanalysis.
In *Analysis Terminable and Interminable*, he in 1937 returns ostensibly
to questions of psychoanalytic technique that he had not discussed for
some twenty years. But this essay is far more than a discussion of how the

analyst should handle the elusive termination of analysis—elusive in part because the dynamics of the transference create a resistance to ending, and the discovery, or creation, of fresh material to be dealt with. One is reminded of Henry James's famous line, in the preface to his novel *Roderick Hudson*: "Really, universally, relations stop nowhere, and the exquisite problem of the artist is eternally but to draw, by a geometry of his own, the circle within which they shall happily *appear* to do so."[11] That is, all of human life ramifies into connections, and the art of the novelist is to create the *apparent* termination, the comprehensible narrative account of a life in its significant connections to others, and to the world.

Beyond the question of ending the inherently unending, Freud encounters a "theory of mine in the writings of one of the great thinkers of ancient Greece," Empedocles of Acragas (Agrigentum, in Sicily) (*SE* 23:245). This pre-Socratic philosopher turns out really to be a pre-Freudian. He saw the universe as determined by the conflict of *philia* and *neixos*, love and strife. Freud notes that the former corresponds to his own Eros, then recharacterizes the latter—the force of destructiveness and aggression in humans and their culture—by tracing it to the death instinct, Thanatos. He thus completes his *Beyond the Pleasure Principle*, published in 1920, not so much by any substantive addition as by his grandiose identification and naming of the basic drives at work in the individual, and in the world. The work of psychoanalysis is in essence a miniature of this unending struggle.

After inscribing psychoanalysis under this ancient authority, Freud abruptly returns to issues of therapy and technique in the final two sections of *Analysis Terminable and Interminable* to declare famously that along with education and government, psychoanalysis may be the third of the "'impossible' professions, in which one can be sure beforehand of achieving unsatisfying results" (*SE* 23:248). Here Freud addresses the ethics of psychoanalysis and the psychoanalyst. If an analysis is to be brought to a successful close, that depends not only on the personality and the work accomplished by the patient, but also on the skill and self-mastery of the analyst. The analyst cannot be perfect, but he or she needs to know his or her own imperfections—a knowing that can only be accomplished through the experience of undergoing psychoanalysis. This is the pedagogic imperative, the liminal requirement to become an analyst. Yet of necessity "this analysis can only be short and incomplete. . . . It has accomplished its purpose if it gives the learner a firm conviction of the existence of the unconscious, if it enables him, when repressed material emerges, to perceive in himself things which would otherwise be incredible to him, and if it shows him a first sample of the technique which has proved to be the only effective one in analytic work" (*SE* 23:248). The analyzed person will then bring "the processes of remodelling the ego" into analytic work, and indeed into all experience.

But something much more negative can happen: the analyst can set up defense mechanisms, and withdraw from the "critical and corrective influence of analysis" (*SE* 23:249). Freud here reaches for "a disagreeable analogy with the effect of X-rays on people who handle them without taking special precautions." And here the wayward analyst becomes comparable to the patient under treatment—a Sherlock Holmes identifying with Professor Moriarty, the Napoleon of crime:

> It would not be surprising if the effect of a constant preoccupation with all the repressed material which struggles for freedom in the human mind were to stir up in the analyst as well all the instinctual demands which he is otherwise able to keep under suppression. These, too, are "dangers of analysis", though they threaten, not the passive but the active partner in the analytic situation; and we ought not to neglect to meet them. There can be no doubt how this is to be done. Every analyst should periodically—at intervals of five years or so—submit himself to analysis once more, without feeling ashamed of taking this step. This would mean, then, that not only the therapeutic analysis of patients but his own analysis would change from a terminable into an interminable task. (*SE* 23:249)

So at the last we come back to the analyst—here, the man who invented psychoanalysis through his own self-analysis—in the admission that all the repressed material he struggles with in the other, in his patients, lies within himself as well, may indeed be activated in the analysis of patients, and can be counteracted only through submitting the "subject supposed to know" (Jacques Lacan's appropriately knowing and skeptical term for the analyst) to further analysis himself, in a circular and unending process. Analysis itself, it turns out, is a kind of struggle between Eros and Thanatos, an unending dialogic structuring and restructuring of human personality in the world. And it is to that dialogic process that Freud will return in what is essentially his last essay, *Constructions in Analysis*, published in December 1937.

Yet before bringing his essay on the interminable to an end, Freud in a brief final section reaches—as if in an attempt precisely to arrest the flow of the unending—to "two themes" that are especially prominent in psychoanalyses, and give the analyst "an unusual amount of trouble" (*SE* 23:250). The two themes turn out to be distinctly gendered: on the side of women, an irreducible penis envy, and for men what Alfred Adler called the "masculine protest," which Freud would prefer to call "repudiation of femininity"—which is in fact a repudiation of passivity toward another male. On these two topics, the resistance of patients can remain resolutely unaltered, so that no change can be produced: "We often have the impression that with the wish for a penis and the masculine protest we have penetrated through all the psychological strata and have reached bedrock, and that thus our activities are at an end. This is probably true, since, for the psychical field, the biological field does in fact play the part of the underlying bedrock" (*SE 23:252*). For Freud, the archaeologist who has dedicated his life—in emulation of his childhood hero Heinrich Schliemann—to digging through the layers of repression to reach some buried psychic Troy, the biological bedrock is an end, much in the manner of a blank wall. Biology is there to be acknowledged—much of *Beyond the Pleasure Principle* was spent in pursuing what biology might have to teach us about the origin of sexual reproduction—but biology has yet to speak on the underlying nature of humanity. Its revelations, Freud says in *Beyond the Pleasure Principle*, lie in the future. For now, it is silent on the subjects that interest us most. In the absence of its answers, there is only conjecture.

And the dialogue. *Constructions in Analysis* returns us to the dialogic relation of analyst and patient. It, too, is a paper on therapeutic technique, and what one might call the ethics of psychoanalysis. And like *Analysis Terminable and Interminable*, it appears to give away the magician's art—like Prospero breaking his wand in *The Tempest*—by citing the quip of "a certain well-known man of science" who saw in psychoanalysis a realization of the famous principle of 'Heads I win, tails you lose' " (*SE* 23:257). (The phrase is in English in Freud's text.) That is, a refusal on the part of the patient to say "yes" to the analyst's interpretations isn't to be trusted or even accepted: the patient's "no" may be simply the product of resistance, the refusal to accede to the truth. The essay then announces itself as an investigation of the ways in which analysis assesses the value of "yes" and "no."

What it in fact becomes is a final reflection on the relation of analyst to analysand in the space of the analytic transference. The work of analysis, writes Freud, "involves two people, to each of whom a distinct task is assigned" (*SE* 23:258). The patient, of course, is assigned the task of remembering, even that which has been "forgotten." But the analyst? "The analyst has neither experienced nor repressed any of the material under consideration; his task cannot be to remember anything. What then *is* his task? His task is to make out what has been forgotten from the traces which it has left behind or, more correctly, to *construct it*" (*SE* 23:258–59; emphasis in the original). Those "traces" revive in Freud his recourse to his favorite analogy in archaeology, where the reconstitution of an ancient site involves using the remaining debris to reconstruct the whole. "Both of them [the archaeologist and the psychoanalyst] have an undisputed right to reconstruct by means of supplementing and combining the surviving remains" (*SE* 23:259). Yet the analyst has this distinct advantage over the archaeologist: the material he deals with, though buried, is still alive, and "even things that seem completely forgotten are present somehow and somewhere, and have merely been buried and made inaccessible to the subject" (*SE* 23:260).

Yet the construction of past events is only the beginning of the task of psychoanalysis. The analyst needs to convey his constructions to the patient, to see how they will work on her or him. Here, we deal with the *no* that may merely be the sign of resistance, but also with the *yes*, that may in itself prove valueless unless it is confirmed by other signs, unless it is productive of more narrative from the patient. There is a continuing dynamic dialogue, where the analyst "finishes a piece of construction and communicates it to the subject of the analysis so that it may work upon him; he then constructs a further piece out of the fresh material pouring in upon him, deals with it in the same way and proceeds in this alternating fashion until the end" (*SE* 23:260–61). The "alternating fashion" (*Abwechslung*) becomes the key, the centerless center of psychoanalysis, the place of the construction of a truth that can never be verified other than through its interpretive effects. "The path that starts from the analyst's construction ought to end in the patient's recollection; but it does not always lead so far. Quite often we do not succeed in bringing the patient to recollect what has been repressed. Instead of that, if the analysis is carried out correctly, we produce in him an assured conviction of the truth of the construction which achieves the same therapeutic result as a recaptured memory" (*SE* 23:265–66).

It would be a moment to reflect on the path traveled since the invention of the "talking cure" in the 1890s. The premise of *Studies in Hysteria*, which Freud coauthored with Josef Breuer and published in 1896, was always that the pathogenic story from the past uncovered in what was not quite yet psychoanalysis was true, verifiable like a Sherlock Holmes case, if one could take oneself back to the scene of the crime. Now, however, truth is an effect produced by a later construction (Freud earlier in the essay uses the term "reconstruction," but this seems to be set aside for the more radical "construction") which can only be known through the "assured conviction" it produces in the patient. Things *must have been this way*: that is all you know, and all you need to know. And Freud at this point refers to instances in which his constructions produce "ultra-clear" recollections of collateral details associated with a memory—details displaced from the central event. Sometimes these resemble true hallucinations, like those of psychotic patients. And now Freud is willing to believe that such hallucinations contain "a frag-ment of *historical truth*" (*SE* 23:267). He is back to the obsessive topic of *Moses and Monotheism*, as the last paragraph of *Constructions in Analysis* makes clear: delusions "which are inaccessible to logical criti-cism and which contract reality" nonetheless exert great power over hu-manity. It is because "They owe their power to the element of *historical truth* which they have brought up from the repression of the forgotten and primaeval past" (*SE* 23:269; emphasis in the original). Back to that ineradicable trace of the murder of the primal father.

It is here that *Constructions* ends. But the next-to-last paragraph contains an astonishing assertion provoked by the discussion of hallu-cinations and delusions. Freud says that he has "not been able to resist the seduction of an analogy." Here it is: "The delusions of patients ap-pear to me to be the equivalents of the constructions which we build up in the course of an analytic treatment—attempts at explanation and cure . . ." (*SE* 23:268). So it is that the delusional patient and the theory-building analyst come to resemble one another, both mad in the pursuit of explanation and cure. Not only is psychoanalysis an im-possible profession but it is a delusional one as well—if we are willing to understand that the quest to understand the meaning of the past of the self, and to narrativize it, proceeds without any hope of confirma-tion from a lost reality—which does not matter since the truer reality is psychic truth, the story that makes sense of things, the tale that tells us how things must have been, which may have first been laid down by the Delphic oracle. We just have then to enact it. Proust's Marcel says something very similar at the end of the *Recherche*, where he tells us that "la vraie vie est ailleurs": true life is elsewhere, it lies in the deci-pherment of our inner hieroglyphs, and in the writing of the story we could not understand in living it.

At the very end of his life—just before he asked his physician Max Schur to fulfill a long-held promise to inject him with a lethal dose of morphine when the pain of his cancer had become unbearable—Freud finished what was to be his final reading. It was of a novel by Honoré de Balzac, *La Peau de chagrin* (*The Fatal Skin*, in the best translation

I know).[12] Freud remarked to Schur that it was an appropriate text for the end of life: all about shrinking and starvation. Balzac's novel is indeed about that, but shrinking and starvation are the result of desire and its fulfillment. The young hero of the novel, Raphaël de Valentin, on the verge of suicide from despair at his utter destitution and his failure to make his chosen woman love him, is given a magic wild ass's skin, a *shagreen*, by an old antiques dealer (who has reached the age of 102). The magic skin realizes any wish one makes on it. Yet with every realized wish it shrinks. The metaphor is overtly sexual—the skin is like the penis after its realization of desire—but this is largely generalized in the lesson given to Raphaël by the antiques dealer when he presents the skin: "*Desire* sets us aflame, and *Power* destroys us" (*Vouloir* nous brûle, et *Pouvoir* nous détruit). So that the realization of desire, or Eros, always at the same time does the work of Thanatos, leading us more quickly to destruction. But there is an alternative, says the old man: "but KNOWLEDGE leaves our frail organism in a state of perpetual calm" (mais SAVOIR laisse notre faible organisation dans un perpetual état de calme).[13]

In fact, this flamboyant, parabolic tale already contains within itself not only the essential struggle posited by Empedocles but also the adumbration of Freud's *Beyond the Pleasure Principle*. For once Raphaël discovers the power of the talisman given to him by the old antiques dealer (for whom he wishes a passion for a dancer from the opera, contradicting the dealer's choice of knowledge and calm passivity—a wish that will, of course, be realized, to the old man's destruction), he plunges headlong into the world of desire and power, summoning up a drunken orgy peopled with beautiful women. The morning after, he discovers that he has inherited an immense fortune from an unknown uncle in Calcutta. At once, he sets the magic skin against the outline he traced of it the night before—to measure the shrinkage this realization of desire has produced: "A horrible pallor brought into relief every muscle of the haggard face of this heir to a fortune, his features tensed in a frown, and blanched, while the furrows of his face darkened, his eyes stared fixedly out from a livid mask. He saw DEATH" (10:209).

The discovery of the realization of desire, in all its fullness, is equally the discovery of death, as the inevitable outcome of desiring. If the death drive serves the pleasure principle, assuring the discharge of libido, in a deeper sense the pleasure principle is the servant of the death drive, assuring that the organism is led back to what Freud in *Beyond the Pleasure Principle* calls primal quiescence, the death that precedes and follows life. At the tail end of the orgy, all Raphaël can pronounce is "*I desire nothing.*"

To desire is ultimately to choose death. As Freud readily acknowledges in *Beyond the Pleasure Principle*, the philosopher Arthur Schopenhauer had already discovered this, as well as many a poet before him. If, as Wallace Stevens would later say, "Death is the mother of beauty," the desire to defeat death becomes the cultivation of ugliness. In his desperate attempt to prolong his existence, Raphaël tries to live will-lessly, all his needs taken care of by a servant who is never to ask what his master wants. He has made for himself a set of opera glasses that purposely distort the lines of the world, rendering everything seen through it ugly— in particular, transforming women from objects of desire into monsters. Yet it can't work. Life without desire is sterile. When Raphaël's old love from his student days, Pauline, reappears, he tosses away the talisman and devotes himself to a life of loving. But the death drive quickly does its silent work—the talisman reappears, now reduced to the size of a leaf, and Raphaël begins coughing his life away. He retreats to mountain spas, to no avail. At the last, Pauline reappears again, and he calls to her, overcome by desire. She now is holding the skin:

> Lit by the flickering light that shone on both Raphaël and the talisman, she studied very attentively both the face of her lover and the last morsel of the magic skin. Seeing her beautiful from terror and love, he was no longer master of his thoughts: memories of scenes of caresses and the delirious joys of passion triumphed in his long-sleeping soul, and awoke like an unquenched fire.
>
> "Pauline, come! Pauline!"

> A terrible cry came from the throat of the young woman,
> her eyes dilated, her eyebrows arched violently from an
> unbearable anguish, she read in Raphaël's eyes one of those
> unbridled desires which once had been her glory; but as this
> desire grew great, the magic skin, shrinking away, tickled the
> palm of her hand. (10:291–92)

Raphaël, with an inarticulate cry that becomes a death rattle, dies on her breast. It is an appropriately melodramatic and gothic ending to a highly colored tale of what is at stake in desire, power, knowledge, and death.

If *La Peau de chagrin* is about "shrinking and starvation," as Freud said to Schur, it's also about everything on the way to that finality. It is a rich allegory of life choices in an economy of desire governed by the ultimate arbiter of death. It has aspects of a tale from the *Arabian Nights* beloved of Proust, but also of the spiritual autobiography, as Raphaël courts a "woman without a heart" (who is apparently also a woman without a sex), tries gambling (in violation of a stern paternal interdiction), and attempts to write a treatise on the will. Freud was at times ungenerous to his intellectual precursors—many readers have noted his apparent repression of the influence of Friedrich Nietzsche—but his expression of appreciation for Balzac's novel, though we only have Schur's brief report, may suggest a recognition that once more "the poets" have been his true precursors. All of Freud's late system of thought lies in this first of Balzac's great novels. And the mode of Balzac's novel somehow, in a retroaction that Freud might have appreciated, brings out the melodramatic and gothic elements of psychoanalysis as the impossible but necessary, though unending, quest for knowledge of one's identity. Late Freud seems to move, though perhaps unconsciously, from Oedipus of Thebes to Oedipus at Colonus. "Do not try to be master in everything," Creon says to Oedipus at the end of *Oedipus the King*. "All is ordered for the best," the chorus concludes in *Oedipus at Colonus*. If one takes this as a message of consolation, it is not Freud's final position. If one takes it rather as unblinking recognition of an inevitable outcome, grim but ineluctable, then we are with the late Freud.

Think back to the ending of Freud's *A Disturbance of Memory on the Acropolis*, where he refers to his old age, his immobility, his need of forbearance. Like Yeats, like Cézanne and Matisse, Freud's response more deeply is to reject forbearance, to assume the posture of Yeats's wild old wicked man, to write the most provocative stuff of his long and provocative career. The lesson one might want to take away, from all these examples, and the many other I have not discussed (of which late Beethoven seems to me the most to cry out for analysis—but of a kind beyond my competence) may be that Rousseau struggles with in the unfinished Tenth of his *Reveries*: the sameness yet difference of the self over time, its capacity to alter radically its contours through its creative work on itself, along with the affirmation that it is still the same—-indeed, that it is more than ever itself. If, in Benjamin's haunting phrase, "Death is the sanction of everything the storyteller has to tell," it is in facing the imminence of their own death that these creators most assert the right to remake themselves, in words, in images, through metaphors or in identification with great (murdered) heroes. They end, at very least, in the restlessness of identity.

# Epilogue | The Identity Paradigm

As Marlow famously says of Kurtz, in Joseph Conrad's *Heart of Darkness*, "He had summed up; he had judged." But then when we come to Marlow's report of Kurtz's summing up, it turns out to be the dark utterance: "The horror, the horror!" Which may not only figure a loss of personal identity and morality on the part of the colonial exploiter in the Congo—which comes close to undermining the forthright seaman's morality that Marlow thinks he subscribes to—but also a more general modernist suspicion of summing up. It's not surprising that Kurtz's death reappears in T. S. Eliot's *The Waste Land*. One of the things that is most modern in modern literature is the suspicion of and resistance to endings—something that Conrad noted in his masterful essay on Henry James: "One is never set at rest by Mr. Henry James's novels. His books end as an episode in life ends. You remain with the sense of the life still going on; and even the subtle presence of the dead is felt in that silence that comes upon the artist-creation when the last word has been read."[1]

Conrad's meditation on James's restless endings might serve to a further commentary on the problem of the self faced with and refusing to accept its extinction, or rather—since it has no choice in the matter—refusing to let its extinction mute its strident claim to selfhood and self-recreation in the madness of art. I want to use it also as an excuse for my own inconclusiveness in this book. For what I have reached, I think, is not any possibility of a summing up, a lesson drawn from the itinerary followed, but simply a reflection on the critical importance of the identity paradigm—and especially the identificatory paradigm—in our culture. It seems useful to point to the contours of that paradigm, and to some of the items it comprehends. To see the identificatory paradigm at work, in a range of cultural and social contexts—in legal settings and debates, in fictions from low and high culture, in confessional and psychoanalytic discourse—is to bring to attention something characteristic and important about our lives, singly and collectively. To grasp the predominance and the importance of the identity paradigm is to recognize something ineradicable and significant in our culture.

We have had since 1979 a magazine called *Self*, which claims to reach five and a half million readers and has spawned a number of imitators. It can stand as emblematic of a culture obsessed with the self, the individual body and psyche, the first-person confessional narrative, and a narcissistic valuation of all that gratifies the ego. The collectivist ideal of socialist societies, and utopian thinkers throughout history, seems to have largely disappeared from sight in favor of an economic and hedonistic agent whose decisions are based on selfishness rather than altruism. Yet when we talk about identity, as in "identity theft," we tend to refer to the self as represented in the digits of our Social Security numbers and our credit cards—as if the theft of these constituted a direct threat to our selfhood, seen as defined by the state and the financial nexus. We come, once again, on something of a contradiction: the self sees itself from the inside, as a place of depth, meaning, and as the center of the universe, whereas the self viewed from the outside is merely the point of intersection of impoverished data. We are forced, I think, to accept that both images of the self are true, though we can't really reconcile them.

I began by noting that it matters crucially to be able to say who we are, why we are here, and where we are going. We also know that like Jean-Paul Sartre's boy in the train, in his recurrent nightmare, when asked by the conductor for our ticket, we can't find it. We know we don't have it, and have no means of buying it. That doesn't mean we won't keep looking for it and producing various excuses for occupying our seat in the train. We need to keep saying what our identity might be and where it might lie, and how we might find it authenticated by other identities. That is an anxiety-laden quest, and one that brings no true ending, no resolution, but perhaps rather the sense of life going on along with the "subtle presence of the dead" that Conrad ascribes to James's endings. It's very much a part of who we are.

# | Acknowledgments

I have been helped by many friends and colleagues: fellow teachers, professors of law in particular; those who invited me to lecture, and thus forced me to move forward on the project; those who asked pertinent questions of the lecturer; and my habitual companions in dialogue. Thanks, then, to Kerry Abrams, Jeff Alexander, Carol Armstrong, Megan Becker-Lekrone, Sandra Bermann, Rachel Bowlby, Gordon Braden, Helena Buescu, Elizabeth Emery, Paul Gewirtz, Laure Goldstein, Marilyn Heller, David Hollander, Michael Holquist, Hilary Jewett, Michael Levenson, Robert J. Lifton, Joseph Luzzi, Maria Rosa Menocal, Bernadette Meyler, D. A. Miller, Martha Nussbaum, Dan Ortiz, Robert Post, George Rutherglen, Maurice Samuels, Kim Lane Scheppele, Michael Seidman, Garrett Stewart, Steve Wasserman, Hanne Winarsky, and Suzanne Wofford—with my apologies for the woeful inadequacy of this unannotated list. An early version of chapter 5 appeared in *Yale Journal of Law and the Humanities* 15:1 (2003), 101–29, as "'Inevitable Discovery'—Law, Narrative, Retrospectivity"; my thanks to its editors.

I had at various times very helpful research assistance from Lindsay Minnis and Justin Schwab. I benefited from a tranquil and productive stay at the Rockefeller Foundation's Bellagio Study Center, and thank in particular its resident director, Pilar Palacio.

My research has been supported and encouraged by the Andrew W. Mellon Foundation, and I express my especial gratitude to Joseph Meisel and Harriet Zuckerman.

# | Notes

To Begin

1. Jean-Paul Sartre, Les Mots (Paris: Gallimard, 1964); English trans. Bernard Frechtman, *The Words* (New York: Vintage, 1981), 110–11.

Chapter 1. Marks of Identity

1. The first Pollak opinion comes in *United States v. Llera-Plaza*, 179 F. Supp. 2d 494, (E.D. Pa. 2002), vacated by 188 F. Supp. 2d 549 (E.D. Pa. 2002); see also *Daubert v. Merrell Dow Phamaceuticals, Inc.*, 509 U.S. 579.

2. *Maryland v. Bryan Rose* (Circuit Court, Baltimore County, MD), K06-0545 (2007), 4.

3. See Simon A. Cole, "A Little Art, a Little Science, a Little 'CSI,'" *New York Times*, December 31, 2006. Cole, whose *Suspect Identities* is the best book on fingerprinting that I know, touches lightly on some of the issues that interest me in this chapter. On a number of court cases in which judges have rejected Pollak's views in his first *Llera-Plaza* decision (in some of which Simon Cole was a witness for the defense), see the "Daubert Links" website: http://onin.com/fp/daubert_links3.html.

4. Jean-Jacques Rousseau, *Les Confessions*, in *Confessions. Autres Textes Autobiographique: Oeuvres completes* (Paris: Bibliothèque de la Pléiade,

1959–95), 1:1; my translation. My references to Rousseau will all use the Pléiade edition, giving volume and page number. The best available English translation of the *Confessions* is by Angela Scholar (Oxford: Oxford World Classics, 2000).

5. Michael de Montaigne, "Du Repentir," in *Essais* (Paris: Bibliothèque de la Pléiade, 1950), book 3, chap. 2, 900; English trans. Donald M. Frame, *The Complete Essays of Montaigne* (Stanford, CA: Stanford University Press, 1965).

6. John Locke, *An Essay Concerning Human Understanding* (1689), book 2, chap. 27, "Of Identity and Diversity" (London: Penguin, 2004), 303; emphasis in the original.

7. Nathalie Z. Davis, *The Return of Martin Guerre* (Cambridge, MA: Harvard University Press, 1983).

8. *Blade Runner* (1982) derives from the novel by Philip Dick, *Do Androids Dream of Electric Sheep?* (New York: Doubleday, 1968).

9. See Louis Chevalier, *Classes laborieuses et classes dangereuses* (Paris: Plon, 1958); English trans. Frank Jellinek, *Labouring Classes and Dangerous Classes* (London: Routledge and Kegan Paul, 1973).

10. It is worth noting that in 1792, the revolutionary government established the civil registry—replacing and, it hoped, improving the earlier church parish records—and thus inaugurating the modern state bureaucracy charged with knowing who you are. See Gérard Noiriel, "L'identification des citoyens: Naissance de l'état civil républicain," *Genèses* 13 (1993): 3–28. On the history of earlier forms of identifying signs and documents, see Valentin Groebner, *Who Are You? Identification, Deception, and Surveillance in Early Modern Europe*, trans. Mark Kyburz and John Peck (New York: Zone Books, 2007).

11. See Alain Corbin, *Les Filles de noces: misère sexuelle et prostitution (19e et 20e siècles)* (Paris: Aubier-Montaigne, 1978).

12. Charles Dickens, *Great Expectations* (New York: Signet Classic, 1998), 317.

13. Carlo Ginzburg, "Spie. Radici di un paradigma indizario," in *Miti Emblemi Spie* (Torino, Italy: Einaudi, 1986), 166; English trans. John and Anne C. Tedeschi, "Clues: Roots of an Evidential Paradigm," in *Myths, Emblems, Clues* (Baltimore: Johns Hopkins University Press, 1989), 103. I have modified the Tedeschi translation in order to give a more literal rendition. Many of the large implications of Ginzburg's "indicial paradigm" are developed in the far-ranging book by Terence Cave, *Recognitions* (Oxford: Clarendon Press, 1988).

14. Arthur Conan Doyle, "The Red-headed League," in *Sherlock Holmes: The Complete Novels and* Tales (New York: Bantam Dell, 2003), 1:287.

15. Balzac, *Le Colonel Chabert* [1832, 1844], in *La Comédie humaine* (Paris: Bibliothèque de la Pléiade, 1976), 3:317; translations are mine, but a good English version by Carol Crossman is available (New York: New Directions, 1997). There is also an effective screen version from 1994, directed by Yves Angelo, with Gérard Depardieu as Chabert, Fanny Ardent as the Comtesse Ferraud, and Fabrice Luchini as Derville.

16. See Jerome Bruner, "The Transactional Self," in *Actual Minds, Possible Worlds* (Cambridge, MA: Harvard University Press, 1986), 67.

17. D. A. Miller, *The Novel and the Police* (Berkeley and Los Angeles: University of California Press, 1988). In the background of Miller's study, and my own, looms the work of Michel Foucault, especially his *Surveiller et punir* (Paris: Gallimard, 1975); English trans. Alan Sheridan, *Discipline and Punish* (New York: Pantheon, 1977).

18. Ronald R. Thomas, *Detective Fiction and the Rise of Forensic Science* (Cambridge: Cambridge University Press, 1999), 11.

19. See Tony Tanner, *Adultery in the Novel: Contract and Transgression* (Baltimore: Johns Hopkins University Press, 1979).

20. Alphonse Bertillon, quoted in Simon A. Cole, *Suspect Identities: A History of Fingerprinting and Criminal Identification* (Cambridge, MA: Harvard University Press, 1986), 45; emphasis in the original.

21. See Cole, *Suspect Identities*, 103–7. Cole's article, "A Little Art, a Little Science, a Little 'CSI'" (see note 2, above) mentions that identification of a fingerprint left by Leonardo da Vinci has, for some investigators, tended to confirm the hypothesis that his mother was of Central European descent.

22. On the untested nature of fingerprint technical expertise, see Jennifer L. Mnookin, "Fingerprint Evidence in an Age of DNA Profiling," 67 *Brooklyn Law Review* 13 (2001): 19. See also the recent report of the National Research Council, *Strengthening Forensic Science in the United States: A Path Forward* (Washington, DC: National Academies Press, 2009).

23. Arthur Conan Doyle, "The Adventure of the Cardboard Box," in *The Complete Sherlock Holmes* (New York: Doubleday, 1930), 52–53.

24. The Supreme Court said yes in *Kyllo v. United States*, 533 U.S. 27, in 2001, but this area of Fourth Amendment jurisprudence remains divisive and subject to changing court majorities.

25. Marcel Proust, *In Search of Lost Time*, trans. C. K. Scott Moncrieff and Terence Kilmartin, rev. D. J. Enright (New York: Random House, 2003), 2:310–11; I have made some modifications to the translation. For the orig-

inal, see *A la recherche du temps perdu* (Paris: Bibliothèque de la Pléiade, 1988), 2:152.

## Chapter 2. Egotisms

1. John Locke, *An Essay Concerning Human Understanding* (1689), ed. Roger Woolhouse (London: Penguin, 2004), book 2, chap. 27, 297.
2. Stendhal, *La Vie de Henry Brulard*, in *Oeuvres intimes* (Paris: Bibliothèque de la Pléiade, 1982), 2:532; English trans. John Sturrock, *The Life of Henry Brulard* (New York: New York Review Books, 2002).
3. Stendhal, *Souvenirs d'Egotisme*, in *Oeuvres intimes*, 2:430; English trans. Andrew Brown, *Memoirs of an Egotist* (London: Hesperus Classics, 2003).
4. See Jean Strobinski, "Stendhal pseudonyme," in *L'Oeil vivant* (Paris: Gallimard, 1961); English trans. Arthur Goldhammer, *The Living Eye* (Cambridge, MA: Harvard University Press, 1989).
5. Freud's reasons for "forgetting" the name Signorelli are ostensibly different; see his extended analysis of this memory lapse in the first chapter of Sigmund Freud, *The Psychopathology of Everyday Life* (1901), in *The Complete Psychological Works of Sigmund Freud (The Standard Edition)* (London: Hogarth Press, 1955–74), 6:1–7.
6. Émile Benveniste, "De la subjectivité dans le langage," in *Problèmes de linguistique generale* (Paris: Gallimard, 1967), 260; English trans. Mary Elizabeth Meek, *Problems in General Linguistics* (Coral Gables, FL: University of Miami Press, 1971).
7. Here is the first page of Rousseau's *Confessions*, in French and in English:

> Je forme une entreprise qui n'eut jamais d'exemple, et dont l'exécution n'aura point d'imitateur. Je veux montrer à mes semblables un homme dans toute la vérité de la nature; et cet homme, ce sera moi.
>
> Moi seul. Je sens mon coeur, et je connais les hommes. Je ne suis fait comme aucun de ceux que j'ai vus; j'ose croire n'être fait comme aucun de ceux qui existent. Si je ne vaux pas mieux, au moins je suis autre. Si la nature a bien ou mal fait de briser le moule dans lequel elle m'a jeté, c'est ce dont on ne peut juger qu'après m'avoir lu.
>
> Que la trompette du jugement dernier sonne quand elle voudra, je viendrai, ce livre à la main, me présenter devant le souverain juge. Je dirai hautement: Voilà ce que j'ai fait, ce que j'ai pensé, ce que je fus. J'ai dit le bien et le mal avec la même franchise. Je n'ai rien tu de mauvais, rien ajouté de bon; et s'il m'est arrivé d'employer

quelque ornement indifférent, ce n'a jamais été que pour remplir un vide occasionné par mon défaut de mémoire. J'ai pu supposer vrai ce que je savais avoir pu l'être, jamais ce que je savais être faux. Je me suis montré tel que je fus: méprisable et vil quand je l'ai été; bon, généreux, sublime, quand je l'ai été: j'ai dévoilé mon intérieur tel que tu l'as vu toi-même. Être éternel, rassemble autour de moi l'innombrable foule de mes semblables; qu'ils écoutent mes confessions, qu'ils gémissent de mes indignités, qu'ils rougissent de mes misères. Que chacun d'eux découvre à son tour son coeur au pied de ton trône avec la même sincérité, et puis qu'un seul te dise, s'il l'ose: je fus meilleur que cet homme-là.

I am resolved on an undertaking that has no model and will have no imitator. I want to show to my fellow-men a man in all the truth of nature; and this man will be myself.

Myself alone. I feel my heart and I know men. I am not made like any that I have seen; I venture to believe that I was not made like any that exist. If I am not more deserving, at least I am different. As to whether nature did well or ill to break the mould in which I was cast, that is cometing no one can judge until after thay have read me.

Let the trumpet of judgement sound when it will, I will present myself with this book in my hand before the Supreme Judge. I will say boldly: 'Here is what I have done, what I have thought, what I was. I have told the good and the bad with equal frankness. I have concealed nothing that was ill, added nothing that was good, and if I have sometimes used some indifferent ornamentation, this has ever only been to fill a void occasioned by my lack of memory; I may have supposed to be true what I knew could have been so, never what I knew to be false. I have shown myself as I was, contemptible and vile when that is how I was, good, generous, sublime, when that is how I was; I have disclosed my innermost self as you alone know it to be. Assemble about me, Eternal Being, the numberless host of my fellow-men; let them hear my confessions, let them groan at my unworthiness, let them blush at my wretchedness. Let each of them, here on the steps of your throne, in turn reveal his heart with the same sincerity; and then let one of them say to you, if he dares: *I was better than that man.* (Rousseau, *Confessions*, trans. Angela Scholar)

8. See, as exemplary of the anti-Rousseau position, Irving Babbitt, *Rousseau and Romanticism* (Boston: Houghton Mifflin, 1919).

9. See Bernard Williams, "The Self and the Future," in *Problems of the Self: Philosophical Papers 1956–1972* (Cambridge: Cambridge University Press, 1973); and Derek Parfit, *Reasons and Persons* (Oxford: Oxford University Press, 1984), 204–9.

10. Eric T. Olson, "Personal Identity," in *The Stanford Encyclopedia of Philosophy*, winter 2008 ed., ed. Edward N. Zalta, at http://plato.stanford.edu/archives/win2008/entries/identity-personal/.

11. Sigmund Freud, "The Ego and the Id," in *Standard Edition*, 19:48.

12. Jacques Lacan, *Ecrits* (Paris: Editions du Seuil, 1966), 417–18; 524; 864; my translation.

13. Charles Taylor, *Sources of the Self* (Cambridge, MA: Harvard University Press, 1989), 409.

14. See Erik Erikson, *Childhood and Society* (New York: W. W. Norton, 1950). A very useful summary of the twentieth-century revival of the term *identity* can be found in Elizabeth Lunbeck, "Identity and the Real Self in Postwar American Psychiatry," *Harvard Review of Psychiatry* 8 (2000): 318–22.

15. Erik Erikson, *Identity: Youth and Crisis* (New York: W. W. Norton, 1968), 22; emphasis in the original.

16. Taylor, *Sources of the Self*, 36.

17. See Robert J. Lifton, *The Protean Self* (New York: Basic Books, 1993).

18. Alain Badiou, *Saint Paul: La fondation de l'universalisme* (Paris: Presses Universitaires de France, 1998); English trans. Ray Brassier, Saint Paul: The Foundation of Universalism (Stanford, CA: Stanford University Press, 2003), 17.

19. Sophocles, *Oedipus the King*, trans. Robert Fagles, in *Three Theban Plays* (New York: Penguin, 1984), ll. 1492–95.

20. Some of these questions are discussed in Marshall Berman, *The Politics of Authenticity: Radical Individualism and the Emergence of Modern Society* (New York: Atheneum, 1970).

21. Louis de Saint-Just, "Institutions républicaines," in *Oeuvres choisies* (Paris: Gallimard, 1968), 327: "*Le gouvernement républicain aura pour principe la vertu; sinon, la terreur.*"

22. See André Malraux, "Laclos," in *Tableau de la littérature française, XVIIe–XVIIIe siècles* (Paris: Gallimard, 1939), 426–27.

Chapter 3. The Outcast of the Universe

1. *In re Soper's Estate*, 264 N.W. Minn. 427, 428.

2. Adeline in fact received four further suicide notes by mail the next day. One read, "Dumplins—Hate to do it, but noodle is wrong. Be good. God knows I love you. Sope." See *Louisville Times*, August 23, 1921.

3. Nathaniel Hawthorne, "Wakefield," in *Tales and Sketches* (New York: Library of America, 1982), 290.

4. Jerome Bruner, "The Transactional Self," in *Actual Minds, Possible Worlds* (Cambridge, MA: Harvard University Press, 1986), 57–69.

5. *In re Soper's Estate*, Plaintiff's Brief, in *Soper Record* (Cochran and Adeline Johnson Soper v. Gertrude Whitby and First Mutual Bank), 30564 State of Minnesota, Supreme Court, 7. I was able to consult this complete file of the case thanks to the generosity of the Minnesota Supreme Court, and the diligent research of David Hollander of the Princeton University Library; my gratitude to both.

6. See J. L Austin, *How to Do Things with Words* (Cambridge, MA: Harvard University Press, 1962).

7. Adeline Soper on cross-examination: "I never felt he was dead." *Soper Record*, 84.

8. Henry James, *The Beast in the Jungle*, in *Selected Tales* (London: Penguin, 2001), 437.

9. John Banville, *The Untouchable* (London: Picador, 1997), 46-47; emphasis in the original.

10. John Le Carré, *A Perfect Spy* (1986; reprint New York: Scribner, 2008), 287.

11. Helene Deutsch, "The Impostor: Contribution to Ego Psychology of a Type of Psychopath" (1955), in *Neuroses and Character Types* (London: Hogarth Press, 1965), 329.

12. Jorge Luis Borges, "Tlön, Uqbar, Orbis Tertius," in *Ficciones*, ed. Anthony Kerrigan (New York: Grove Press, 1962), 34.

13. I have recourse here to the most recent such dictionary, that of the Pléiade edition of *La Comédie humaine*, vol, 12, comp. Ferdnand Lotte (Paris: Bibliothèque de la Pléiade, 1981),

14. See, in particular, Erich Auerbach's classic study *Mimesis*, trans. Willard Trask (Princeton, NJ: Princeton University Press, 1959).

15. Honoré de Balzac, *Le Père Goriot*, in *La Comédie humaine* (Paris: Bibliothèque de la Pléiade, 1976), 3:55. All references to Balzac will be from

the Pléiade edition, with volume and page number, in parentheses in the text; my translations.

16. Le Carré, *A Perfect Spy*, 310–11.

## Chapter 4. Discovering the Self in Self-Pleasuring

1. *Griswold v. Connecticut*, 381 U.S. 479, 485–86.

2. Thomas Laquer, *Solitary Sex: A Cultural History of Masturbation* (New York: Zone Books, 2003), 277. Readers of Laquer's major study will recognize my debt to it throughout this chapter—a debt that has much to do with our joint understanding of the importance of Rousseau on this matter. For a brisk and useful history of attitudes toward masturbation, see also Jean Stengers and Anne Van Neck, *Histoire d'une grande peur, la masturbation* (Le Plessis-Robinson: Institut Synthélabo pour le progrès de la communication, 1998); English trans. Kathryn A. Hoffman, *Masturbation: The History of a Great Terror* (New York: Palgrave, 2001).

3. See Jean-Jacques Rousseau, *Discours sur l'inégalité*, in *Oeuvres complètes*, (Paris: Bibliothèque de la Pléiade, 1964), 3:157–58. For English translations of this and other texts of Rousseau, see *The Collected Writings of Rousseau*, ed. Roger D. Masters and Christopher Kelly (Hanover, NH: University Press of New England, 1990–2009).

4. See Jean-Jacques Rousseau, *Émile*, in *Oeuvres complètes*, 4:502.

5. Jean-Jacques Rousseau, *Confessions*, in *Oeuvres complètes*, 1:67.

6. See Jacques Derrida, *De la grammatologie* (Paris: Editions de Minuit, 1967); English trans. Gayatri Chakravorty Spivak, *Of Grammatology* (Baltimore: Johns Hopkins University Press, 1976).

7. Laquer notes that a popular sex education guide for young women—Mary Wood-Allen, *What a Young Woman Ought to Know* (1899)—made the point that "feelings awakened by the imagination were by their nature morally wrong and more dangerous physically than actual deeds." See Laquer, *Solitary Sex*, 215.

8. Jean-Jacques Rousseau, *Lettre à d'Alembert sur les spectacles*, in *Oeuvres complètes*, 5:73.

9. Jan-Jacques Rousseau, *Julie, ou La Nouvelle Héloise*, in *Oeuvres complètes*, 2:5.

10. Marcel Proust, *A la recherche du temps perdu*, ed. Jean-Yves Tadié (Paris: Bibliothèque de la Pléiade, 2001), 1:4.

11. Much later in the novel, Gilberte Swann—now married to Saint-Loup—reveals that at the time evoked in Marcel's first masturbation reveries she was playing sexually charged games with peasant boys, precisely in the

ruins of the Roussainville castle, and would only have been too happy to satisfy Marcel's desires. This knowledge comes, of course, too late to be of any use—and too-late knowledge in the *Recherche* is itself a form of fiction.

12. See Jacques Lacan, *Le Séminaire*, vol. 8, *Le Transfert* (Paris: Editions du Seuil, 2001).

13. Sigmund Freud, "Contributions to a Discussion on Masturbation" (1912), in *Standard Edition*, 12:251.

14. See Sigmund Freud, "Creative Writers and Day-Dreaming" (1908), in *Standard Edition*, 9:143. See my discussion of this model of literary analysis in Peter Brooks, *Psycho-Analysis and Storytelling* (Oxford: Blackwell, 1994).

15. Freud, "Notes upon a Case of Obsessional Neurosis" (1909), in *Standard Edition*, 10:245.

16. See Taylor, *Sources of the Self*; Laquer identifies the author of *Onania* as one John Marten, a medical quack.

17. See Georges Bataille, *La Part maudite, essai d'économie générale* (Paris: Editions de Minuit, 1949). Bataille argues for the study of waste, extravagance, the unproductive—including sexuality—as an entry into understanding of society.

18. See Michel Foucault, *Histoire de la sexualité, 1: La volonté de savoir* (Paris: Gallimard, 1976); English trans. Robert Hurley, *The History of Sexuality, 1: The Will to Knowledge* (New York: Vintage, 1988). Among many novelistic examples of the hereditary ravages of venereal disease, one could cite Jacques de Mortsauf, in Balzac's *Le lys dans la vallée* (1836), who is debilitated and headed toward a premature death, on account of his father's syphilis.

19. See the account by Stephen Greenblatt of the reactions of the staff of the History and Literature Program at Harvard University upon the announcement that Thomas Laquer would visit to talk about his new book on masturbation; Greenblatt, "Me, Myself, and I," *New York Review of Books* 51:6 (April 8, 2004): 32–36.

## Chapter 5. Inevitable Discovery

1. See *Kyllo v. United States*, 533 U.S. 27 (2001), in which Justice Scalia for the majority finds the technology does result in a "search" in Fourth Amendment terms, whereas Justice Stevens dissents on grounds that the technology doesn't penetrate the exterior walls of the house.

2. *Boyd v. United States*, 116 U.S. 616 (1886).

3. *Griswold v. Connecticut*, 381 U.S. 479, 486 (1965).

4. See *Lawrence v. Texas*, 539 U.S. 558 (2003).

5. *Semayne's Case*, Coke's Rep 91a, 77 Eng Rep 194 (KB 1604).

6. Louis Brandeis and Samuel Warren, "The Right to Privacy," 4 *Harvard Law Review* 193, 196 (1890).

7. *Olmstead v. United States*, 277 U.S. 438, 478 (1928).

8. For a probative discussion of Fourth Amendment doctrine, see Silas J. Wasserstrom and Louis Michael Seidman, "The Fourth Amendment as Constitutional Theory," 77 *Georgetown Law Journal* 19 (1988).

9. *Brewer v. Williams*, 430 U.S. 387, 392–93.

10. The quotations are from the transcript of "Hearings on Motion to Suppress" in *State v. Williams*, and are cited in *Nix v. Williams*, 467 U.S. 431, 448–49.

11. The "exclusionary rule" essentially dates back to *Weeks v. United States*, 232 U.S. 383, in 1914. Its rationale was succinctly stated by Justice Oliver Wendell Holmes in *Silverthorne Lumber Co. v. United States*, 251 U.S. 385, 392: "The essence of a provision forbidding the acquisition of evidence in a certain way is that not merely evidence so acquired shall not be used before the court, but that it shall not be used at all."

12. It should be noted, however, that the habeas petition—though not the trial records—in Williams's case suggests that the body might not have been so inevitably subject to discovery: that it was covered with snow, and in a culvert not visible from the road. See Phillip E. Johnson, "The Return of the 'Christian Burial Speech' Case," 32 *Emory Law Journal* 349, 372–73 (1983).

13. See, for example, Jean-Paul Sartre, *La Nausée* (Paris: Gallimard, 1947); Frank Kermode, *The Sense of an Ending* (New York: Oxford University Press, 1967); Roland Barthes, *S/Z* (Paris: Editions du Seuil, 1970); and Peter Brooks, *Reading for the Plot* (New York: Alfred A. Knopf, 1984).

14. Anton Chekhov, *Literary and Theatrical Reminiscences*, trans. S. S. Koteliansky (1974), 23. I find another version of Chekhov's remarks in an important essay by the Russian formalist Boris Tomachevsky, in a discussion of narrative "motivation"—that is, the narrative economy by which all properties and episodes must be made functional: "Chekhov referred to just such compositional motivation when he stated that if one speaks about a nail being beaten into a wall at the beginning of a narrative, then at the end the hero must hang himself on that nail." See Tomachevsky, "Thematics," in *Russian Formalist Criticism*, trans. and ed. Lee T. Lemon and Marion J. Reis (Lincoln: University of Nebraska Press, 1965), 79.

On a similar concept of "motivation," see my quotation from Gérard Genette, below.

15. *United States v. Andrade*, 784 F.2d 1431.

16. *United States v. Levasseur*, 620 F.Supp. 624; *State v. Butler*, 676 S.W. 2d.

17. *Feldhacker v. United States*, 849 F.2d 293, 296 n. 4.

18. See, for example, the superintendent's contemptuous remark: "There *is* such a thing, Sergeant, as making a mountain out of a molehill. Good day." And Cuff's reply: "There is such a thing as making nothing out of a molehill, in consequence of your head being too high to see it." Wilkie Collins, *The Moonstone* (1868; reprint Oxford: Oxford University Press, 1999), 104.

19. Jorge Luis Borges, "Funes the Memorious," trans. James E. Irby, in *Labyrinths* (New York: New Directions, 1962), 59–66; see also Borges's meta-detective story, "Death and the Compass," in the same volume, 129–41.

20. Doyle, "The Red-headed League," 83.

21. Arthur Conan Doyle, "Silver Blaze," in *Sherlock Holmes: The Complete Novels and Stories* (New York: Bantam Dell, 2003), 1:534.

22. Kim Lane Scheppele has argued that American evidence law embodies a "ground zero" theory of evidence—very much like Holmes's "you might have been there." See Scheppele, "The Ground Zero Theory of Evidence," 50 *Hastings Law Journal* 321 (1998).

23. Gérard Genette, "Vraisemblance et motivation," in *Figures II* (Paris: Editions du Seuil, 1969), 94; English trans. Alan Sheridan, *Figures of Literary Discourse* (New York: Columbia University Press, 1982).

24. Ginzburg, "Spie," 158–209; English trans. John and Anne C. Tedeschi, "Clues," 96–125. I have modified the Tedeschi translation in places in order to give a more literal rendition.

25. Terence Cave, *Recognitions: A Study in Poetics* (Oxford: Clarendon Press, 1988), 250.

26. I am grateful to Simon Stern for bringing this parallel to my attention. Langdell hoped that his approach would lead to the discovery of large legal principles that would serve to adjudicate cases in the future, making case study obsolete. Time has suggested that his method belonged rather to the hunter's paradigm.

27. See Justice Souter's opinion in *Safford United School District v. Redding*, no. 08-479 (2009), the case in which a school principal ordered what was virtually a strip-search of a thirteen year old girl suspected of hiding ibuprofen tablets on her person—where he concedes the right of a school to search for drugs on the grounds of "reasonable suspicion," a

lower standard than "probable cause." He glosses the terms: "probable cause" means a "fair probability" of finding what you are looking for; "reasonable suspicion" only a "moderate chance." The search of Savanna Redding was found unconstitutional even under the more lax standard, in an 8–1 decision.

28. See *United States v. Andrade*, 784 F.2d 1431 (9th Cir. 1986). But see also *United States v. Six Hundred Thirty-Nine Thousand Five Hundred and Fifty-Eight Dollars in United States Currency*, 293 U.S. App. D.C. 384 (1992).

29. See *United States v. Levasseur*, 620 F.Supp. 624 (E.D.N.Y.1985); *State v. Butler*, 676 S.W.2d 809 (Mo.1984).

30. See Louis Chevalier, *Classes laborieuses et classes dangereuses* (Paris: Plon, 1958); English trans. Frank Jellinek, *Labouring Classes and Dangerous Classes* (London: Routledge and Kegan Paul, 1973).

31. Sartre, *La Nausée*, 59–60; my translation.

32. Roland Barthes, "Introduction to the Structural Analysis of Narrative" (1966), trans. Richard Howard, in *The Barthes Reader*, ed. Susan Sontag (New York: Hill and Wang, 1982), 266.

33. See Jerome Bruner, "The Narrative Construction of Reality," *Critical Inquiry* 18, no. 1 (1991): 6.

34. *Old Chief v. United States*, 519 U.S. 172.

35. Sophocles, *Oedipus the King*, trans. Fagles, ll. 1531–35.

36. Sophocles, *Oedipus the King*, trans. and ed. Thomas Gould (Englewood Cliffs, NJ: Prentice-Hall, 1970), comment on ll. 1398–1402.

Chapter 6. The Derealization of Self

1. Sigmund Freud, *A Disturbance of Memory on the Acropolis*, in *Standard Edition*, 22:240–41.

2. See Claude Lévi-Strauss, "The Structural Study of Myth," in *Structural Anthropology* (New York: Basic Books, 1963), 206–31.

3. Jean-Jacques Rousseau, "Deuxième Promenade," *Les Rêveries du Promeneur solitaire*, in *Confessions. Autres Textes Autobiographiques* (Paris: Bibliothèque de la Pléiade, 1959), 1005; my translation. I have consulted with profit the translation by Peter France (London: Penguin, 1979).

4. See Sigmund Freud, *Civilization and Its Discontents*, in *Standard Edition*, 21:64–69, on the "oceanic feeling" that some take as a religious experience but which he traces back to this neonatal oneness with the mother's body.

Rousseau's loss of consciousness after being struck by the dog, and his return to consciousness without knowing who he is, recalls (once again) Michel de Montaigne's similar accident (a fall from his horse, struck by another rider) recounted in "De l'exercitation" (in *Essais*, book 2, chap. 6). But the ensuing analysis is quite different from Rousseau's: for Montaigne the near-death experience becomes a text on the unreasonableness of our fear of death.

5. Rousseau, "5ème promenade," *Rêveries d'un promeneur solitaire*, in *Oeuvres Complètes*, 1045: "Le flux et reflux de cette eau, son bruit continu mais renflé par intervalles frappant sans relâche mon oreille et mes yeux, suppléaient aux mouvements internes que la rêverie éteignait en moi et suffisaient pour me faire sentir avec plaisir mon existence sans prendre la peine de penser."

6. Rousseau, *Rêveries*, "5ème promenade," 1047: "De quoi jouit-on dans une pareille situation ? De rien d'extérieur à soi, de rien sinon de soi-même et de sa propre existence, tant que cet état dure on se suffit à soi-même comme Dieu."

7. See Geoffrey Hartman, "Romanticism and Anti-Self-Consciousness," in *Beyond Formalism* (New Haven, CT: Yale University Press, 1970), 298–310.

8. See Sigmund Freud, *From the History of an Infantile Neurosis*, in *Standard Edition*, 17:89.

9. See Lévi-Strauss, "The Structural Study of Myth."

10. Sigmund Freud, *Analysis Terminable and Interminable*, in *Standard Edition*, 23:249.

11. Henry James, *What Maisie Knew* (London: Penguin, 1985), 43.

12. Marcel Proust, *A la recherche du temps perdu*, ed. Jean-Yves Tadié (Paris: Bibliothèque de la Pléiade, 1987), 1:5; for this first part of the novel, *Du Côté de chez Swann* (Swann's Way), I have generally followed the new translation by Lydia Davis (New York: Viking, 2003), though I have introduced my own modifications. Henceforth I give the French reference followed by reference to the English translation (here, 1:5).

13. On *le sentiment de l'existence* in Rousseau, see especially the "5ème promenade" of the *Rêveries du promeneur solitaire*.

14. For Proust's *Time Regained*, I use (with my own modifications) the translation by Andreas Mayor and Terence Kilmartin, revised by D. J. Enright (New York: Modern Library, 2003).

15. On this question, see Gérard Genette, *Narrative Discourse*, trans. Jane E. Lewin (Ithaca, NY: Cornell University Press, 1980).

16. Walter Benjamin, "The Storyteller," in *Illuminations*, trans. Harry Zohn (New York: Schocken, 1978), 94.

17. John Milton, *Paradise Lost* (Oxford: Oxford University Press, 2008), 10:1443–47.

Chapter 7. The Madness of Art

1. James Joyce, *The Dead*, in *Dubliners* (New York: B. W. Huebsch, 1917), 287–88.

2. Gustave Flaubert, *Un Coeur simple*, in *Trois Contes* (Paris: Garnier, 1969), 73: "Les mouvements du coeur se ralentirent un à un, plus vagues chaque fois, plus doux, comme une fontaine s'épuise, comme un écho disparaît; et, quand elle exhala son dernier souffle, elle crut voir, dans les cieux en-trouverts, un perroquet gigantesque, planant au-dessus de sa tête." The translation in the text is my own.

3. William Shakespeare, *King Lear*, 5.2.11–13.

4. Paul Cézanne to Émile Bernard, 21 September 1906, in Cézanne, *Correspondance*, ed. John Rewald (Paris: Grasset, 1978), 327.

5. Paul Cézanne to Émile Bernard, 23 October 1905, in Cézanne, *Correspondance*, 314–15.

6. Philip Conisbee, "The Atelier des Lauves," in *Cézanne in Provence*, ed. Philip Conisbee and Denis Coutagne (New Haven, CT: Yale University Press, 2006), 240.

7. Henry James, *The Middle Years*, in *Selected Tales*, ed. John Lyon (London: Penguin, 2001), 254.

8. Jean-Jacques Rousseau, *Les Rêveries du promeneur solitaire*, in *Oeuvres complètes*, 1:995.

9. On this point, and for many other interesting comments on Freud's text, see Yosef Yerushalmi, *Freud's Moses: Judaism Terminable and Interminable* (New Haven, CT: Yale University Press, 1991). Yerushalmi notes, for instance, on the secret of religious tradition to Freud, "Its power lies precisely in the return of the repressed, in the triggering of hitherto un-conscious memories of real events from the remote past" (33).

10. See, in this connection, Robert Cover, "Violence and the Word," 95 *Yale Law Journal* 1601 (1986).

11. Henry James, preface to *Roderick Hudson*, in *Literary Criticism* (New York: Library of America, 1984), 2:1041.

12. See Peter Gay, *Freud: A Life for Our Time* (New York: W. W. Norton, 1988), 650.

13. Honoré de Balzac, *La Peau de chagrin* (1831), in *La Comédie humaine*, 10:85; English trans. Atwood H. Townsend, *The Fatal Skin* (New York: Signet, 1963).

Epilogue: The Identity Paradigm

1. Joseph Conrad, "Henry James—An Appreciation" (1905), in *Notes on Life and Letters* (London: J. M. Dent, 1921), 19.

# Index